DEVELOPMENT CENTRE SEMINARS

MICROFINANCE FOR THE POOR?

Edited by
Hartmut Schneider

DEVELOPMENT CENTRE
OF THE ORGANISATION FOR ECONOMIC CO-OPERATION AND DEVELOPMENT

ORGANISATION FOR ECONOMIC CO-OPERATION AND DEVELOPMENT

Pursuant to Article 1 of the Convention signed in Paris on 14th December 1960, and which came into force on 30th September 1961, the Organisation for Economic Co-operation and Development (OECD) shall promote policies designed:

- to achieve the highest sustainable economic growth and employment and a rising standard of living in Member countries, while maintaining financial stability, and thus to contribute to the development of the world economy;
- to contribute to sound economic expansion in Member as well as non-member countries in the process of economic development; and
- to contribute to the expansion of world trade on a multilateral, non-discriminatory basis in accordance with international obligations.

The original Member countries of the OECD are Austria, Belgium, Canada, Denmark, France, Germany, Greece, Iceland, Ireland, Italy, Luxembourg, the Netherlands, Norway, Portugal, Spain, Sweden, Switzerland, Turkey, the United Kingdom and the United States. The following countries became Members subsequently through accession at the dates indicated hereafter: Japan (28th April 1964), Finland (28th January 1969), Australia (7th June 1971), New Zealand (29th May 1973), Mexico (18th May 1994), the Czech Republic (21st December 1995), Hungary (7th May 1996), Poland (22nd November 1996) and the Republic of Korea (12th December 1996). The Commission of the European Communities takes part in the work of the OECD (Article 13 of the OECD Convention).

The Development Centre of the Organisation for Economic Co-operation and Development was established by decision of the OECD Council on 23rd October 1962 and comprises twenty-four Member countries of the OECD: Austria, Belgium, Canada, the Czech Republic, Denmark, Finland, France, Germany, Greece, Iceland, Ireland, Italy, Japan, Korea, Luxembourg, Mexico, the Netherlands, Norway, Poland, Portugal, the United States, Spain, Sweden and Switzerland, as well as Argentina and Brazil from March 1994. The Commission of the European Communities also takes part in the Centre's Advisory Board.

The purpose of the Centre is to bring together the knowledge and experience available in Member countries of both economic development and the formulation and execution of general economic policies; to adapt such knowledge and experience to the actual needs of countries or regions in the process of development and to put the results at the disposal of the countries by appropriate means.

The Centre has a special and autonomous position within the OECD which enables it to enjoy scientific independence in the execution of its task. Nevertheless, the Centre can draw upon the experience and knowledge available in the OECD in the development field.

Publié en français sous le titre :

MICROFINANCE
POUR LES PAUVRES ?

*
* *

Foreword

This book was produced in the context of the Development Centre's 1996-98 research programme on "Good Governance and Poverty Alleviation". The seminar on which it was based was organised in co-operation with the International Fund for Agricultural Development (IFAD) in April 1996.

Table of Contents

Preface

In developing countries, the poorer sections of the population have little or no access to financial resources. Consequently, their participation in economic development is either limited or denied. Many specialised financial institutions created in the 1950s and 1960s proved unable to meet the dual challenge of institutional and financial sustainability on the one hand, and outreach to large numbers of poor people on the other hand. Over more recent years, a variety of initiatives of microfinance have been taken, often combining financial and social intermediation in both urban and rural areas.

In the framework of its research on participatory development, the Development Centre undertook to analyse that experience, focusing on two main aspects. The first involved special attention to transaction costs which have often been seen as an obstacle to reach the poor. The second related to issues of institutional development and sustainability. To broaden the range of experience covered, and to deepen the insights that could be drawn, the Development Centre subsequently joined hands with the International Fund for Agricultural Development (IFAD) which has been active in the provision of financial resources to the rural poor since its inception in the 1970s.

In its introductory overview chapter, this volume draws on the broad review of experience that took place at an Expert Meeting on the subject. It further contains a selection of papers which delve into some of the general issues associated with microfinance as well as in specific cases from Africa, Asia and Latin America. The overall analysis shows that there is no single model that can be prescribed for all circumstances. Rather, adjusting financial institutions and their operations to local conditions implies diversity and innovation.

Some general policy conclusions can nevertheless be derived to offer broad guidance to national and international sponsors and to promoters of microfinance enterprises. First, demand-driven strategies have many advantages compared to the earlier, often donor-driven, supply-side approaches. Second, subsidised finance (via low interest rates) is an inappropriate instrument for reaching large numbers of poor people in a sustainable way. However, there is still considerable need for grant financing to develop efficient and sustainable institutions. This process may stretch over longer periods than the usual duration of development assistance projects. In any case, institutional development should be supported by participatory, client-oriented approaches rather than by "old-style" technical and financial assistance.

Institutional and financial innovation can go a long way to provide the poor with access to financial services. Many of the poorest of the poor live in such conditions of destitution and vulnerability that they may be unable to take immediate advantage of the opportunities offered by microfinance initiatives. We are confident that the analysis in this volume will stimulate debate and policy formulation, helping to extend the frontiers of microfinance for the poor. Moreover, it should give an impetus to the design of complementary policy instruments serving specifically those of the poor who are presently beyond the reach of microfinance.

Jean Bonvin
President
OECD Development Centre
Paris

Fawzi Al-Sultan
President
IFAD
Rome

December 1996

Introductory Overview: Principles and Perspectives

J.D. Von Pischke, Hartmut Schneider, and Rauno Zander

Creating financial mechanisms so that the poor can participate fully in market and political processes is a major objective of contemporary development assistance. The strategic relevance of this objective arises from a new awareness that institutions are most likely to be sustainable when they function for a majority in a society, or serve purposes that are perceived as at least indirectly benefiting most people. A related fact is that rural savings are generally much greater than has been assumed, for poor people need to save to make ends meet and cope with uneven income flows over time. In addition, recent comparative field studies (Zander, in this volume) have shown that informal financial arrangements benefit many people and that formal financial institutions can also expand their outreach greatly (Germidis *et al.,* 1991).

Advances in financial intermediation and infrastructure, stimulated by deregulation of financial sectors and facilitated by modern technology, have also put the spotlight on participatory mechanisms for integrating the poor into the economic mainstream. The advances in financial intermediation include recent efforts to design and deliver very small loans to poor borrowers, often women organised into small groups, providing more accessible deposit facilities, and much greater attention to risk management.

This volume and the conference on which it is based represent contributions by the International Fund for Agricultural Development (IFAD) and the Organisation for Economic Co-operation and Development (OECD) towards achieving more sustainable outreach to the poor. They also are in the spirit of the priority now accorded to microenterprise finance by bilateral and multilateral development assistance agencies, and the extraordinary interest in and support for participatory approaches to development assistance in recent years (Schneider with Libercier, 1995).

The conference aimed at facilitating learning from experience, based on selective or focused treatment of issues of outreach and sustainability in finance for the poor, which includes "poverty lending" operations targeting economically productive persons in poor households. The conference was intended to increase the visibility of the major issues identified and explored by a circle of specialists, making them more accessible to the wider development community. This increased accessibility is intended to pave the way for more effective initiatives by OECD Members' donor agencies and policy makers for improving opportunities for the poor in developing countries, enabling them to participate in shaping their own economic destinies[1].

The conceptual framework of the conference embraced a multiplicity of approaches, based on the realisation that there is no best single model or panacea for providing financial services to the poor. The conference explored how financial mechanisms can be developed to assist this mission.

The central dynamic in the provision of financial services to the poor is reconciling outreach and sustainability (Schneider, conference; Zander, in this volume). Outreach is the extent to which financial systems and their instruments reach the poor directly, increasing their participation in market processes and, by this empowerment, in political processes. Outreach must be the ultimate objective because reduction of poverty necessitates the empowerment of large numbers of people. Also, programme growth involves economies of scale, although the potential for savings in the context of providing cost-effective financial services has not yet been explored much in the microfinance literature. An expensive service approach with high transaction costs per client will not necessarily increase overall cost-effectiveness. However, economies of scale are possible if client-staff ratios can be increased within the institutional service structure.

Sustainability is a necessary but not a sufficient condition for empowerment. Gonzalez-Vega *et al.* emphasize that sustainable growth is a signal to the intermediary's potential borrowers (microclients) and to potential lenders (banks) about the programme's strength and purpose. Its effect, in turn, serves to attract loanable funds for additional growth and to increase customers' willingness to repay loans. Because sustainability underpins perceptions of permanency, it generates mutually compatible incentives for all those such as clients, managers and staff who are interested in the microfinance organisation's survival.

The importance of sustainability is demonstrated, so to speak, by its absence in many officially sponsored development assistance projects for providing credit for poor people during the past 35 years (Ijioma, Lucano, Yaron, conference). Schemes and institutions flower and die, leaving most poor people without access to formal savings facilities, credit or insurance (Zander, in this volume). These experiences have been widely documented in the development finance literature, rather limited in 1970 but now quite extensive. Authors on microfinance are responsible for a large proportion of recent development finance literature (see, for example, Bennett and Cuevas, 1996, and Gentil and Hugon, 1996).

There are highly contrasting views about the interaction of outreach and sustainability, and the relative emphasis to be accorded to each. Gonzalez-Vega takes a long-term view by noting that "sustainability today is outreach to the poor tomorrow". Conversely, others might argue that outreach today is essential for finding formulae for sustainability tomorrow, including economies of scale.

Economic logic offers a framework for this debate. Financial intermediaries in a competitive system would be expected to lower their costs continuously to reach out to an expanding number of clients with an increasing range of services. But is this actually occurring with the deregulation of finance in many countries? Under what conditions is it most likely to occur?

Country-specific case studies assisted the discussion and debate. Bangladesh probably offers the best-documented and most varied efforts to reach the poor through financial mechanisms (Hashemi, in this volume; Choudhury, conference). The case of Bangladesh is particularly interesting because of the country's low per capita income; success in reaching poor women who are greatly constrained by poverty, law and culture; and a formal financial sector of primarily nationalised commercial banks that face high risks and are not known for innovativeness. Bolivia offers another instructive case because it includes an NGO that gave birth to BancoSol, a commercial bank, and a specialised microlender (Gonzalez-Vega *et al.* in this volume). Examples from other countries were also presented at the meeting, providing perspectives on what may be achieved in different situations.

In general, it seemed apparent that the state should be a facilitator rather than a provider. This view of the state's role is based on information and incentive concerns and on principal agent problems which have precluded the development of sustainable state-owned development finance institutions in most poor countries.

The conference was oriented around three themes: outreach, sustainability and the design of efforts to intervene in finance on behalf of the poor. The rest of this introductory chapter will be devoted to the conclusions with respect to these three themes.

Expanding Outreach

Expanding outreach requires an orientation towards the client and an effort to address the limitations facing the poor and those who would serve them. In finance this orientation and "assault on the frontier" (Von Pischke, 1991) requires innovation which provides new services or instruments that are cheaper, better, or both better and cheaper. In addition, increasing outreach to the poor can also be facilitated by demographic trends, primarily by increases in the population density of hitherto sparsely populated areas.

Financial innovation can be defined in different ways. Von Pischke (1991) identifies three. The first is by lengthening the term structure of financial markets. This is described most simply by noting that a loan granted against the next harvest, paycheck or artisanal product is unlikely to exceed the value of the harvest, paycheck or product. A loan that is granted against a succession of expected harvests, paychecks or products can be repaid over a longer time period, but extending the term or time horizon of the market by offering loans with longer maturities also increases risk. The reasoning is simple: more things can go wrong in a longer period than in a shorter one, requiring more advanced risk management techniques.

The second is by lowering transaction costs. These costs are borne by all concerned: savers, intermediaries and borrowers. Transaction costs are the admission tickets to financial markets (Von Pischke, 1991). Although they may not by themselves govern the access of the poor to financial services (Zander, 1994), they are a crucial decision variable for improving financial systems. When transaction costs are high, they exclude many potential savers and borrowers who cannot afford them, and make financial institutions less likely to reach out to serve more poor people because the costs of doing so are regarded as excessive. The reduction of high transaction costs can have a dramatic effect on access (McGuire and Conroy, in this volume).

The third form of financial innovation involves refining valuation processes. The valuation process is the means a lender uses to identify good business prospects and determine how much credit can be offered to a loan applicant. The valuation process is essentially based on the lender's view of the prospect of reimbursement. Alternative valuation criteria that could be used for a classical agricultural input loan include:

— one harvest;

— a succession of harvests, especially if one fails;

— household income;

— the borrower's character;

— collateral.

Loan size and conditions vary depending on lender's view of who and what stands behind a loan request.

Refinements in valuation processes can occur in existing institutions and by establishing new institutions with an innovative view of value. In fact, poverty lending provides examples of some of the most striking refinements in valuation processes. The Grameen Bank, assisted from its early experimental stages for more than a decade by the IFAD, lends to some women who have never before even held money in their hands. Grameen's organisational framework and the incentives it provides enable women's promises to be exchanged for cash. The women obtain loans which they fully repay, with very few exceptions. Risk is well-managed but containing service costs remains a challenge (Hashemi, in this volume).

These technical forms of innovation — longer term structures, lower transaction costs and refinements in valuation processes — are almost always associated with social innovations that provide incentives for repayment and financial controls;

economic innovations that increase incomes, broaden markets and permit better management of real risk; and institutional innovations that lower transaction costs and increase returns on investment.

Client Orientation

Client-oriented providers with superior management of costs and risks are required for the development of financial services that are attractive to the poor (Zander, in this volume). Adoption of a client orientation is reflected in new financial services and products often specifically dedicated to serving the lower end of the market. These new services strive to combine incentives and opportunities for the poor to improve their productivity and economic performance with risk management and other requirements for survival as financial intermediaries. The latter see their own survival as essential to maintaining the confidence of their clientele over the long term, recognising that the road out of poverty is a long one.

A client orientation is also reflected in a willingness to undertake market research. The IFAD has been instrumental in promoting relevant studies in Asia and Africa (Audinet, conference). Bank Rakyat Indonesia has used social scientists to help design savings account terms and conditions for its village unit operations. Grameen Bank uses market research in its staff training and for the opening of new offices. Market research accounted for about 20 per cent of the project cost in the KfW-funded promotion of *caisses villageoises* in Mali. This research identified appropriate financial services and management structures and techniques for the *caisses* (Chao-Béroff, in this volume).

The more successful institutions appear to be effective because they focus more on opportunity and capacity than on the deprivation and misery of their clients. They seek to create market niches that they can profitably fill. This requires realistic assessments of debt capacity and not promoting credit where it is unlikely to be viable or relevant (Zander). In this respect innovation based on local participation is very attractive. However, donors tend to base their justification for poverty lending on market failure arising from information problems that limit lending to the poor, and on incentive problems, including those arising from lack of competition in financial markets that lead mainstream financial institutions to avoid serving the poor.

Attacking Limits and Financial Frontiers

Few financial intermediaries serving the poor see their mission as being limited to finance. They generally also provide non-financial services, linking the poor with larger markets and opportunities through facilitating measures. These include training in business decision making, literacy classes, health education, social organisation and networking, and linking up with relevant marketing and management development institutions (Kiriwandeniya).

Financial intermediation has simple yet demanding requirements for sustainability, i.e. the market test of performance is that costs are fully covered. In credit projects this requires very high loan recovery rates. Intermediation is unlikely to work well if there is insufficient attention to detail, appropriate business accounting and internal and external supervision and control procedures.

Social services generally work on different perceptions and objectives, based on transfers from the "rich" to the poor, often through the state and its fiscal mechanisms. Funding for social intermediation related to credit projects can be provided by official donors as well as by private sources. Activities include training in financial awareness and thrift, skills development, and other related areas. Sustainability requires a consensus among donors that the particular venture in social intermediation is worthwhile and that it continues to deserve funding. The objectives of social intermediation may be achieved slowly, at best, or few of the intended beneficiaries fully attain the goals supported by a programme's sponsors. This is often characteristic of social work, which nonetheless continues because it is supported by a broad consensus within the community and because it provides outreach to the poor which is considered a moral imperative or social good.

The differing priorities and expectations associated with financial intermediation and social goals can easily conflict. They can also be managed and complement each other when the specific functions of each are respected and kept sufficiently apart in the organisation of outreach to the poor.

Financial intermediaries serving the poor can also support the creation of new economic opportunities for their beneficiaries or intended beneficiaries. These include the introduction and promotion of new technologies, efforts to remove legal barriers to informal trade like that of street vendors or jitney operators, and facilitating links with large buyers such as governments and with export markets through charities like OXFAM.

At the same time, limits are usually imposed by the internal organisation of financial intermediaries and by law. The former involve incentives that are inconsistent with outreach; principal-agent problems that lead people providing financial services in the field to behave differently from the intentions of project designers and senior management; asymmetric information that enables a lender to have, at best, no more than a partial view of the intentions and competence of the borrower and hence of lending risks; enforcement problems arising from imperfect information and relationships; and weaknesses in the reliance on third parties to ensure compliance with financial contracts. Successful financial innovation creates confidence that offsets these risks as shown by examples discussed at the conference, including BancoSol in Bolivia, SANASA in Sri Lanka, Grameen Bank in Bangladesh and the *caisses villageoises* in Mali.

Limits imposed by law and regulations may pose greater problems because they are beyond the control of financial intermediaries. Laws often limit entry into finance by specifying the types of organisations that can accept deposits, defined by their ownership and the services they provide, and also the minimum capital requirements for establishing a new financial institution. Laws or regulations may also limit lending interest rates, often below the rates required for sustainable outreach to the poor. Moreover, in some countries judicial systems are often reluctant to deliver judgements favourable to creditors, and the judicial system's slowness is also a widespread problem. Finally, land tenure law may preclude poor people from using what little land they may own as collateral.

A client orientation based on service requires identification of target groups of potential clients. An interesting change in this approach became apparent at the conference. Target groups were formerly based on economic, ethnic, locational and other variables. They were provided a financial service or package of services that was more or less standard, depending on the donor. The new approach is to design financial services or packages that will attract the poor. Under this new approach, clients are self-selected. One means of achieving this is to organise groups of clients who do peer screening and monitoring, which is complemented by professional loan appraisal and follow-up procedures of financial institutions. This enables all concerned to identify and manage risks much more effectively than was possible using the older, one-size-fits-all format.

Specific Innovations

Loan and Deposit Contract Design

In remote, sparsely populated areas a lack of access to formal financial services may simply reflect the absence of formal financial intermediaries. In other instances, there are branches of banks in rural towns but their outreach is restricted. The poor may be discouraged from opening savings accounts by relatively high minimum balance or transaction requirements. Also, they may be excluded from access to credit by high minimum loan sizes, high transaction costs required to obtain a loan, and a lack of collateral or guarantors to support loan applications (Zander, 1994).

Facilitating access for the poor requires deposit and lending facilities that are attractive to them. This means that deposit account balances and transactions can be small, and that transaction costs must be minimised by convenient office locations and by prompt service, by loans that are small, and by a desire on the part of savers, borrowers and financial intermediaries to create lasting relationships characterised by repeat business. This lowers information costs and helps control risk. It also gives borrowers an incentive to repay so that they can obtain additional and generally larger loans in the future. These conditions can be realised only when operating costs are well managed and when operations are reasonably efficient.

BancoSol provides an example of creating relationships based on powerful incentives for having a flawless repayment record. These incentives include continued access to credit, in successively larger amounts, with longer maturities and with less frequent instalments (Gonzalez-Vega et al., in this volume). These business-like procedures contribute to effective risk management and reduce transaction costs as a percentage of loan size for both borrower and lender. Borrower groups, for people ineligible for individual loans, offer peer monitoring. BancoSol refuses to accept any repayment from a group less than the amount due. Non-repayment is followed up within 24 hours.

Evidence from India and the Philippines suggests that links among different types of institutions providing financial services to the poor can achieve economies. Self-help groups and NGOs can perform certain functions such as initial selection of borrowers and forming groups at a lower cost than commercial banks, and can also reduce the transaction costs of poor borrowers and savers (McGuire and Conroy, in this volume). Links enable loans to be provided in much smaller amounts than could be considered by commercial banks.

Creating access requires financial services or instruments that are appropriate for the target clientele and remunerative to the service provider. This can be achieved through financial innovation, offering new types of financial contracts and of their respective loan and deposit components.

Decentralisation

Decentralised decision making has a potential for reducing costs and increasing efficiency. Efforts to enhance decentralisation of business procedures, in particular the authority to approve loans, however, are often resisted in financial institutions because of a concern about preventing misappropriation of funds. In general, decentralisation may be resisted because of bureaucratic precedent that favours hierarchy, centralisation of power and restricted flows of information. However, decentralisation should be explored as an alternative that can improve performance, save time, empower staff, create profit, and perhaps most importantly, increase the outreach of institutions to lower-income households (Camara, conference).

Decentralisation is also increasingly required in a modern or modernising economy in which competition is a driving force for change and efficiency. Decentralisation requires transparency and accountability, as well as sanctions against insiders who abuse it.

Credit decision making can be decentralised if branch managers and lending officers are given clear guidelines and procedures, if there are effective controls and individual lending limits, and if management information systems are sufficiently robust to permit measurement of performance and results. The advantages of decentralised credit decisions include lower transaction costs for all concerned and loans that are crafted in response to information available to branch decision makers. Borrower self-selection by groups is a critical decentralised risk management tool. In co-operative or other collective types of credit institutions, the general assembly or meetings of the entire membership can be used to obtain guidance about the nature of demand for financial services, and acceptable terms and conditions. This gives members of lower-income households an opportunity to participate in decision making and express their concerns and needs to others. Elected committees and officers have to inform the membership about the likely outcome of different lending and deposit terms and conditions, ensuring that the organisation does not become dominated by borrowers acting in their own selfish interests to the detriment of savers or the organisation's future. This danger is greater to the extent that such organisations are politicised or subsidised.

Risk-Hedging Arrangements

The provision of financial services is risky by nature. Failures of banks and other financial institutions have been relatively common in the history of modern industrial society. Credit exposes lenders to a possibility of non-recovery of the principal amounts of loans outstanding and the interest due. This risk threatens a lender's liquidity, which is the ability to honour financial commitments. It also threatens a lender's capital or solvency, the extent to which the lender's assets exceed its liabilities, measured in financial terms. The lender's protection against these risks is ultimately its capital, which provides a cushion for creditors. Capital is created by owners' contributions to the organisation, by retained profits or surplus and also by grants. Capital adequacy, as well as stability over time, adds another dimension to the elements governing institutional sustainability.

The United Nations Capital Development Fund (UNCDF) argues that a necessary condition for successful group lending is capital accumulation by borrower groups. Otherwise, a default by one group member has to be made good immediately by others under the rules of group credit. This can eventually destroy groups, causing lenders to cease dealing with otherwise good clients who refuse to cover their contingent liabilities, as well as with the bad clients whose defaults precipitated the group's collapse (Garson).

Other means of dealing with risk include guarantees offered by third parties. While requiring third-party guarantors for individual borrowers is an established technique, a newer financial instrument is a guarantee for an entire portfolio or portfolio segments. These are increasingly provided by development assistance agencies. Their costs are generally not fully disclosed and their effects are not yet fully explored, in part due to difficulties in measuring additionality, the extent to which a specific intervention by a development assistance agency, for example, changes the behaviour of the guaranteed party, in this case a lender, towards the target group of beneficiaries such as poor borrowers. Part of the difficulty in measuring additionality is counterfactual, the problem of estimating what might have happened in the absence of a guarantee, for comparison with performance supported by a guarantee.

Enhancing Sustainability

The financial definition of sustainability is quite simple: it is denoted by a positive net present value of an investment or an institution. According to this definition, financial institutions, programmes and instruments do not have to last forever, although sustainability is emphasized because of the need for stable institutions with viable prospects beyond the short term. Sustainability implies that institutions have to recover their costs plus a surplus at least equal to the opportunity cost of capital. This calculation is clouded by subsidy, which is inherent in development finance from official sources. Accordingly, the definition of sustainability may be redefined as "achieved when the return on equity, net of any subsidy received, equals or exceeds the opportunity cost of funds" (Yaron, 1994).

Essentials for reducing subsidy dependence and hence achieving sustainability are simply covering costs — including the costs of inflation — through lending rates and fees, so that capital is maintained in real terms; recovering a very high percentage of amounts falling due from borrowers; offering attractive deposit interest rates to build a good source of loanable funds; and controlling costs through a continual search for more efficient means of doing business (Yaron, 1994).

A complementary approach of dealing with sustainability at the institutional level is to identify and manage risks in all aspects of operations: lending, funding, and administration. This is the task of good bankers; precedent and tools from established financial market operators are available to those who would adapt or reconstruct them in financial relationships with poor people. However, effective financial institutions reaching out to the poor must be able to deal with small borrowers who keep no accounting records and who have little, if any, tangible collateral to offer (Gonzalez-Vega *et al.*, in this volume).

A third approach is to view the challenges to sustainability as consisting of governance, investment and socio-economic issues. Sustainability is a governance concern because it requires viable organisational strategies and structures. It is an important investment consideration because investment tends to be incremental in nature and has a long time horizon. Sustainability is a socio-economic issue because the purpose of outreach to the poor is not fully realised until the structure of the formal financial market is changed in such a way that the poor have broad access. This structural change, when attained voluntarily and through innovation, constitutes a social good as well as a source of profit to intermediaries serving the poor and also to their clients. Programmes that are unsustainable tend to lead to a withdrawal from changes introduced in business structures that do not meet the test of cost reduction or increases in business efficiency. These unsuccessful attempts at innovation result in avoidance or evasion by lenders that have been pressured or coerced into deals that they otherwise would not undertake.

The dimensions of sustainability — covering costs, managing risks and the complex of governance, investment and socio-economic issues — are discussed next in terms of the major issues in the presentations and discussion at the conference.

Internal Governance Issues

Governance for sustainability requires competent management and good operational and programme design. Much of the conference discussion was devoted to this. Issues include corporate form, local participation and financial controls.

Corporate Form and Objectives

BancoSol was formed in part to transcend the limitations of the NGO responsible for its existence. This NGO, PRODEM, found it difficult to manage cash flows because of donor disbursement procedures. It was also limited in its capacity to raise funds from the market. As a bank, these constraints could be and have been overcome, providing scope for flexibility and growth. However, BancoSol's corporate objectives are not purely market-driven, as suggested by its ownership, which includes NGOs, foundations, the Inter-American Investment Corporation, private banks and firms, and five prominent businessmen, including the country's president. The status of the owners is a major asset for BancoSol from the standpoint of internal decision making expertise and in its relations with the rest of the financial community, donors, and clients. A useful board should behave in a manner consistent with sustainability. Davalos notes that attitudes may be affected by board members' interpretations of corporate objectives.

Board members of many NGOs, although successful business persons in their own private lives, seem to lose a sense of rigour when they enter the NGO boardroom. Cost structures are not openly scrutinised, inefficiencies are tolerated, and interest rates are set without regard to financial parameters. Governance is indeed a problem when managers are unwilling to change and boards are not prone to make substantial changes. Those that do make changes immediately start to show healthy improvements, which in turn, induce changes in other (NGOs') boards.

FondoMicro in the Dominican Republic made it a point to have bankers on its board from the very beginning, and this has proved to be extremely important. The problem of governance is not that NGOs have no real owners, but that boards do not behave "as if" they were real owners. When boards perform their responsibilities in a professional fashion, governance problems are reduced or eliminated.

Local Participation

Voluntary input from the community, especially by borrowers organised into groups through decentralised co-operatives or village banks, can greatly reduce lending costs while creating incentives for businesslike behaviour by all concerned. In Mali, for example, only two of 56 *caisses villageoises* in the KfW-funded project failed. Voluntary input includes the functions of elected officeholders and the activities of members in the establishment and operation of their groups of borrowers. Members' commitment to their financial institution can permit better risk management, although this requires continued training and vigilance (Camara, conference). Cost reductions achieved in Mali arose from donated labour for the construction of *caisse* offices, prudent criteria for credit access and expectations governing savings mobilisation, as well as volunteer leadership and greatly reduced safekeeping costs.

Experience in Africa suggests that villagers' voluntary participation is likely to be greatest where poverty is greatest, i.e. where locations are remote and distant from markets (Chao-Béroff, in this volume). Local participation, of course, is easiest to enlist when the intervention responds effectively to local priorities and values and reduces the costs of participants, possibly providing opportunities for the poor for the first time that were considered beyond their reach. In these cases participation may also lower costs by permitting decentralisation based on local solidarity.

Control Mechanisms

Sustainability requires good accounting and internal financial control procedures. Planning becomes more difficult when management information is low quality, while deficient financial reporting opens the door to irregularities. Efforts to ensure good controls in local financial institutions such as co-operatives and credit unions are easiest when members have a strong sense of solidarity based on the perception that their stake in the enterprise is a meaningful one. Institutional measures that facilitate control include making the internal auditor part of the executive committee, establishment and maintenance of internal audit procedures that are transparent and enforced, and also by using the services of government auditors for external audits. There are many good, simple bookkeeping systems that are designed for or that can be adapted to small-scale credit operations. However, records must be kept up to date to be useful.

External Governance Concerns

Government Relations

Sustainability is also affected by a lender's stance vis-à-vis the government. Many poverty lenders, especially NGOs headquartered in wealthy countries, are dependent upon governments and create a space for themselves in public policy forums by acting as self-appointed advocacy groups for the poor. They often do this successfully and with considerable imagination and flair. One result has been a wholesale reorientation of major aid programmes toward microenterprise finance and away from older interests in agricultural and rural finance, promoting small and medium-sized enterprises, capital markets and industrial and co-operative finance.

NGOs in poor countries may also cultivate the public policy route, as in the Philippines. Even if they do not achieve favourable recognition, they may be well received in governmental circles because of the stature of their sponsors, the funds they bring to the country and the employment they create, and the infrastructure they leave behind as a result of successful projects.

In other cases, relationships between NGOs and governments may be strained or even hostile. Government officials may believe that NGOs are providing services that are fundamentally the government's province, that they encourage the poor to put even greater strain on government finances, that they are conduits for alien values, and that they obtain development assistance that should be allocated more in accordance with government objectives and priorities. These perceptions are basically about power and control. The good that NGOs do may be perceived as a threat to the government and their organising of people at the grassroots for an economic or social objective may also be interpreted as an unwelcome political act. In other cases, government relationship to NGOs suggest the opposite. NGOs are government agencies in all but name, while others exist only on paper to mobilise donor funds.

The case is different with savings-based decentralised financial intermediaries, notably thrift and credit co-operative societies. Many networks of financial co-operatives operating on the principles of the outstanding innovation of self-help groups that began with Raiffeisen more than a hundred years ago, usually prefer to obtain legislation that facilitates their legal existence, and then to be left alone to work out their programmes through co-operative governance procedures, often assisted by experienced, officially funded experts from abroad. Some credit unions have enlisted banking regulatory authorities to examine their members for safety and soundness. Credit union officials defend their approach to regulators by citing competitive concerns. If banks are regulated and therefore perceived as safe, while credit unions do not have this seal of approval, larger deposits will tend to flow to banks rather than to credit unions, especially when a few credit unions experience difficulty.

The quest for sustainability is easily derailed by politicisation. This has been reflected in the past in relationships between government-initiated co-operatives that were far from Raiffeisen's original idea of self-help, and governments in many developing countries. It is also seen in the problems encountered by many state-owned lenders to agriculture and to industry. Lending programmes were designed to promote government priorities such as food self-sufficiency, export growth and development of backward or favoured regions. Individual loans were provided to the rich and powerful or to others who might provide support to the government. Patronage overwhelmed financial discipline and lending institutions declined as a result, precluding sustainability.

An extreme form of politicisation is represented by government decisions to forgive loans on a broad scale, or statements to this effect by politicians or candidates for political office. Changes of government in Sri Lanka (1977, 1995) have led to major debt forgiveness programmes. Moreover, the loans in some priority lending programmes imposed on village-level financial institutions were cancelled only a few years after being granted. In 1988, for example, the government of Sri Lanka cancelled all outstanding housing loans. This step threatened the autonomy and the viability of the thrift and credit societies which had been compelled to extend these loans that were outside their ordinary lending business (Kiriwandeniya, conference).

Legal Infrastructure

Another type of governance issue with deep socio-economic roots is the extent to which government encourages and provides for compliance with contracts. Timely enforcement of creditors' claims reduces the transaction costs of financial intermediaries, which influences their approach to and evaluation of risks attached to outreach. While laws can be promulgated, it is quite often extremely difficult for governments to improve the operation of the legal infrastructure because of entrenched customary power.

In many situations a poverty lender has to accept the way business is done and work within whatever limitations this may impose. Successful cultivation of relationships with clients through innovative financial arrangements is the key to good contracts. Several poverty lenders such as Grameen Bank have been able to thrive and achieve satisfactory loan collections by establishing new ways of doing business in otherwise inhospitable formal and legal environments. Good credit culture can be created locally and on an institution-specific basis, as demonstrated in Mali's *caisses villageoises*.

Macroeconomic Environment

The government has a major role to play in creating a macroeconomic environment conducive to rural financial institutions. Reaching the poor not only requires macroeconomic stability, but also sound financial sector policies, as well as non-distortionary policies in other areas as, for example, agriculture.

Effective monetary policies to control inflation rates instil confidence in the financial system and can significantly increase domestic savings, while reductions in the fiscal deficit lower the level of public borrowing. With high rates of inflation, financial calculation becomes problematic and incentives are greatly skewed, often towards speculation and opportunism. Some donors have taken the position that they will not support credit operations in countries experiencing high inflation.

Financial sector policies, above all the market determination of interest rates, have an important bearing on the access of marginal clients to financial services. The general arguments in favour of positive on-lending interest rates are underlined in Jacob Yaron's contribution. Interest rate subsidies are easy to introduce but hard to phase out. They undermine institutional viability and promote leakage to borrowers other than to those intended.

Liberalised exchange rates can raise agricultural prices and may lead to increased aggregate agricultural production. Similarly, revisions in the tax regimes for agricultural export commodities can open up additional opportunities for small and primarily subsistence-oriented farmers.

Financial Management Issues

Provision of financial services for the poor encounters the same types of risks that other lenders face as well as some that are more common at the lower end of the market. These issues may be thought of as internal governance challenges and also as technical problems that have to be managed.

Interest Spreads

Experience has shown that dependence on subsidies is usually inconsistent with sustainability in the long run (Yaron, in this volume). This is true for a number of reasons as illustrated by donor experience with agricultural and industrial finance: *a)* the priorities of the providers of subsidy are likely to change over time, requiring abandonment of existing programmes; *b)* subsidy brings politicisation and control, which easily overwhelm efforts to ensure that loans get repaid; *c)* the lender devotes efforts to maintain subsidies at the expense of efforts to learn more from borrowers, savers and potential clients; *d)* subsidised programmes based on perceptions of deprivation rather than on visions of empowerment often provide incentives for borrowers not to repay in full and on time.

To be sustainable, lenders need to charge interest rates and fees that are sufficient to cover their costs, including the costs of risk as reflected in arrears and bad debt losses. The spread between lenders' cost of funds and their lending rates have to be quite large if the poor are to be reached, because the costs of reaching the poor are high and because the poor are often subject to extraordinary risks. In Mali, local participation in *caisses villageoises* is considered by CIDR as a means of ensuring adequate spreads, based on an understanding of their purpose and good returns to credit use. The *caisses'* spreads have averaged about 25 per cent.

However, large spreads can also mask inefficiency. The best controls over excessive spreads is a competitive financial market in which intermediaries are sufficient in number and their products or services sufficiently varied to give the poor a possibilty of choice. Developing a competitive financial sector requires explicit and implicit public policy that provides relative freedom of entry, offers incentives for good conduct, supports legal systems that provide low-cost contract enforcement, and limits reserve requirements so that they are not excessively costly to deposit-taking financial institutions. High reserve requirements coupled with zero interest paid on reserves deposited with the central bank contribute to excessively large spreads charged by lenders.

Managing Covariant Funds Flows

The most probable reason why many informal moneylenders do not accept deposits and become bankers is the problem of covariance. In a relatively small area, clients' fortunes are often closely linked to a major economic activity, commonly agriculture. If agricultural yields and prices are not favourable for producers, for example, their incomes tend to decline and their liquidity dries up. This makes it more difficult for them to repay their loans. At the same time, it is precisely in such situations that they would want to withdraw their deposits.

Any formal financial intermediary that attempts to deal in areas marked by high covariance will be subject to these forces, especially if the lender is guided by a strategy that is inconsistent with risk diversification (Garson, conference). Successful management of covariance risk requires sufficient liquidity to see borrowers through a bad season, year or cycle. Liquidity is required in order to preserve relationships with clients, who will value credit most highly in the period immediately following the crisis or misfortune, when their own resources are most thinly stretched.

The lender's access to additional liquidity by refinancing from larger financial networks can be highly useful for this purpose. This access is commonly provided through other banks or lending institutions with different risk exposures as in the Philippines (FSSI), apex lending institutions for microlenders or co-operatives, or from the central bank. Apex lenders may emerge from relatively highly developed networks of village institutions as in Sri Lanka (Kiriwandeniya), but may still face massive risk covariance, especially in small countries, because of the nature of their clients (Davalos, conference).

The Role of Savings

The case for stimulating savings mobilisation is well established. The poor want to save because the risks they face are large. The poor often save in relatively unremunerative ways, such as investment in livestock that is held for sale in times of distress, which often exhibit covariance that depresses livestock prices as many households attempt to liquidate their stock at the same time. Savings deposits enable deposit-takers to have a window on depositors' savings capacity, which is a good basis for determining their debt capacity. Depositors have to have a certain degree of confidence in their financial institution, which also gives them incentives to behave responsibly as borrowers when deposits are provided voluntarily. Deposits may also provide loanable funds, giving lenders an incentive to treat depositors well. Successful deposit-taking institutions that also lend to the poor tend to have many more depositors than borrowers. This reflects the fact that most people want to save most of the time, while they do not want to borrow all the time. Many people may not want to borrow at all because they have few things that they would like to borrow for, because they feel that saving before undertaking major expenditures is less risky, or for moral or religious reasons. These concerns led one participant to observe that, "Savings-based systems are more empowering for the poor than credit-based systems." AFRACA (the African Rural and Agricultural Credit Association) argues for "savings mobilisation first, credit next" (Ijioma, conference).

The Regional Agricultural Credit Associations (RACAS)

Established by the Food and Agriculture Organisation of the United Nations (FAO) in the 1970s and currently supported by the IFAD and other donor agencies such as the GTZ and ILO, the Regional Agricultural Credit Associations (RACAS) provide a training and management development forum for rural finance institutions. The RACAS organise seminars and training programmes at national and regional levels, attended by practitioners and policy makers to learn from other member institutions' experience. The IFAD's grants are focused primarily on facilitating the reach of rural finance institutions to poorer households with innovative financial products.

The Near East and North Africa Regional Agricultural Credit Association (NENARACA) is based in Amman, Jordan. NENARACA's seminars focus on increasing the reach of banks to rural customers through training programmes on issues like lowering the transaction costs, simplifying lending procedures, relaxing traditional collateral requirements and tackling risk management issues. NENARACA has been able to accumulate considerable amounts of its own funds while using the IFAD grant to cover its programme and operational costs as well.

The African Regional Agricultural Credit Association (AFRACA) in Nairobi, Kenya, has 44 active members. It mainly fosters innovative financial technologies to broaden the customer base of traditional rural finance institutions and to promote financial intermediation with integration of demand-based deposit products together with conventional lending business of its members.

The Asian Regional Agricultural Credit Association (APRACA), whose Secretariat is in Bangkok, with similar objectives as its counterparts in Africa and the Near East and North Africa, has decentralised to a considerable degree, establishing separate bodies in countries other than Thailand for implementation of specific programmes. CENTRAB in the Philippines manages all APRACA training activities, while "APRACA Consultancy Services" in Indonesia assists in programme implementation and offers consultancy services to other organisations. A recently approved IFAD grant aims at improving financial services to poor rural households and developing successful building blocks of member institutions' and IFAD promoted financial products for the poor for replication on a wider scale in Asia.

Institutions that provide loans only and that appear weak or do not seem to be viable, provide the community with an incentive to destroy them, which is most effectively done by failure to repay loans. These lenders, wholly dependent on outside funding, usually not on commercial terms, often have relatively little information about their borrowers and are ineffective at screening loan applicants while facing high information costs.

Experience with credit projects that include savings and donor funding, usually through co-operative forms of financial intermediaries, indicates that beneficiary groups or members tend to make qualitative distinctions between funding based on the source (Ijioma, conference). For example, funds provided by members as savings are treated as "warm" money, alive and vibrant and hence requiring good stewardship. Funding provided by outsiders such as donor agencies is perceived as being "cold," in the sense of being distant, aloof or alien, implying less of an obligation to repay.

Credit unions, the Credit Mutuel System and thrift and credit co-operatives scrupulously manage "warm" money. They often have simultaneously presided over the disappearance of "cold" money invested in loans that do not get repaid. This incentive issue is tremendously important. Borrowers and the intermediaries funding them must have a stake or sense of ownership or responsibility in the funds being loaned if high collection rates are to be achieved.

The sequencing of saving and credit in poverty lending is a source of debate. In the event that donor funding is reduced or terminated, decentralised financial institutions such as thrift and credit co-operatives that begin with saving activities and that are dependent upon deposits as a source of loanable funds are likely to be least affected. In this sense, deposit-taking is a means of blending or reconciling concerns for outreach with the requirements for sustainability. However, these institutions also take a long time to grow, as deposits are accumulated and as the dynamics of member control are collectively explored and developed by the members of the new organisation. But once established and experienced, they can expand savings services at a rapid rate and serve large numbers of people (Camara, Kiriwandeniya).

Others argue that it is quicker and managerially more effective to begin with an externally funded lending programme and to work toward becoming self-sufficient in the sense of developing income sources that cover all operating costs through efficiency and the realisation of economies of scale. In addition, deposit-taking is a high-cost activity, especially relative to the short-run perception of the easy terms on which donor funding is usually provided for poverty lending. However, operational self-sufficiency has been reached by only a very limited number of those poverty lenders starting out as externally funded lending programmes.

Operating Costs

The control of operating costs is clearly required for sustainability. Above all, tendencies to expand staffing have to be balanced against cost considerations. This is an area in which donors were not very deeply involved in the past, although agencies like the IFAD increasingly require business plans as a condition for co-operation in a project. Such plans are drawn up together with the institution to be supported, with annual performance targets for critical cost elements such as specific bad debt provisions and total operational costs against operational incomes. Financial co-operatives and credit union assistance projects have developed standards relating operating costs to income and assets, and many NGOs have done the same.

Innovative financial institutions serving the poor have discovered interesting ways of controlling costs. In Bangladesh and Sri Lanka, for example, there is an abundant supply of local graduates who face uncertain employment prospects. This low-cost resource has been used by Grameen Bank and ASA in Bangladesh and by SANASA in Sri Lanka. In the case of Bangladesh, however, wages are determined by the government on a sectoral basis. Wage increases decreed for the banking sector in 1991 forced Grameen Bank to increase its staff costs by 40 per cent. BancoSol drastically reduced its overhead in relation to its total expenses, from 84 per cent in 1992 to 59 per cent at the end of 1994, through economies of scale and improved business practices (Gonzalez-Vega *et al.*, in this volume).

Sri Lanka: The SANASA Thrift and Credit Co-operative Societies

Established as early as 1906, this single-purpose savings and credit cooperative movement has experienced a remarkable revival during the last two decades. Due to voluntary management and meeting facilities provided by members, village-based primary co-operatives operate at exceptionally low costs. Loan and deposit contract components vary from village to village, since primary co-operatives establish their upper borrowing limits and interest rate spreads individually. Village groups provide loans exclusively from savings capital. The district and national umbrella structures service the needs of village co-operatives in the areas of auditing, training and liquidity management. The movement is vulnerable to outside interference, in particular externally imposed lending programmes. However, many co-operative societies continued providing deposit and credit services even during a period of political unrest in southwestern Sri Lanka during the latter 1980s.
Source: Kiriwandeniya, conference.

Credit unions and other co-operatives have customarily relied on volunteer ("honorary") leadership, including elected officers and committee members. (The *caisses villageoises* in Mali have done likewise [Chao-Béroff, in this volume].) Group lending imposes costs on group members, relieving the lender of certain tasks. The functions of group members include screening of loan applicants and loan purposes and enforcement of loan contracts through peer pressure and the application of other social control mechanisms based on custom and social norms. In addition, certain costs have been externalised, such as the use of banking regulators and examiners to review the safety and soundness of credit unions. ASA in Bangladesh enlists the middle class and wealthy to support efforts to improve the lot of the poor. External assistance is of course the ultimate in externalisation because of the very large sums available.

Managing Growth Rates

The experience of FUCEC in Togo (Camara, see Box 3) illustrates the difficulties a decentralised financial system may encounter in trying to reconcile growth and sustainability. Much poverty lending supported by donors, specifically microenterprise finance, is governed by the objective of scaling up operations quickly so that outreach is greatly expanded. This is held to be a condition for meaningful poverty alleviation. It may also be good management if there are economies of scale that facilitate embracing large number of clients as experienced by BancoSol. However, diminishing marginal returns apply (Gonzalez-Vega *et al.*, in this volume). Again, the will to keep growth within limits as determined by managerial capacity, internal control and sensitivity to risk may be viewed as a governance issue. Can the lender find its own balance and resist donor pressures to disburse funds ever more rapidly?

Paradoxically, caution is important in financial innovation because risks take time to discover. All lending programmes begin with negligible arrears, but repayment performance tends to decline after the initial momentum of newly initiated lending programmes. Many of the donor-supported programmes in the past have eventually been brought down by the accumulation of arrears. It is deceptive to proclaim success in the early years of a programme before it has seasoned (Von Pischke, Yaron and Zander, forthcoming). Financial innovations are hard to price *ex ante* because of the sluggishness and inevitability of risk. This basic uncertainty presents the largest challenge to sustainability. Risks are unlikely to be managed well in the absence of effective risk-oriented information systems. Risk management in response to information makes it possible for sustainable expansion to occur more rapidly than is otherwise possible, providing a basis for continuing innovation and responsiveness.

Maximising the Effect of Donor Support

Support for enhanced outreach and sustainability should avoid the mistakes of the past which range from the clearly dysfunctional to the mildly ineffective, and make best use of recent insights at the conceptual and operational levels. To achieve this requires changes in donor governance, defined as the structures which create incentives. Meaningful monitoring of relevant results and avoiding the repetition of actions that threaten sustainability are the starting points for reform. Lessons highlighted during the conference are as follows:

Sustainable Programme Size and Growth Rates

A participatory development approach, by its very nature, has to be based on demand articulated by the people and institutions concerned (Schneider with Libercier, 1995). Supply-driven disbursement targets, a major governance issue in many donor organisations, should not be the force behind the provision of financial services for the poor. Demand-driven programmes and development strategies diminish the probability that interventions are inappropriate. For example, when conditions for sustainable financial intermediation are not present, or are not very likely to occur over the life of a project or disbursement cycle, demand driven-initiatives would tend to uncover these more quickly and accurately than supply-driven ventures. Impediments also include a credit culture that encourages non-repayment by borrowers, incompetence or abuse by those in control, and the existence of controls and regulations that undermine innovation and sustainability.

The Example of the *Fédération des unions coopératives d'épargne et de crédit du Togo* (FUCEC - Togo)

The FUCEC was established in 1983 by forming a federation of 93 existing savings and credit co-operatives (*coopératives d'épargne et de crédit* — COOPECs). This network is the largest decentralised financing system in Togo. It is structured in three levels: individual COOPECs, which organise the collection of savings and the distribution of credit among their members; regional unions, each of which supervises and monitors the COOPECs located in a certain area (they have no financial function); and the federation, whose main tasks are expanding the network throughout the country and managing financial resources. For the latter function, the federation is endowed with a central fund which refinances the COOPECs and collects their excess cash.

As of 1995, the network had 155 COOPECs and nearly 50 000 members. The volume of deposits and loans had risen steadily, except in 1993 when the country experienced major social unrest. During this period, when the entire banking system was disrupted, the maintenance of lending even at a lower level than in preceding years was beneficial for the members and their families.

The fairly positive socio-economic impact of the network's activities was offset, however, by its poor financial results. From 1983 to 1993, the network received substantial financial assistance from abroad, mostly from USAID through the World Council of Credit Unions. The 1983-88 period was a start-up/promotion phase. A second phase (1988-93) was devoted to consolidation of the network's activities. For this second phase alone, USAID financial support was $4.8 million, covering not only the costs of technical assistance and investment in equipment for the central services but also those of developing the base-level COOPECs.

Comparative analysis of accounts underscores the flaws in the federation's management. In particular, it seems that the network did not know how to manage its expansion. The fact is that a change of dimension in a financial system involves increased needs for human and material resources, and hence supplementary costs. In the case of the FUCEC, this supplementary cost could not be covered by the federation's own earnings, and the central structure became even more dependent on external subsidies during the consolidation phase. The individual COOPECs recorded a profit without any subsidies, but this result should be interpreted with caution. Their provision for bad debts is insufficient, and they are not billed for the inspection, monitoring and training services provided by the federation. Moreover, an increase in the number of financial operations carried out by the COOPECs was accompanied by a drop in their efficiency. The weaker co-operative spirit of new members and the inability of administrators and managers to cope with the growing complexity of operations caused a rise in the number of bad debts. Finally, members and elected officers became less deeply involved in the various organs (administrative board, lending board and so on), which hurt the functioning of the entire system.

The founders of the FUCEC had emphasized the need to achieve financial autonomy, but it seems that this objective was forgotten during the network's phase of expansion. At the end of 1994, the unexpected withdrawal of USAID (for political reasons) forced the FUCEC to adopt a management policy aimed at making the system permanent. The three-year plan for 1995-97 provides for the decentralisation of technical services at the level of the regional unions, better control of overhead costs (particularly personnel costs), an increase in revenue (with the head office progressively billing the COOPECs for its services, and diversification of the federation's activities) and better control of bad debts in the base-level COOPECs. These measures are to be supplemented by training for the COOPECs' managers so that they will have a better grasp of management principles and techniques and will favour the appropriation of the system by the beneficiaries.

Source: Camara, *conference.*

Demand-driven strategies also temper the enthusiasm for rapid replication of programmes that are successful in one set of circumstances in areas where other conditions prevail. Another perspective on replication is that risks may not be similar across areas, populations, cultures, target groups and donors or other sponsors. Seasoning, which occurs when a programme is tested by risk and masters risk by finding ways of controlling or avoiding it, is important for sustainability. Unseasoned programmes are not mature: the viability of their culture and lifestyles, however promising, cannot be confirmed. Measurement of results is crucial to the control of risks and to the design of risk management innovations.

Another means of using demand-driven strategies is for donors to work only with local innovators rather than attempting to be innovative themselves or simply replicating innovations (Feige, in this volume). This approach is more consistent with the exploration of specific risks and builds on the specific strengths of local experiments, institutions and leaders. Donors following this approach should look for synergistic combinations of local resources and also for situations that are receptive to changes that are consistent with local values and opportunities.

One dimension of the scope for demand-driven progress is found in the research on BancoSol reported at the conference. This work lists three ways in which microenterprise lenders can increase sizes of loans to established clients. Policy-induced increases reflect changes in the lender's strategies, often based on cost calculations. Information-induced increases reflect experience that permits lenders to manage risks more effectively, increasing clients' debt capacities. Client-induced increases occur when borrowers improve their repayment capacities and seek larger loans (Gonzalez-Vega et al., in this volume).

Donors may seek to reinforce financial infrastructure, including development and supervisory capacity. This is a frequent donor priority, but it is not yet clear whether this, too, works only when it is demand-driven rather than transplanted through the internationalisation of banking norms and regulatory models. When intervention at this level is contemplated, attention should be focused on how the additional information such as on safety and soundness will be used, by whom and for what purpose. Donors should also be aware that procedures that deal with conflicts of interest and other perverse incentives may be culture-specific. These may be relatively simple to manage in large, diversified countries such as many donor nations, but not in small countries led by a small é•elite.

Forms of Donor Funding: Loans versus Grants

There is an emerging consensus that donors should fashion their interventions in such a way that competitive market forces are stimulated rather than suppressed, so that cost-reducing efficiency can determine market structure. From this perspective, subsidy is clearly seen as only a temporary phenomenon, as not being sustainable in the long-run (Zander, in this volume). The case for subsidy is strongest when nonmarket or social work aspects of assistance are stressed, such as health and education, although even here there are dangers of creating levels of activity that cannot be sustained without continued dependence on donors.

Another role frequently advocated for subsidy is that of initial investment costs, including financing the learning curve of local institutions attempting to innovate. Subsidy is most effective economically when it supports investments that would not otherwise be made, at least within a fairly long time frame. The objectives of such investments should include their phase-out as local recipients become capable of self-financing, independent of subsidy.

An example of this strategy are the *caisses villageoises* in Mali (Chao-Béroff, in this volume). Start-up costs may be extremely large because of the location and situation of the poor. CIDR estimates that costs associated with rural poverty, training, motivating women, transport, market research and special equipment required for computerised operations in hot, dusty and remote places amounted to about 45 per cent of total project costs. In other words, dealing with the illiterate, tradition-bound poor in remote and difficult locations is almost twice as costly as working with the somewhat more fortunate urban poor.

Apex Lenders and Institution Building

One form of investment subsidy is in apex or wholesale financial institutions that can serve numerous retail institutions that serve the poor directly. Structures involving apex financial institutions are common in co-operative finance and also in banking where city banks provide services to country banks and central banks work closely with city banks to maintain a healthy banking system. Donors are currently supporting several contemporary efforts to establish apex or "second floor" financial institutions that would lend to specialised retail financial institutions and would also be open to NGOs. Examples are the Palli Karma Shahayok Foundation established in Bangladesh with encouragement from the World Bank (Choudhury, conference) and FondoMicro in the Dominican Republic (Davalos, conference).

FondoMicro is a vibrant apex lender that started as a wholesaler of external funds to microlenders in the Dominican Republic. Access to subsidised funds enables FondoMicro to be financially self-sufficient while providing lines of credit to microlenders at about 85 per cent of the local commercial prime rate (Davalos, conference). However, its lending rate forecloses the possibility of raising funds from local banks, which would provide funds only at or above the local prime rate. This makes FondoMicro's long-run usefulness problematic because it is not in a position to obtain intermediate market resources or to have well-distributed risks on both sides of its balance sheet.

FondoMicro lends based on the business plans of its retail microlender clients, especially forecasted cash flow and expected performance. It exercises a commercial lender's customary power of control and has discontinued lending, without taking any losses, from microlenders in which it has lost confidence.

A focused approach to subsidy for institution building is found in the "self-administered capital funds" provided by German Federal Ministry for Economic Cooperation and Development (BMZ) (Feige, in this volume). These funds are provided as grants to NGOs or other private agencies lending to the poor that are judged to have good prospects for viability based on performance to date and the adoption and use of banking practices. The grant is intended to promote outreach while sustaining or improving good practice. The grant is not linked to technical assistance because the recipient institution is judged not to require it or to be sufficiently competent to engage technical assistance directly if needed. Likewise, the grant has no conditions requiring changes in the *modus operandi* of the lender. The recipient has complete discretion in the use of the grant to achieve efficiency and outreach within a broad general agreement with BMZ. Assuming satisfactory performance, the grant passes unconditionally and irrevocably to the lending agency at the end of the agreed project period.

"Market" Rates to Ultimate Borrowers

Subsidised interest rates on loans to target-group borrowers is usually dysfunctional. Its unfortunate results take time to become apparent, depending in part on the amount of the subsidy. Essentially, the damage of subsidies is to distort financial markets. Interest rates that are not rational in the economic sense of being sustainable and efficient misallocate resources. Low rates on loans also lead to low rates on deposits, depriving potential savers from investing in remunerative financial instruments, while precluding intermediation of savings by low-rate lenders.

Cheap funds provided by noncommercial sources make it difficult or impossible for an unsubsidised local financial innovator to be a low-cost supplier, retarding the growth of the financial sector. Competition from unduly low-priced loans can devastate the informal commercial financial sector, which may even be a programme objective. Given the unsustainability of donor-funded programmes and institutions in the past, however, one wonders whether that sector will re-emerge to serve the target group after the donor-funded activity lapses.

Subsidy also invites lack of diligence in lending, if not outright abuse, which in finance includes broken loan contracts. When nonrepayment becomes common practice, not to say an art, the consequences are twofold. The first is the unsustainability and destruction of the lender or lenders concerned. The second becomes obvious in the longer run: the costs of developing sustainable financial arrangements are greatly increased. Any innovator has to overcome the widespread assumption that a loan is a grant, or that a significant part of it is.

For these reasons, donor funded credit should be loaned to target group members at reasonable rates of interest. This proposition is now widely accepted but perhaps not always thoroughly understood within the framework of sustainability requirements. Attempts have often been made to charge "market rates," using a formal sector reference point such as the commercial bank prime rate on loans to good commercial clients. This rate is not reasonable on loans to the poor, however, because they are a different market than good commercial clients of commercial banks. Also, where poverty lending is an innovation, by definition, there is no existing formal market. The project creates its own market, an entirely new one, and requires its own appropriate rate or rates.

The only sustainable rate is one that covers the lender's costs in the long run. A reasonable strategy could even include initial rates higher than the rate that is estimated to be sufficient. The premium could cover unexpected risk. Its removal with experience showing that it is excessive results in tremendous goodwill and favourable publicity and provides a continued competitive edge to the lender.

Concern for risk leads to attention to a lender's permanent capital, the portion of its balance sheet that ultimately shoulders risk. Davalos implies that subsidies should be directed at capital and that paradoxically they can be debilitating to sustainability.

Grants and other soft funds, when handled properly and used to form a capital base, may aid in achieving break-even results and preparing institutions for further growth. But often their conditionalities do not induce financial discipline and know-how. At the other end of the spectrum, as sustainability is stressed, some policy designers forget that a capital base is necessary in order to cover basic costs and leverage properly. Grants are not evil *per se*, but when an institution's viability depends solely on them, they become a double-edged sword.

In microfinance, often a first priority is covering the cost of funds and administrative expenses out of interest income (Rhyne and Otero, conference). The deficiency of this approach is that it ignores the cost of risk when this cost is not fully reported in financial statements. The cost of risk is found in loans in arrears and in bad debt losses, which may be difficult to project and which are sometimes underreported in practice by insufficient provisioning for these losses. The conceptual flaw in starting with administrative cost coverage as the proxy for self-sufficiency is that these costs are qualitatively different from bad debt losses. The former are almost fully under the control of the lender, while the latter are only indirectly so. Losses on bad debts are much more likely to put a lender out of business than administrative costs.

Debt Conversion as a Source of Funds

An initiative that attracted attention at the conference was the possibility of using debt conversions as sources of funds for participatory development activities, defined as involving decentralised financial intermediaries and NGOs with outreach to the poor (Libercier, in this volume). Several debt-for-development swaps have occurred, using nonofficial developing country foreign debt purchased by Northern NGOs at large discounts in secondary markets. The debt is then sold by the NGO to the issuing country's central bank for local currency at a price in excess of the local currency equivalent of the cost of the purchase. The NGO then uses the local currency for activities in the debtor country, usually in collaboration with a local NGO as partner.

These deals require agreement among a number of parties: the debtor government has to agree to buy the debt at a favourable rate and has to have the funds to do so. The willingness of the government is usually forthcoming only if the Northern and local NGOs are considered trustworthy and professionally competent, and if the activities to be undertaken are consistent with government priorities. The Northern NGO has to have a plan acceptable to its local partner and to the government, as well as the ability to purchase the debt in the secondary market.

Several Northern governments have used variations on this type of transaction. For example, the Swiss government has forgiven LDC debt obligations that it officially guaranteed for imports of Swiss goods (Blesse-Venitz et al.). Counterpart funds equal to some fraction of the amounts forgiven have been set up by beneficiary governments for uses agreed by the Swiss and the NGOs concerned. In the Philippines, for example, proceeds of a debt swap were used by the Swiss to endow a foundation that provides funds to NGOs and community groups (FSSI, conference).

Debt-for-participatory-development swaps have involved a relatively insignificant amount of developing country debt, but they remain attractive because they offer a win-win outcome for participatory development once the loss in the value of the debt, a sunk cost, is recognised in the secondary market. More widespread use requires deals that are attractive to all concerned. Their net effectiveness is influenced by the additionality they include, i.e. activities that would not have been carried out using alternative means of funding.

Donor Commitments

Little sustainable progress can be expected to result from donor intervention unless donors' time horizons are consistent with those required for meaningful change, for the introduction and seasoning of innovations. In finance, this can require considerable time (Schmidt and Zeitinger). Accordingly, donors should take a long view. Commitments should also embrace change, so that they are continually renewed with better practice.

There remain two threats to the development of better practice. One is reluctance by donors to embrace risk explicitly. To do so may temporarily diminish the amounts that can be disbursed. In the long-run, however, experience with risk and its management is essential to sustainable financial arrangements. Dealing with risk in this manner requires a shift in attitudes towards development finance. However, it is a relatively straightforward extension of donors' concerns about the legal framework for financial development and the appropriateness of financial institutions, instruments and delivery systems (Lucano, conference).

Dealing with risk as a major organising principle for credit projects would also help define an appropriate time horizon for donors and their clients. No specific number of years can be prescribed as adequate or satisfactory. From the standpoint of sustainability, donors should remain with an initiative through at least one major cycle defined by risk. The cycle may be economic, political, climatic or whatever other type of change is reasonably likely to occur that would have an adverse impact on the credit scheme. The effects are probably most likely to occur at the level of the poor, but also include those that would affect the financial intermediary lending to the poor, such as organisational changes relating to scale or to client turnover as old clients leave and new ones enter.

Donor commitment should also be synchronised with the length of time required for the lending activity or institution to become independent of subsidy (Yaron, in this volume).

The second major threat to better practice and sustainability arises from shortcomings in donor supervision, specifically the failure to measure the impact of their interventions on the financial intermediaries that use donor funds to lend to the poor or to other target groups and assume the credit risk of doing so. Such institutions either make money, break even or lose money using donor funds. Knowing which of these possible results actually occurs, and quantifying it as precisely as possible, is tremendously important in the quest for sustainability and risk management.

Donor priorities change, and proposals for change should be weighed against the time horizon required for successful innovation in finance. Change creates the possibility that recipients may be abandoned and that commitments promised by donors may be revised downward. Such changes result from new political agendas in donor governments, adverse economic developments in donor nations and changes in relationships between a donor and recipient nations. Clearly, such changes can have a material or even devastating impact on subsidy-dependent programmes, which is another reason for working diligently for reducing dependence on subsidy.

Donor co-ordination is achieved to a considerable extent in microfinance practice, although one case in which a donor was displaced by another offering cheaper funds was reported at the conference (Davalos). There is a considerable consultation among microfinance providers and their bilateral and multilateral sponsors. The recent formation of CGAP, the Consultative Group to Assist the Poorest, (Al-Sultan, 1995) attests to this movement toward co-ordination, as does the identification of performance and reporting standards. However, much remains to be done on the identification of risk and the measuring of financial results.

Conclusion and Perspective

The conference confirmed that financial mechanisms in support of participation by the poor are a topic of great interest. A few agencies such as the IFAD, and an increasingly broader group of financial institutions faced with a daily challenge of cost-effectiveness and sustainability, have acquired a fund of insights that can contribute to current and future discussions. The field which is now focused on microfinance is expanding very rapidly. Several conclusions and perspectives can be drawn from the conference.

First, it is not easy to provide financial services for the poor which meet the dual challenges of sustainability and outreach. However, it does appear worthwhile when efforts are made to manage risks successfully over the long term. Strong political will can be helpful in shaping appropriate donor and local government commitments for development of these small financial markets. Good management of financial institutions is also important if operating losses are to be avoided and if fraud is to be minimised.

A conclusion for public policy is that no single model works best. A number of approaches have achieved varying degrees of success, and much has yet to be learned about comparative performance as microfinance becomes more seasoned by the risks it clearly faces.

Donor co-ordination does not seem to have reduced the range of efforts used to provide financial services to the poor. Retaining and even supporting diversity is important. The experts convened for this conference agreed that successful models cannot simply be replicated in social and economic environments that may differ greatly. Thus, no single model offers a panacea.

Second, demand-driven strategies have many advantages that are absent in donor-driven or supply side approaches. Demand-driven operations naturally facilitate local participation and tend to be decentralised, creating a sense of ownership or holding a stake that reduces cost and facilitates innovation. Appropriate social intermediation can provide a tremendous boost to financial intermediation, through group formation and establishing trust between group members. Emphasis on measurement of results, incorporating quality of financial intermediation as well as quantity, is a central concern of demand-driven practitioners. This requires more attention by donors and also by their clients.

Third, innovation is essential for creation of sustainable financial institutions serving the poor. The case of Grameen Bank suggests that while financial markets can be used to exploit the poor, innovative approaches in these markets can empower the poor. Financial innovation takes time because its result is a function of confidence and trust, as well as of risk. Donors should take a long view in their provision of support. Innovation requires delivery systems, which means that emphasis should be on the development of institutions rather than simply the implementation of programmes. Institution building should also be viewed broadly, including legal systems, the requisites of sustainable finance, such as good governance and controls, and responsiveness to clients as embodied in participatory systems. The ultimate client and his or her specific situation should guide development interventions. All of these concerns meet in pricing strategies applied in the provision of financial services for the poor.

Finally, it is difficult to evaluate the success of finance in combating poverty. It is clear, however, that poverty alleviation cannot be achieved by financial sector activities alone. This is because the causes of poverty are complex and stubborn. They also change over time and place. While finance can provide an extremely useful tool when it achieves outreach and sustainability, it remains only one of many instruments required to improve the welfare and productivity of the poor. For this reason, many providers of financial services to the poor also offer related forms of participation and assistance.

Even Grameen Bank reaches only the better-off among the poor. The lower half of the poor — the hard core poor — rarely participate in its programmes. In addition, Grameen Bank branches in poorer parts of Bangladesh are much less likely to be profitable than those in less poor locations. Microcredit is not the way out of poverty for many of the truly destitute, and the usefulness of credit to many of them may be limited.

Note

1.   The poor are so numerous that no simple definition can provide specific guidance to their identity. As far as financial markets are concerned the poor can be viewed as those who have no or little access to formal financial services (Schneider, conference).

Bibliography

Papers Presented at the Conference:

AUDINET, J.P., "Selected Lessons Learned from Evaluation of IFAD Projects in Southern Asia, West Africa and Southern Africa".

BALKENHOL, B. "The Social Dimension of Finance".

CAMARA, I.F. « Coût, performances et perspectives de pérennisation de la Fédération des unions coopératives d'épargne et de crédit du Togo ».

CIDR (Centre International de Développement et de Recherche), « Développer des services financiers en milieu défavorisé : le cas de caisses villageoises d'épargne et de crédit autogérées du pays Dogon ».

CHOUDHURY, S.H. "Wholesale Financial Services by Palli Karma Shahayok Foundation (PKSF) to Retail Micro-Credit Providers in Bangladesh: A Case of Partnership with ASA".

DAVALOS M., "Innovative Mechanisms for Funding of Capacity Development: The Case of FondoMicro in the Dominican Republic".

FEIGE, T., "Innovative Mechanisms for Funding of Capacity Development: The Case of the Self-Administered Capital Fund Instrument in German Bilateral Cooperation".

FSSI (The Foundation for a Sustainable Society, Inc.), "Debt for Development Swaps as an Additional Resource for Capacity Development".

GARSON, J., "Issues in Microfinance".

GONZALEZ-VEGA, C., M. SCHREINER, R.L. MEYER, J. RODRIGUEZ AND S. NAVAJAS, "Banco Solidario S.A.: The Challenge of Growth for Microfinance Organizations".

HASHEMI, S.M., "Building Up Capacity for Banking with the Poor: The Grameen Bank in Bangladesh".

IJIOMA, S.I., "Financial Mechanisms in Support of Participation of the Poor".

KIRIWANDENIYA, P.A., "Financial Mechanisms of the Participation of Poor: SANASA Movement in Sri Lanka".

LIBERCIER, M.-H., « La conversion de dette en programmes de développment local: mécanisme, expériences et potentiels ».

LUCANO, F., « Pérennisation des institutions de financement de la micro et petite entreprise: perspectives en Amérique Latine ».

MCGUIRE, P.B. AND J.D. CONROY, "Bank-NGO Linkages and the Transaction Costs of Lending to the Poor through Groups: Evidence from India and thePhilippines".

SCHNEIDER, H., "A Note on Main Issues".

YARON, J., "Performance of Development Finance Institutions: How to Assess It?"

ZANDER, R., "Integrating the Poor into the Rural Financial Mainstream: Issues and Options".

Other Materials:

AL-SULTAN, F. (1995), Opening Statement of IFAD President at the June 27 Meeting of the Consultative Group to Assist the Poorest (CGAP), Excerpts, CGAP Newsletter No. 1, December.

BENNETT, L. AND C. CUEVAS, eds. (1996) , "Sustainable Banking with the Poor," Special Issue of the *Journal of International Development*, 8,2, March-April.

BLESSE-VENITZ, J., A. GUGLER AND R. HELBLING (1995), *The Swiss Debt Reduction Facility: A State of the Art*, Swiss Coalition of Development Organizations, Bern.

GENTIL, D. AND P. HUGON, eds. (1996), « Le financement décentralisé : Pratiques et théories », *Revue Tiers Monde*, No. 145, January-March., D. GERMIDIS, D. KESSLER AND R. MEGHIR (1991), *Financial Systems and Development: What Role for the Formal and Informal Financial Sector?* OECD Development Centre, Paris.

KRAHNEN, J.P. AND R.H. SCHMIDT (1994), *Development Finance as Institution Building: A New Approach to Poverty-Oriented Banking,* Westview Press, Boulder.

SCHMIDT, R. AND C-P. ZEITINGER (1996), "Prospects, Problems and Potential of Credit-Granting NGOs," in L. BENNETT AND C. CUEVAS, eds, "Sustainable Banking with the Poor," Special Issue of the *Journal of International Development*, 8,2, March-April.

SCHNEIDER, H. WITH M-H. LIBERCIER, eds. (1995), *Participatory Development: From Advocacy to Action,* OECD Development Centre, Paris.

RHYNE, E. AND M. OTERO (1994), "Financial Services for Microenterprises: Principles and Institutions," in M. OTERO AND E. RHYNE, eds., *The New World of Microenterprise Finance: Building Healthy Financial Institutions for the Poor,* Kumarian Press, West Hartford, CT.

VON PISCHKE, J.D. (1991), *Finance at the Frontier: Debt Capacity and the Role of Credit in the Private Economy*, The World Bank, Washington, D.C.

VON PISCHKE, J.D., J. YARON AND R. ZANDER (forthcoming), *Why Credit Project Repayments Decline.*

YARON, J. (1992), *Successful Rural Finance Institutions*, World Bank Discussion Paper 150, Washington, D.C.

YARON, J. (1994), "Successful Rural Finance Institutions," *Finance & Development*, 31,1.

ZANDER, R. (1994), "Barriers to Credit Access in Rural Sri Lanka", in F.J.A. BOUMAN AND O. HOSPES, eds., *Financial Landscapes Reconstructed: The Fine Art of Mapping Development*, Westview Press, Boulder.

ZANDER, R. (forthcoming), *Rural Finance in Sri Lanka: A Comparative Analysis of Rural Finance Systems with Particular Emphasis on Informal Systems.*

PART ONE. FOCUS ON MAIN ISSUES

Integrating the Poor into the Rural Financial Mainstream: Issues and Options

Rauno Zander*

This chapter focuses on technical issues relating to the role of finance in rural development and alleviating rural poverty, highlighting the scope for and constraints on integrating the poor into rural financial markets. It contains a comprehensive checklist of sustainability potentials in project credit interventions. Annexes I and II provide five "best practices" and elaborate on "technical modules".

From Agricultural Credit to Rural Finance

Development thinking has undergone important changes during the past 40 years, although the basic requirements for successful rural financial intermediation remain the same, i.e. a clear orientation towards demand for financial services at the rural household level, successful management of costs and risks at the institutional level, and an enabling legal environment.

Since the 1950s, agricultural credit has been viewed as the primary tool for increasing farmers' productivity, and specialised rural credit institutions were promoted to provide input financing and raise agricultural production. In the 1970s, problems became apparent in the supply-led credit provided by newly established state-owned agricultural credit institutions with quickly expanding loan portfolios. Subsidised interest rates led to credit rationing in favour of rural élites, banking incomes did not cover service costs, and financial products were imposed on rural clients regardless of customer requirements. Lending without mobilising deposits also led to dependence on government or donor funds and thus made the institutions vulnerable to changing political environments and donor priorities.

During the 1980s, reform of the existing state-owned agricultural finance institutions became unavoidable after mounting foreign debt reduced the ability of governments to finance agricultural credit, donor emphasis shifted from credit to other priorities and many of the agricultural finance institutions were decapitalised and kept alive only through government budget allocations for loan write-offs or capital injections.

Major issues emerged which continue to influence policy objectives for developing rural financial markets to the present. These include charging interest rates for loans and deposits over and beyond the inflation rate with an adequate spread to cover service costs, improving the self-reliance of rural finance institutions through increased mobilisation of deposits, promoting decentralised institutions at the village level, and a governance structure that ensures sustainability through professional management of costs and risks.

Donors focused on furthering the outreach of financial institutions to low-income rural households by lowering the access barriers for the poor to rural financial services and replicating successful models such as the BRI Indonesia, the Grameen Bank, and the thrift and credit co-operatives. The active participation of villagers in their local institutions also received more attention. In order to reach these strategic objectives, financial innovation became a matter of prime importance for officially sponsored development efforts.

Providing Financial Services to the Poor: Emerging Technical Issues

IFAD's Role

Providing financial services has become a major concern of projects of the International Fund for Agricultural Development (IFAD). Support for savings and credit services by IFAD is based on the conviction that the rural poor can be bankable. Credit and deposit services properly managed to protect participants can contribute to their economic and social advancement.

IFAD projects seek to reconcile the conflicting views inherent in the conventional approach to financial development: a) that of the financial intermediary for which IFAD's target group represents a major challenge because of perceived cost and risk implications of banking with the poor; and b) that of the poor household with its specific requirements for deposit and credit services. A basic test of a project's quality is how well it has harmonized the objectives of the institution and targeted clients.

The Three Levels of Intervention

When planning rural financial services projects, it is not sufficient to focus solely on the institution and the financial sector's environment. The project participant, with his/her specific demands for financial services, constitutes the starting point for formulating a project. The exclusive emphasis on institutional development of many conventional development projects could result in neglect of the demand side of financial services. However, the institution is simply a means to an end, that of meeting client demands. Thus institutional support is not an end in itself in the context of poverty alleviation.

Similar considerations apply to financial services. A field assessment of the requirements among targeted project participants may show that the demand for deposits, insurance services, leasing and hire-purchase exceeds their requirements for credit, or that demand for medium- and long-term credit outstrips lending facilities which are mainly short-term. The conventional notion that demand for credit among the poor is infinite, turns out to be untrue, particularly if loans are offered at positive real rates of interest with an adequate spread to cover costs, including risks.

In identifying the key technical issues for providing financial services to the poor, it is therefore necessary to distinguish between three different levels of intervention:

a)   the project client, as the prime target;

b)   the institutions, as the key instrument; and

c)   the policy, legal and regulatory framework, as the enabling environment.

Client/Household Level

Access

Improving access to financial services for low-income clients has been one of the overriding concerns of donors. However, experience shows that quantitative aspects have figured more prominently than the qualitative dimension of improving access to financial services. Development projects operate with fixed targets, which may not have the flexibility to adapt to changing environments during project implementation, and performance objectives that are limited to the implementation period of a project. As a result, clients from low-income households often have services for the duration of a project only, while a lasting customer relationship with improved access beyond the duration of a development project does not materialise.

Addressing the qualitative issue of improved access requires a sound grasp of financial contract components. Barriers to institutional credit are found in loan contracts in the form of collateral or guarantor requirements, which make it impossible for the poor to take out a loan, repayment terms that do not coincide with cash flow patterns, conditions for use of loans or loan sizes that do not match the effective demand. These contractual barriers to access by the poor have to be identified as an integral part of project design. Many of the IFAD-supported innovations have introduced credit or deposit products with contract stipulations that facilitate poor people's access to financial services.

Sustainability at the Client Level

Sustainability issues of rural finance arise at the institutional level (see below), but are equally important at the level of the rural household. Investments must generate an adequate, risk-adjusted financial rate of return in order to allow for a credit intervention. If a loan does not finance a viable investment, it is not sustainable at the client level.

Financial Services for Women

Women, especially those who head households in remote rural areas, are a particularly vulnerable segment of the rural population. IFAD focuses on facilitating access of women to financial services. Experience shows that women are reliable borrowers with a strong sense of dedication to a rural institution that provides the financial services they require. Depending on the social, cultural and economic situation, the framework for support to women may operate through ensuring equal access to female and male clients or through specific credit windows for women.

Realistic Assessment of Credit Demand

The resource limitations and liquidity constraints of low-income households do not necessarily translate into an effective demand for project-supported credit. The professional skills and management capacities of credit clients may be inadequate. Marketing opportunities might not be available. In other cases, production factors other than capital are limiting economic advancement: a line of credit will not automatically lead to benefits, unless there is assured access to inputs, cultivable land and appropriate technology.

Project lending operations can result in low rates of repayment because of inadequate assessments of the loan applicants' creditworthiness. The success or failure of a loan is largely determined by a competent initial appraisal of the borrower's debt repayment potential. Lack of professional analysis of the extent to which a resource-poor household can service loan repayments leads to over-ambitious credit programmes with low rates of repayment.

The Link between Financial Services and Poverty Alleviation at the Household Level

Production and consumption loans. Distinguishing between production and consumption loans may appear artificial in a subsistence environment, where the poor household forms an integral system with money being fungible. However, non-productive use of credit does not create income and can lead to problems in loan repayment. Improving the status of a poor borrower thus requires that loans are invested productively. Additional income can increase client assets and lead the way out of poverty.

Term structure of development credit. In many developing countries, practically no medium and long-term lending is available for smallholders. In the few cases where rural households have access to medium-term loans, mostly to finance small rural industries or petty trading, they have to pay floating rather than fixed rates of interest, thus constraining investment decisions based on expected net future cash flows. A potential mismatch of deposit and lending maturities is another reason for the short supply of term-lending since banks in rural areas do not mobilise sizeable deposit funds with a maturity of more than one year.

Asset creation. While increased income is an important indicator of reduced poverty in the short-term, asset-building of low-income clients represents the most sustainable way out of poverty. Assets such as land, livestock and agricultural equipment may be directly productive, while housing and household furniture increase the social status of the poor.

When effective demand for credit in a group targeted by IFAD is evaluated in marginal and remote rural areas, financial services — in particular credit — may turn out not to be the primary constraint within the rural economy. Financial services should be promoted cautiously in areas with a low savings potential, in economies with limited monetisation, and when the target group is already overindebted or cannot be expected to generate surpluses that permit capital accumulation. Deposit and credit activities should be complemented by support activities in the areas of marketing, skill training and development, with a sequencing that allows a phasing-in of financial services after essential preconditions in other areas have been met.

Institutional Level

Costs and Risks of Servicing the Poor

The dimension of risk. There are several kinds of risk that can impede the success of a development project, but here we will focus on lending risk, the probability of non-repayment of loans. Compared to conventional collateralised lending, loans to low-income borrowers certainly appear more risky, even though the poor may be more motivated to repay. In many instances, loan instalments are paid at the cost of decreasing the household's asset base, if low-income borrowers repay regardless of the level of incremental income generated by the investment. However, the different ways of securing loans to the poor, through guarantors, small assets, hypothecating the investment item, joint liability or by loaning partly on deposits and providing the remainder unsecured, are less straightforward than lending against tangible collateral.

Although recent success stories have shown that the risk of banking with the poor may be more preconceived than real, expectations of a greater default rate are a major factor deterring financial institutions from dealing with the poorer strata of the village society. It is worth noting that the risk aversion of many rural financial institutions led to heavily distorted deposit-to-loan ratios at the branch level, resulting in an outflow of capital from rural areas, thus contributing to a scarcity of investment capital in rural areas rather than helping provide investment funds for rural development.

However, the viability of a lending programme depends on repayment performance. Non-repayment can result from wilful default or inability of the borrower to repay. While wilful default can be reduced through strengthened enforcement measures or stronger peer pressure, non-repayment by a poor client is often due to circumstances beyond his/her control. Many externally sponsored programmes promoted investment packages which subsequently proved to be unprofitable. Credit should finance robust investments with cash flow prospects allowing for profits and margins for loan repayment. Professional vetting of loan applications can go a long way towards minimising the risk of non-repayment.

The cost dimension. The costs of providing financial services to the poor are another key consideration determining the degree of outreach by rural financial intermediaries to the poor. Small transactions with higher unit costs for processing and monitoring can restrict the outreach. Defaults also constitute costs for the intermediary in the form of reserves to be built up and provisioning for bad debts.

Forced expansion as a consequence of policy priorities or donor interventions may lead to a temporary increase in outreach to the poor. For example, subsidised lending or institutional support may enhance outreach only until these subsidies are terminated and the programme is exposed to market forces. Therefore, a lasting process of developing new customer segments from the poorer strata of society will only materialise if business procedures that reduce the overall costs and risks of banking with the poor are developed.

Managing Costs and Risks in Benin

IFAD financed the savings and loan co-operative system in a project co-financed with the World Bank. Credit recovery rates have been more than 97 per cent under the IFAD component at the time of project completion. The IFAD credit line under the project generated a positive financial spread for the savings and loan network and continues to be implemented given the sustained high credit recovery rates. A recent project completion report by the World Bank concludes that the IFAD line of credit is sustainable, and that the rural poor have developed an exceptional commitment to their microfinance institution.

Financial Innovation

Financial innovation enhances sustainability of institutions and their outreach to the poor.

Schrieder (1995) and von Stein (1991) recently proposed a useful distinction between different types of financial innovations:

a)   *Financial system/institutional innovations.* They can affect the financial sector as a whole, relate to changes in business structures, to the establishment of new types of financial intermediaries, or to changes in the legal and supervisory framework. Important examples include the use of the group mechanism to retail financial services, formalising informal finance systems, reducing the access barriers for women, or setting up a completely new service structure such as the Grameen Bank.

b)   *Process innovations.* They cover the introduction of new business processes leading to increased efficiency, market expansion, etc. Examples include office automation and the use of computers with accounting and client data management software.

c)   *Product innovations.* These include the introduction of new credit, deposit, insurance, leasing, hire purchase and other financial products. Product innovations are introduced to respond better to changes in market demand or to improve the efficiency of the financial intermediary. More diversified deposit services, formal insurance facilities and specialised term-lending products for the agricultural sector are but a few of the many examples for product innovations in the financial sphere.

Institutional Innovation in Indonesia: The P4K Project

IFAD initiated a new approach to credit for the poor through member-managed self-help groups. Credit from the main rural bank in the country is channelled cost-effectively to these groups for investments in viable micro-enterprise activities. Field extension workers serve the groups and help strengthen the link between the commercial bank and village groups. The loans to small farmers and landless people are accompanied by technology packages and extension services, and resulted in exceptionally high repayment rates of more than 95 per cent throughout the project's duration. Initial loans are as low as Rp 100 000, or $50, per month. The project is known in Indonesia as P4K, and the government recommended its replication through local resources on a national scale, leveraging out an additional $600 million with the PK4 approach for microcredit for the poor.

Changes in business processes or new financial products will have a better chance to reduce costs if the institution operates in a competitive financial market and is fully exposed to market pressures. Credit quotas, centralised and inflexible financial products and a disregard for services oriented towards effective demand constitute major current weaknesses, but also opportunities for efficiency-oriented innovation.

Deposit services need to be accessible in terms of minimum initial and running balance requirements, savings should be easy to withdraw and administrative procedures for opening and utilising savings accounts kept to a minimum. Demand-oriented credit services should reconcile the cost and risk considerations of the financial institution with customer preferences. Interest rates reflecting costs and risks will ensure better access to loans than subsidised credit lines which tend to be used more by wealthier villagers. Repayment periods matching positive cash flows of investments, timely availability of loans, and collateral arrangements which take into account the asset limitations of resource-poor households, should be tailored to customer needs in loan contracts and at the same time contribute to institutional viability.

Aspects of Participation in Financial Services Promotion

Two developments have enhanced participatory elements in financial services promotion: *a)* the organisation of project participants into groups as a retailing mechanism for credit, and *b)* the re-emergence of the co-operative model from a government-sponsored top-down model to a member-owned and controlled institution. This trend away from centralised lending institutions to decentralised financial intermediaries at the village level offers entry points and opportunities for participatory institutional governance.

Technical issues related to participation in informal credit-retailing groups concern: rules governing the group, to be determined and approved by its members; procedures for electing group officers and for soliciting the views of members in decisions affecting the group; and adequate controls with reporting to the group on financial status and irregularities in transactions affecting group members. Transparency is essential in group accounting procedures as it facilitates corrective actions. However, this element of participatory governance is often lacking in informal groups.

Participation is embodied in the co-operative institution. Modern rural co-operatives with a bottom-up "back to basics" approach, stressing the co-operative idea of help through self-help, have a better chance of making member participation work. The participatory elements in co-operative governance may carry more or less weight, depending on the overall functioning of the primary co-operative society. In essence, members of a co-operative have equal rights to vote, independent of the volume of their deposits. They approve the by-laws, the basic set of rules governing their institution. Members of the group are elected to the board of directors, and thus the group exercises indirect control over the affairs of their co-operative. In general, co-operative movements with functioning internal audit and control procedures that stay clear of government dominance in staffing and lending programmes have shown promising results as decentralised financial intermediaries in countries as diverse as Sri Lanka, Kenya and Paraguay, to name but a few of the many examples throughout the world.

Participatory aspects also figure prominently in providing access to financial services for rural women. While experience with separate institutions serving women exclusively is scarce and may not be cost-effective in many cases, support is generally directed towards broadening the female client base of existing institutions according to the following principles: *a)* where women can be assured equal access to financial services, a service structure exclusively for female clients should not be pursued; *b)* in cases where mixed groups of women and men are likely to fail, and where the institutional service structure requires specific staff skills to increase the outreach to women, lines of credit specific to women are the best option. These financial products should be integrated into the ordinary business structure of the institution over time, with specific training and management development activities by the project to create the necessary staff skills to serve female customers.

Sustainability at the Institutional Level

The sustainability of a rural financial institution depends on its financial performance. The determinant parameters are the management of costs and risks, the positioning of the institution in the market and its capacity to respond quickly to changing client demand. Equally important are professional skills and effectiveness of staff, operational efficiency, independence from subsidies, and a well-enforced legal and supervisory framework.

The IFAD "Financial Institutions Performance Assessment" contains a one-page set of performance parameters for institutional appraisal in project development and implementation. Focusing on isolated benchmarks can lead to misinterpretations when assessing institutional sustainability or prospects for attaining it. High repayment rates may be the result of a non-viable, cost-intensive approach, while low operational costs can imply high-risk business without a broad client base. High net profits may be due to inadequate provisioning, and a positive net worth may result from considerable, though singular, capitalisation by grant inflows. Therefore, it is important to look at overall financial performance and not confuse single benchmarks with the overall financial status of an institution.

In providing financial services to the poor, financial discipline is even more important than when dealing with a broader mix of rural deposit and credit customers. A temporary strengthening of weak institutions or, on the other hand, a permanent weakening of strong institutions may be the result of financial assistance without consideration of the cost and risk dimensions of providing services to the rural poor. There are many instances where financial institutions view additional customers from lower income groups as a market segment worth developing. If market outreach considerations of existing financial institutions is also the basis for donor assistance, donor-sponsored financial services will be in step with the business interests of financial intermediaries.

Macro Level[1]

The government has a major role to play in creating a macroeconomic environment conducive to rural financial institutions. Effective monetary policies to control inflation rates instil confidence in the financial system and can significantly increase domestic savings, while reductions in the fiscal deficit lower the level of public borrowing. Liberalised exchange rates can raise agricultural prices and may stimulate aggregate agricultural output. Similarly, revisions in the tax regimes for agricultural export commodities can open up additional opportunities for small and primarily subsistence farmers.

Financial sector policies, above all the market determination of interest rates, have an important bearing on the access of more marginal clients to financial services. The general arguments in favour of positive on-lending interest rates put forward by Gonzalez-Vega are well known, and are also emphasized in Jacob Yaron's contribution. Interest rate subsidies are easy to phase-in but hard to phase out. They undermine institutional viability and promote leakage to borrowers other than the intended project participants. However, directed credit, for specific types of borrowers or utilisation in situations where market finance is not readily forthcoming, should not be confused with subsidised credit.

Safeguarding equal access for women to financial services constitutes an important issue for policy dialogue. Ensuring commitment at the highest political level paves the way for instituting legal reforms and adjusting financial institutions towards increasing their outreach to female clients.

IFAD investments are project-specific with no direct lending for Structural Adjustment Programmes or Financial Sector loans. Therefore, IFAD project formulation aims at identifying strengths and weaknesses in institutional structures and existing financial sector policies and at defining opportunities and possible constraints for the prospective project. A country's legal and prudential framework influences the design of innovative and catalytic projects. The legal form and supervisory requirements for NGOs differ from country to country, as do accounting standards and auditing and supervisory requirements for financial intermediaries. While innovative group formation and decentralised financial management may be backed up by the appropriate sector framework in one country, the conditions may not be right in other countries in the same region. The same applies to financial intermediation in financially repressed economies. If deposits of the poor lose purchasing power and loans with administered interest rates have little chance of reaching the poor, project design would have to be adjusted accordingly.

The financial sector and macro conditions therefore set the basic framework for feasible and for "no-go" situations in promoting rural financial services for the poor.

Checklist of Sustainability Potentials in Project Credit Interventions

(A) No or Low Potential	(B) High Potential

I. Project Approach and Design /Household Level

- Overemphasis on credit	- Mobilisation of indigenous financial resources
- No demand assessment for FSs[a]	- Professional demand assessment for FSs
- Dependence on external assistance and subsidy	- Viability of project interventions at all levels
- High external technical assistance	- High indigenous human resource mobilisation
- Top down approach without market orientation	- Demand, market and customer-orientation
- Without involvement of "beneficiaries"	- Village-based genuine co-operative approach
- Projected long-term hypothetical incremental income	- Planned short-term secure incremental income
- High recurrent costs and low or no viability	- Cost-effectiveness and high viability
- Insincere support and low risk aversion	- Professional support and high risk aversion
- Complex external technology	- Improved local and appropriate technology
- Operating under complex alien norms	- Operating under transparent legitimate norms
- Without or against legitimate leadership	- Under legitimate leadership
- Complex project organisation	- Simple and transparent project organisation
- Legal insecurity	- Legal security
	- Distinct project M&E, control and audit.

II. Participating Financial Institution

- Subsidised, directed and limited services	- Viable and customer-oriented services
- Overburdening of PFIs[b] through project credit	- Capacity adequate participation of FIs[c]
- Government-controlled institutions	- Private sector institutions
- High transaction costs (operation & risks)	- Low transaction costs (operation & risks)
- Low productivity and low motivation	- High productivity and high motivation
- Low financial performance (CAMEL)[d]	- High financial performance (CAMEL)
- Lack of cost-effective retailers/intermediaries	- Involvement of cost-effective intermediaries
- Credit based on project models	- Credit based on character and capacities
- Inadequate management information and control	- Adequate management information and control
- Erratic and unprofessional audit	- Regular and professional audit

III. Macro-Policy Environment

- Insufficient political commitment/responsibility	- Firm political commitment/ responsibility
- Centrally planned economy	- Pluralist and market oriented policies
- Low subsidiarity/centralised decision making	- High subsidiarity/delegated political authority
- Negative and subsidised interest rates	- Positive and cost-covering interest rates
- Ineffective regulation and supervision of FIs	- Effective regulation and supervision of FIs
- Limited government/project accountability	- Clear government/project accountability

---

a.   FS: Financial Services.
b.   PFI: Participating Financial Institution.
c.   FI: Financial Institution.
d.   CAMEL: Capital Adequacy, Asset Structure, Management of Risks, Earnings and Liquidity.

Technical Tools and Best Practices

Providing sustainable access to rural financial services for households at the lower end of the income scale constitutes a challenge. Many projects have failed, and the scope for replicating successes can be limited because social and sector conditions vary from country to country. As an institution mandated to design innovative and catalytic interventions, IFAD puts particular emphasis on learning from project experience together with our partners in the field, and distilling elements that contribute to successful financial services promotion. Thematic studies and the compilation of lessons learned are prepared by the IFAD Office of Evaluation and Studies.

IFAD has created a forum for collecting and disseminating best practices in providing financial services to the poor (see Annex I) through its Technical Assistance Grant programmes to Regional Agricultural Credit Associations (RACAs). Our assistance to the RACAs is based on the belief that the best insight into strengths, weaknesses, opportunities and risks in microcredit for the poor derives from the experts most closely involved, bankers who do business with the rural population as a matter of daily routine. Valuable lessons have already been distilled, and the joint programme of identifying best banking practices for serving the poor is continuing. Exchanges with relevant agricultural credit institutions have already yielded results in the areas of collateral substitutes, poverty targeting and customising financial services with a view to including poor households in the portfolio of banks, which have proven useful in developing IFAD projects.

IFAD is synthesising pertinent project design and implementation issues in the form of technical modules. These guiding tools are grouped under different subject clusters, comprising innovative, proven approaches. They will be continuously compiled and updated by experience from projects, and also through workshops with practitioners and experts from the field. Annex II provides some examples of relevant technical tools under the Rural Financial Services Cluster which directly relate to issues highlighted in the first part of this chapter.

Conclusions

IFAD's 18 years of experience in promoting financial services for the poorest of the economically active poor shows that rural low-income clients can be bankable. However, a demand-driven support strategy with the requirements of the ultimate client as the primary focus requires an approach integrating the client and institutional and financial sector issues and options. The failure of many past programmes shows that there are no shortcuts for promoting financial services for the poor. Demand for adequately priced loans for the poor with margins for operating costs and risks for the lending institutions is not unlimited. The effective demand for credit among the poor can be much less than assumed. In addition, if clients' demand is not assessed, support for institutions may not automatically percolate to the intended beneficiaries.

However, professional assistance in assessing effective demand for financial services at the client level and thorough appraisal of the current status and future potential of financial intermediaries can contribute to institutional viability and the economic advancement of rural households.

Note and References

*   Technical Adviser, Rural Credit and Institutions, IFAD. The views expressed are those of the author and should not be attributed to IFAD.

1.   Policy and sector issues related to IFAD's provision of rural financial services will be addressed in an IFAD Policy Paper to be released in 1997.

Annex I: **Five "Best Practices"**

Five essential elements for promoting rural financial services have been identified in an earlier IFAD study on weaknesses, lessons learned and emerging experiences in providing financial services to the poor (Bechtel and Zander, 1994). These best practices summarise basic notions and building blocks for project development, to be complemented by thematic lessons learned and specific technical tools.

(1) Assess costs and risks

Focusing on the costs and risks of existing as well as potential project-induced activities of a participating financial institution (PFI) is a simple starting point for projects to promote financial services. However evident the need for sound cost and risk assessment and management may be, cost and risk considerations often rank far behind targets for providing credit and overly ambitious projects without due regard for the capacity of the PFI to provide services.

(2) Emphasize responsive service structures

Understanding, sharing and incorporating priorities of partner institutions and project participants is another important strategic element. The need for a responsive project design arises at two levels: first, between the financial institution and project design and implementation. An external development intervention that is sensitive to the priorities, constraints and potentials of a PFI should be based on understanding of local institutions by project designers. The second level of responsive service structures is concerned with the relationship between the PFI and project participants. IFAD projects are characterised by a strong emphasis on client demand and beneficiary participation during project planning and implementation. The greater the responsiveness of project-supported institutional services to beneficiary priorities, the greater the prospects for a durable project impact.

(3) Protect clients' interests

Mobilising small-scale deposits is only part of a comprehensive savings service package. Petty savings from resource-poor households need operative protection against loss of deposits. Misappropriation in savings and credit groups as well as imprudent lending from internally generated deposits threaten the security of savings accounts. Borrowers under a project umbrella require customer protection as well. They have to be shielded against the risks of project-induced investments.

(4) Improve borrower screening and loan appraisal

Assessing effective credit demand based on repayment potential requires certain skills in an institution. While local expertise is a useful input for the initial vetting of loan applicants, financial appraisal before sanctioning a loan should be left to the staff of microfinance institutions. The success or failure of a loan depends to a large degree on an accurate appraisal of the customer's repayment capacity. Weaknesses at this early stage of credit management can make the difference between the failure of project-supported credit and achieving high rates of repayment, thus determining the overall viability of the intervention.

(5) Build on institutional potential

Financial institutions with a track record of effectively providing services to resource-poor households are a safer bet than creating new institutions. Possible constraints in terms of training, office automation, accounting and loan supervision should be addressed through the project and assistance provided for fine-tuning planning, management and control techniques.

Annex II. **Technical Modules**

Financial Services Demand Assessment (FSDA)

Focus on the Client. When dealing with marginal and resource-poor households, estimates of the financial return of a credit-financed investment are not the exclusive criteria for phasing in additional lines of credit. Understanding the requirements and constraints of a low-income household also requires knowledge about the financial status of the client's household, income size and structure, and indebtedness before the project. The household's exposure to the informal and semi-formal savings and credit systems can provide valuable information on patterns of demand for financial services. The FSDA also includes a structured method for assessing the investment preferences of the prospective project participants as seen by themselves. Generally, the people themselves know best what type of investment pays off in their village economy.

Integrating Informal Finance Systems

Building on Indigenous Financial Technologies. Informal finance systems are familiar to and fully accessible by the poor. Financial technologies are adapted to the needs of remote and subsistence-based village economies. The very existence of informal finance proves that credit and deposit services can be provided with full coverage of costs and risks, even in isolated and remote rural locations. However, protection for savings deposits is lacking with informal intermediaries, and they can employ exploitative and usurious business practices. Their potential contribution towards enhancing equitable access to financial services on terms attractive for rural people varies. In principle, there are three options for integrating informal finance systems in project development: *a)* modernising existing systems, *b)* integrating technologies of the informal sector into financial products of formal financial institutions and *c)* a direct linkage between informal and formal financial institutions. IFAD has gained the most experience in upgrading informal groups at the village level to retailing institutions for lines of credit from banks or other "wholesale" institutions. (Similar experience is reported by McGuire and Conroy in this volume.

Project Risk Fund (PRF)

Hedging against Non-Repayment Risks. This arrangement provides coverage for part of the expected default risks. Unlike with a conventional guarantee, there are inbuilt incentives for the participating financial institutions (PFIs) to keep the default level low. There are different types of project risk funds to be replenished from part of the on-lending spread, non-banking income from IFAD funds, counterpart funds for technical assistance, etc.

Leveraging out the PFI's Own Resources. The project risk fund facilitates the recycling of loanable funds by intermediaries with excessive deposit-to-loan ratios. In essence, the arrangement foresees coverage of the expected default risk by way of an upfront provision for bad debts. The comparatively small amount of the PRF thus has a high leverage effect by leveraging out locally mobilised capital for lending to the low-income segment of the village economy. The PRF facilitates development of banking with the poor as new market niches by domestic financial institutions.

Bibliography

ADAMS, D.W. (1995), "From Agricultural Credit to Rural Finance", *Quarterly Journal of International Agriculture*, 2.

BECHTEL, P.K.H. AND R. ZANDER (1994), "Providing Financial Services to the Rural Poor: IFAD's Experience, Challenges and Evolving Approaches", Staff Working Paper No. 16, International Fund for Agricultural Development, Rome.

SCHRIEDER, G. AND F. HEIDHUES (1995), "Reaching the Poor through Financial Innovations", *Quarterly Journal of International Agriculture*, 2.

VON PISCHKE, J.D. (1991), *Finance at the Frontier: the Role of Credit in Development of the Private Economy*, EDI Development Studies, Washington, D.C.

VON STEIN, J. (1991), "Finanzinnovationen", *Wirtschaftsstudium* (1).

How To Assess Performance of Development Finance Institutions

Jacob Yaron

The objective of this paper is to provide a comprehensive method of assessing and measuring overall financial costs involved in operating a development finance institution (DFI) and quantifying its subsidy dependence. It suggests moving away from overreliance on financial profitability ratios of conventional accounting procedures for financial analysis of DFIs. A subsidy dependence index (SDI) is proposed for measuring a DFI's financial performance. The SDI tries to provide a public interest analysis of a DFI's financial performance and dependence on subsidies. It involves taking into account the full social costs entailed in operating a DFI, including the complete value of all subsidies received by the institution. The SDI makes explicit the subsidies needed to keep the institution afloat, much of which is not reflected in conventional accounting.

The establishment of formal agricultural credit systems in most developing countries during recent decades was based on the belief that widespread shortages of short- and long-term finance constituted a constraint which slowed down agricultural growth and development. The absence of what was considered affordable formal credit was also blamed for delaying, if not preventing, timely adoption of new production technologies and the dissemination of non-labour intensive inputs such as fertilizer, thereby slowing down the growth and development of the agricultural sector. The "infant industry" argument was frequently used to support intervention in financial markets in favour of the sector as a whole or for specific segments of it (small-scale farmers, promotion of new technologies such as shallow tubewells, etc.)

The World Bank World Development Report 1989 summarises the performance of DFIs as follows:

> The most common type of nonbank intermediary in developing countries is the development finance institution (DFI). Most are public or quasi-public institutions that derive much of their funding from the government or from foreign assistance. Originally, they were intended to provide small- and medium-size enterprises with the long-term finance that commercial

banks would not supply. During the 1970s, that mandate was broadened to include the promotion of priority sectors. Using government funds, DFIs extended subsidised credit to activities judged unprofitable or too risky by other lenders. In practice, the DFIs found it difficult to finance projects with high economic but low financial rates of return and remain financially viable at the same time. (p. 106)

The premise underlying the DFIs' role changed significantly during the 1970s. In many instances, private sector financial institutions were especially weak, and distortions from macroeconomic and financial sector policies adversely affected the emergence and performance of DFIs. International donors increasingly supported state-owned DFIs, which in effect substituted for self-sustaining, private financial institutions. The rationale for administrative intervention in the financial market shifted from resolving a general shortage of investment financing to channelling credit to what were believed to be underserviced priority sectors or targeted clientele.

Intervention in Rural Credit Markets: The "Second Best" Argument

The widespread distortions affecting the agricultural and rural sectors, which were caused by economic policies, provided additional arguments for those favouring state intervention in financial markets to compensate the agricultural sector for the urban-biased macro-policies, such as overvalued exchange rates, price controls on agricultural products, public underinvestment in rural infrastructure, overtaxing of agricultural exports, and overprotection of domestic industrial inputs which were used as agricultural inputs. Many donors began channelling concessional credit to agricultural credit programmes, based on the "second best" argument, i.e., mitigating the impact of "urban-biased" policies. Governments in developing countries have intervened heavily in rural financial markets, and have aimed at supplying affordable credit to small-scale farmers and rural entrepreneurs, who were perceived as a clientele with no alternative access to formal credit markets. Imperfections in rural financial markets led to a discrepancy between social and private costs and benefits, and provided a justification for intervention in rural credit markets. As private returns were estimated to be below the social ones, the intervention was intended to overcome this market failure and spur investments that would not have materialised otherwise.

Imperfections in rural credit markets stem from the characteristics of agricultural production. Agricultural income is markedly influenced by climatic conditions, which expose the rural population to higher risks than in other sectors. In addition, crops may often be subject to drastic price fluctuations, causing further variability in farmers' income and the related repayment capacity. Those risks are typically highly correlated across wide segments of the farming community. Lending in rural areas often implies servicing a widely dispersed clientele, which entails high transaction costs. In many developing countries, an inadequate legal system and enforcement proceedings have contributed to the reluctance of commercial banks to engage in lending to the rural population. A related problem is the frequent lack of secure land tenure, leading to a lack of collateral or limiting possibilities of foreclosure.

When commercial lending institutions have been active in rural areas, in most instances they have focused on large-scale farmers while small-scale farmers have been ignored, due to the significant lending costs of processing and servicing unsecured small loans. The prevailing, often unjustified belief that small entrepreneurs pose a greater risk than large ones has encouraged catering to large borrowers. In the absence of strong formal credit markets, informal credit markets have flourished in many developing countries. These informal markets are characterised by low transaction costs for the borrower and rapid disbursement of funds. These features can be attributed to close familiarity with the borrower's creditworthiness and efficient loan collection mechanisms. As a result, the informal credit market is either the exclusive or the preferred source of credit in rural areas in spite of high interest charges. However, most informal lenders are limited in the term diversification of their portfolio and operate within restricted geographical areas.

Intervention has also been considered justified for reasons of equity. The short-term, high-cost financing by moneylenders was considered an impediment to growth and equity. The social cost of intervening in financial markets was perceived to be minor. Three basic forms of intervention in the rural credit market have prevailed: *(1)* the administrative allocation of funds to agricultural activities and rural areas, *(2)* an imposed interest rate ceiling, and *(3)* regular support for DFIs to cover their usual deficits. These interventions attempted to influence the amount lent in rural areas and the price of loanable funds as well as to control the institutional development and mode of operation of the DFIs.

Overview of DFI Performance

By and large, past performance of the state- and donor-supported agricultural credit operations has been below expectations. Most of the programmes only reached a minority of the farming population, while benefits have been frequently concentrated among wealthier farmers. Many of the institutions established or supported for credit programmes have not developed into self-sustaining credit facilities. Furthermore, in many instances, these institutions have become dependent on large and increasing subsidies, which made credit programmes extremely costly for the sponsoring governments. For example, the agricultural credit systems of the World Bank's three most important agricultural credit borrowers in the 1980s, Brazil, Mexico, and India, have all suffered from severe equity erosion. In Brazil and Mexico, highly negative interest rates in an inflationary environment were responsible, while in India it resulted from dismal loan collection[1]. Administrative interventions in the agricultural credit systems of Brazil, Mexico, and India retarded the development of efficient financial markets and had negative implications for other sectors of the economy by depriving them of loanable funds and increasing their borrowing costs.

A World Bank study of agricultural credit projects in 24 countries points out that they have often failed to become vehicles for upgrading farm technology[2]. The programmes reached a minority of the farming population and benefits were frequently concentrated among wealthier farmers. For example, a study in Costa Rica has shown that income distribution could be significantly improved if credit subsidies were eliminated[3]. Many of the institutions established or supported for delivering credit programmes did not develop into self-sustaining credit facilities.

The disappointing performance of the credit supply-led approach can be attributed to two sets of issues: *(1)* some of the underlying premises of this approach were frequently not valid, and *(2)* the institutions and arrangements for implementing the policy were often unviable, or functioned in a policy and social environment hindering their effectiveness.

Lack of Savings Mobilisation and Misleading Performance Criteria

Many specialised agricultural credit institutions have suffered from innate deficiencies. They were often not designed to function as true financial intermediaries which mobilise deposits to make loans. Instead, these institutions have merely channelled government supplied funds to rural borrowers.

Rural financial institutions have not had to function under financial viability constraints because they had regular access to external funds at below-market interest rates. Together with the lack of competition and limited accountability, this has led to bad loans, extremely inefficient operations, patronage and other irregularities. A report prepared for the World Bank by local experts in India states: "During the election years, there is considerable propaganda from political platforms for postponement of loan recovery or pressure on the credit institutions to grant extensions to avoid or delay the enforcement process of recovery. The wilful defaulters are in general socially and politically important people whose example others are likely to follow." It is therefore not surprising that arrears of about 50 per cent have plagued this system. Furthermore, the report observes that "the general climate in rural areas is becoming increasingly hostile to recoveries."

The DFIs did not use commercial financial performance criteria, so lending institutions did not have incentives for strong loan-collection efforts. Instead, the performance incentives of specialised agricultural credit institutions have often been based on quick loan approval and disbursement, and rapid growth in the lending volume facilitated by rapidly expanding external funding from donors. Inadequate financial reporting practices have made it difficult to determine when and which payments are overdue. Typically, data on arrears (when available at all) only allowed for a partial analysis of the loan portfolio. This led to underestimating the arrears when the portfolio grew rapidly in nominal terms (high inflationary economies), and the loan portfolio contained considerable long-term loans or loans with grace periods. Major World Bank clients such as Brazil, Mexico, and Yugoslavia used stock measures of loan arrears, despite the fact that they were all plagued by high inflation. This resulted in a misleading picture of the quality of the loan portfolio.[4] Sufficient provisions for bad debts were not made and it was often impossible to assess an institution's viability.

As a result, financial data often present rosy scenarios, and, with the lack of adequate provisions for loan losses, the DFI's financial statements are likely to mislead the analyst. The overall cost of maintaining a DFI afloat is almost never presented. Many of the subsidies involved in the DFIs' operations, such as concessional financial resources that were made available by the Central Bank, or state repayment of foreign exchange losses on loans denominated in strong currencies, are not adequately captured in the DFIs' financial statements when the issue is the overall financial cost of maintaining the DFI afloat. Inadequate financial reporting has also contributed to lack of clarity on the DFIs' cost side. In many instances, the subsidies for the DFIs were not transparent and not funded from the budget, so there was little if any public debate on their costs, benefits and social desirability.

This analysis claims that much of the subsidy required to keep DFIs afloat is not covered by conventional accounting procedures, which were not designed for this purpose, and that measures for assessing DFI profitability have provided governments, donors and DFI management with an inadequate picture of the actual cost of DFI operations.

The Subsidy Dependence Index (SDI) of Development Finance Institutions

Two main problems face the analyst who must rely on conventional accounting data to measure the financial performance of development finance institutions (DFIs). First, the difference between the income and expenses (including reimbursement of specific expenses by state or donor) reflected in the DFI's income statement and those not recorded in the income statement, and, second, conventional accounting practices are not designed for all the kinds of subsidies received by a DFI.

The SDI is a user-friendly tool which provides a more comprehensive public interest analysis and assessment of a DFI's financial performance and subsidy dependence. The SDI reflects the overall social costs of operating a DFI, as it accounts for all subsidies received and places a value on the associated opportunity cost of the subsidies. It complements conventional financial analysis and improves the evaluation of financial institutions that receive subsidies. In effect, the SDI goes beyond financial analysis into the area of economic analysis by providing a meaningful picture of the cost side of DFI operations, which is only partly captured in conventional financial data.

The SDI computation enhances traditional financial analysis in three main ways: *(1)* it quantifies the impact of subsidies that affect the DFI's financial performance, making clear that much of the value of the subsidies is not recorded in the DFI income statement; *(2)* it suggests an index that measures the overall subsidy received by the DFI in relation to its primary source of income, the interest earned on its loan portfolio; and *(3)* it imputes the cost of capital of the DFI's equity. This last point resolves the issue of "costless" equity, thereby allowing a more meaningful comparison of the financial and economic costs of DFIs that are characterised by different equity-to-assets ratios.

Conventional accounting practices measure the cost of funds priced at their actual cost. The opportunity cost of a DFI's borrowed funds — that is, the cost the DFI would have to pay for its funds if access to concessional funds were eliminated — is not taken into account. In contrast, the SDI calculation assumes that the volume of the DFI's outstanding loan portfolio remains unchanged. Hence, the change is caused by substituting concessional borrowed funds with voluntary savings obtained at a market deposit interest rate. Thus, if the central bank loans to a DFI at 2 per cent, conventional accounting practices list the cost of the loan at 2 per cent per annum. However, if the cost of alternative nonconcessional funds is 12 per cent per annum, then the SDI allows for the 10 per cent difference in interest rates on those funds and identifies the subsidy the DFI obtains from it. The rationale is that if the subsidised DFI paid only 2 per cent per annum on central bank rediscounting facilities instead of the prevailing market deposit rate of 12 per cent per annum, the accounting profit and the financial ratios measuring the DFI's profitability would not indicate that they were due to the significant subsidy embodied in the cheap central bank rediscounting facilities. Concessional funding is the most common form of subsidy for a DFI, yet calculating the value of the subsidy implicit in the DFI's funds borrowed at concessional rates requires information not included in the DFI's financial statements. The same is true for the DFI's equity.

While a profit maximiser does not differentiate between profit that is dependent on or independent of a subsidy (as long as continued subsidy is ensured), a subsidy is crucial to the DFI's performance. The social cost of DFI operations, of which subsidies represent a significant share, is essential for determining the social justification of their existence, because rural DFIs are often public or quasi-public institutions. To illustrate the irrelevance of the conventional financial reporting system, it may be asked, for example, what is the meaning of a DFI's return on equity of 20 per cent when 50 per cent of the DFI's financial obligations are concessional funds borrowed from the central bank (rediscounting facilities) at an interest rate significantly below market deposit interest rates, and if the government assumes one-third of its payroll cost, 80 per cent of its loan losses and all training expenses.

Furthermore, breaking away from applying financial prices of inputs and outputs and the social cost of investing in the real goods sectors instead of shadow prices have become common practice in assessing and measuring the social desirability of investments. Applying economic shadow prices permits calculation of the economic rate of return (ERR), which often differs from the financial rate of return (FRR). Application of the SDI calculation seeks to achieve a similar goal: to measure more accurately the social cost involved in a DFI's continued operations. However, there is a difference between the ERR and the SDI approaches: the SDI does not claim to evaluate the social benefits of resource allocation through a DFI to the real goods sectors fully. Nonetheless, the SDI provides a better estimate of the social cost of the subsidy by applying approximate market interest rates to the financial resources used by the DFI.

The SDI addresses the need to improve the measurement of progress made towards phasing out credit subsidies, the assumption by the fiscal budget of funding responsibility for any remaining subsidies, and the reduction and/or rationalisation of directed credit lines, as required by the World Bank Policies

Guiding Financial Sector Operations

The dialogue with borrowing countries can be significantly enriched by using the SDI as a routine instrument for measuring a DFI's performance during appraisal, supervision and completion of projects. As with any other financial measurement tool, the SDI is of course only as accurate as the data used to compute it.

In summary, the SDI is instrumental in:

— placing the total amount of subsidies received by a DFI in the context of its activity level, represented by interest earned on its loan portfolio (similar to calculations of effective protection, cost of domestic resources or cost of job creation);

— tracking a DFI's subsidy dependence over time; and

— comparing the subsidy dependence of DFIs providing similar services to a similar clientele.

Calculating the SDI

Calculation of the SDI requires the use of certain procedures as well as judgement. Consistency from period to period is more important than the absolute accuracy of the figures used in the computation. The chapters in this volume by Gonzalez-Vega *et al.* and by Hashemi provide examples of calculation of the SDI for the BancoSol and Grameen Bank. The SDI ratio measures the percentage increase in the average on-lending interest rate required to compensate a DFI for eliminating all subsidies in a given year, while keeping its return on equity equal to the approximate nonconcessional borrowing cost. The index assumes, for simplicity, that an increase in the on-lending interest rate is the only change made to compensate for loss of subsidy. Although removal of subsidies received by a DFI is not always politically feasible or desirable, measurement of any subsidy is always warranted economically and politically.

Calculating the SDI requires aggregating all the subsidies received by a DFI. Then the SDI is simply a ratio of the total subsidy to the DFI's on-lending interest rate multiplied by its average annual loan portfolio, because lending is the primary activity of a supply-led DFI. Measuring a DFI's annual subsidies as a percentage of its interest income yields the percentage by which interest income would have to increase to replace the subsidies and provides data on the percentage points by which the DFI's on-lending interest rate would have to increase to eliminate subsidies.

The annual subsidy received by a DFI is defined as:

$$S = A (m - c) + [(E * m) - P] + K$$

where:

$S =$ Annual subsidy received by the DFI;

$A =$ Annual average outstanding funds borrowed by the DFI at concessional rates;

$m =$ Interest rate the DFI would be assumed to pay for borrowed funds if access to borrowed concessional funds were eliminated;

$c =$ Weighted average annual concessional rate of interest actually paid by the DFI on its annual average outstanding funds borrowed at concessional rates;

$E =$ Average annual equity;

$P =$ Reported annual profit before taxes (adjusted, when necessary, for loan-loss provisions, inflation, etc.);

$K =$ The sum of all other annual subsidies received by the DFI (such as partial or complete coverage of the DFI's operational costs by the state).

The financial ratio that is suggested as an SDI is:

$$SDI = S / LP * i$$

where:

$SDI =$ Index of subsidy dependence of DFI;

$S =$ Annual subsidy received by the DFI (see above);

$LP =$ Average annual outstanding loan portfolio of the DFI;

$i =$ Weighted average on-lending interest rate earned on the loan portfolio of the DFI.

An SDI of zero means that a DFI achieved full self-sustainability. An SDI of 100 per cent indicates that a doubling of the average lending interest rate is required if subsidies are to be ended. Similarly, an SDI of 200 per cent indicates that a threefold increase in the on-lending interest rate is required to compensate for ending the subsidy. A negative SDI indicates that a DFI not only fully achieved self-sustainability, but that its annual profits, minus its capital (equity) charged at the approximate market interest rate, exceeded the total annual value of subsidies, if subsidies were received by the DFI. A negative SDI also implies that the DFI could have lowered its average on-lending interest rate while simultaneously eliminating any subsidies received in the same year.

The SDI by itself does not clarify how the subsidy was used and whether most benefits were accrued to clients or were consumed by an inefficient bureaucracy. The latter question, though important, requires far more detailed data and even then is often subject to interpretation. The advantage of the SDI is its simplicity and, as such, it focuses exclusively on the value of subsidy received by the DFI. The SDI should be seen in some instances as a lower bound because full financing of DFI activities is likely to be difficult at current market borrowing rates (m) if a DFI's financial performance is dismal. However, calculating this lower bound is vital for ascertaining either the DFI's progress toward self-sustainability or the social desirability of continuing its subsidy.

Notes and References

1.   Yaron, J. and P. Siegel (1988), "Bank Lending for Agricultural Credit: FY82-88," Agriculture and Rural Development Department, December.

2.   Document JAC 88-35 of the Joint Audit Committee, "Approach Paper: A Review of Bank Lending for Agricultural Credit (1951-1987)", dated October 5, 1988, para. 6. The study covered the period before 1976.

3.   Vogel , R. (1984), "The Effect of Subsidized Agricultural Credit on Income Distribution in Costa Rica," in Adams et. al., *Undermining Rural Development with Cheap Credit*, Westview Press, 1984.

4.   Yaron, J. and P. Siegel (1988), "Bank Lending for Agricultural Credit: FY82-88," Agriculture and Rural Development Department, World Bank, December.

Bank-NGO Linkages and the Transaction Costs of Lending to the Poor through Groups: Evidence from India and the Philippines

Paul B. McGuire and John D. Conroy*

Transaction costs of lending and borrowing are a major barrier to providing access to microcredit services for the poor on a sustainable basis. Lenders typically incur a range of costs in providing loans, as do borrowers in receiving them. For smaller loans these "transaction" costs can be burdensome in relation to the value of the loan itself, from the perspective of either lender or borrower. A fortiori, in relation to the "micro" loans needed by the very poor, transaction costs typically associated with loans from orthodox financial institutions will almost inevitably prevent any such lending from occurring in the absence of subsidies.

Unless it can be demonstrated that transaction costs can be significantly reduced through innovative forms of financial intermediation, sustainable microcredit will not be possible.

This chapter draws on two case studies[1] to consider a number of issues relating to the transaction costs of lending to the poor, and the transaction costs faced by "micro" borrowers. The next section outlines the key features of the Banking with the Poor (BWTP) approach to microfinance, which involves linkages between banks, NGOs and self-help groups (SHGs). After that, the environment for linkages in India and the Philippines, the two countries considered in the case studies, is discussed. Then we present the findings of the Indian study concerning the impact of linkages on bank transaction costs, and following that we outline the findings of the Philippine study on the transaction costs facing NGOs and the implications for the sustainability of their operations. Finally, we draw on both studies to examine the transaction costs facing borrowers, and lastly, we summarise the key findings and offer some concluding comments.

The Linkage Approach

The Banking with the Poor project stresses the importance of linkages between commercial banks on the one hand, and NGOs and SHGs on the other, as a mechanism for channelling credit to the poor on a sustainable basis. This approach, referred to here as the "linkage" approach, has four key elements. First, it asserts that commercial banks, being the key financial institutions in most developing countries, have a critical role to play in making available some of their resources for providing credit to the poor. Second, it stresses the use of group lending strategies, i.e. organising poor borrowers into small SHGs which provide them with a mutual support network and ensure high repayment rates. Generally speaking, the poorer the borrowers, the more important is the potential role of such SHGs as a means of accessing them and serving their needs.

Third, this approach recognises that community-based NGOs generally have a comparative advantage over commercial banks in actually reaching the poor, reflecting factors such as proximity, trust, commitment, flexibility and responsiveness. Hence, NGOs have a vital role to play in lending to the poor, whether as financial intermediaries which borrow from banks and on-lend to SHGs, or as non-financial intermediaries which identify borrowers and establish and train SHGs. Finally, the approach recognises the importance of establishing lending to the poor on a sustainable and commercially viable basis, and argues that support from donor agencies should be directed specifically to this end. In general, donor support should accord priority to institutional development of microfinance NGOs and SHGs of the poor, rather than provide them directly with loanable funds, which can be obtained in much greater volume from commercial banks and other financial sector institutions.

While most successful programmes originally were established with significant grant funding, there is now a consensus that their further expansion to cover more than a minute proportion of the world's poor requires them to become self-sustaining. To become self-sustaining, programmes need access to commercial sources of finance. By using equity capital or members' deposits as leverage to obtain commercial funds, programmes also can expand their outreach beyond the limits of their own resources. Two main sources of commercial funds are available: deposits from the general public or borrowed funds from the commercial banking system. As a recent USAID study of eleven microfinance institutions (Christen *et al.*, 1994) has shown, these avenues are by no means mutually exclusive, and programmes are likely to rely on varying "mixes" of funds.

A wide variety of influences affects the roles of banks, NGOs, SHGs and other institutions in the microfinance "industry", or subsector, and the modalities of lending within it. Market forces (expressed through the cost and availability of funds from different sources), and the efficiency and effectiveness of the different institutional forms vying for a place in the field, will be important in the further development of microfinancing. Social, cultural, institutional and historical factors specific to each country, or even regions within countries, will also play their roles. Hence it is likely that the institutions adopted will differ significantly between and within countries and regions.

Nevertheless, the linkage approach, which is likely to be appropriate in many cases, offers a number of potential advantages since it:

— enables each institution in the bank-NGO-SHG chain to concentrate on what it does best, in line with its comparative advantage. NGOs and SHGs are able to exercise their comparative advantage in reaching the poor, while commercial banks are able to exercise their comparative advantage in financial management;

— makes use of existing institutions as far as possible. Most developing countries have well-established networks of commercial banks, providing services to a greater or lesser extent throughout the country, including provincial and rural areas. Linkages take advantage of these networks and enable NGOs and SHGs to complement the existing banking system where it is weak;

— helps integrate lending to the poor into the overall banking system, reducing the risk that it will be considered as merely an "add-on", a public relations exercise or a sop to political pressures.

Furthermore, by financing their lending through commercial banks, NGOs and SHGs also subject themselves to market-based quality control. Commercial banks are in a good position to monitor the programmes of NGOs and SHGs to which they lend and impose valuable discipline.

In light of the growing profusion of models for delivering microfinance, it is important to recall the particular advantages of NGOs, with their proximity, trust, commitment, flexibility and responsiveness to the poor, and that SHGs are the best means of organising the poor for microfinance. In combination with the commercial banking system, these people's institutions have the potential to assure sustainable microfinance services for the poor.

The Environment for Linkages

The environment for linkages between banks and NGOs differs in India and the Philippines. In 1991, the Reserve Bank of India issued a circular directive to all Indian commercial banks, encouraging them to deal directly with NGOs and SHGs to serve as financial intermediaries to the rural poor. The National Bank for Agriculture and Rural Development (NABARD) subsequently issued guidelines for a pilot project to link banks with SHGs. This policy support led to a rapid expansion of schemes. The *Best Practice of Banking with the Poor* (Foundation for Development Cooperation, 1995) noted that 2 260 SHGs had already been linked with 16 commercial banks and 12 regional rural banks. Programmes have continued to expand rapidly since then, and as many as 4 000 groups may now be in existence.

The Philippines have also placed greater emphasis on lending to the poor in recent years. For instance, the importance of access to credit in alleviating poverty was further recognised in the Social Pact on Credit, forged in 1993 between government agencies, government financial institutions, private banks, co-operative rural banks and farmers' groups. The Pact recognised the role of NGOs in providing the poor with better access to credit, although the official approach has tended to favour replicating the Grameen Bank for providing credit via state banks with support from government agencies. Nevertheless, the existence of a particularly vibrant NGO community has led to the establishment of linkages between commercial banks and NGOs as well. Early experience of linkages in the Philippines is documented in Banking with the Poor (Foundation for Development Cooperation, 1992a).

Linkages and Bank Transaction Costs

The Indian study (Puhazhendi, 1995)[2] focused on whether the use by commercial banks of NGOs and/or SHGs as intermediaries significantly lowers transaction costs compared to direct lending to the poor. The study compared four different channels of credit:

Model I, where banks lend directly to borrowers without the involvement of NGOs and SHGs;

Model II, where banks lend directly to borrowers but NGOs and SHGs are involved as non-financial intermediaries (e.g., in introducing borrowers to the banks, undertaking training, etc.);

Model III, where banks use SHGs as financial intermediaries to lend to borrowers, with NGOs as non-financial intermediaries;

Model IV, where credit flows from banks to NGOs to SHGs to ultimate borrowers (i.e. both NGOs and SHGs are financial intermediaries).

The analysis of lender transaction costs was based on a sample of 108 accounts from branches of three banks; a regional rural bank (RRB), a public commercial bank and a private commercial bank. The private commercial bank branch selected was the Challakere branch of the Vysya Bank, and part of the sample for Model III was drawn from loans by the branch to SHGs organised by MYRADA. Given the relatively small sample size, especially for some of the models, the results should be interpreted with caution and regarded as simply indicative at this stage. Puhazhendi covered a broad range of transaction costs associated with lending, in particular identification of the borrower; collection of the application and document verification; the pre-approval visit; loan appraisal, approval, disbursement and maintaining the account; the post-approval visit; monitoring, follow-up and recoveries; and other costs. Transaction costs were estimated using the cost allocation method, i.e. multiplying the number of hours bank personnel spent per loan account by salary and allowances per hour. Non-personnel costs were allocated in proportion to personnel costs. Care was also taken to use a constant average loan amount of around Rs 5 000 ($170) when comparing the different models. While this was in the upper range of individual loans to the poor by NGOs and SHGs, it was in the lower range of bank loans.

Estimates of bank transaction costs are provided in Table 1. As can be seen, bank transaction costs were considerably lower where NGOs and SHGs were involved as financial and non-financial intermediaries than where banks lent directly to the rural poor. Costs were lowest where banks used SHGs as financial intermediaries and NGOs acted as non-financial intermediaries (Model III), around 40 per cent lower than in the benchmark case. The percentage reduction was very similar for all three banks. Moreover, Puhazhendhi considered that there was scope for further reduction in time spent as banks expanded their lending to SHGs and NGOs and developed more standardised procedures for the conduct of this relatively novel mode of lending. This was especially the case for Model IV, as this channel of lending was very much in its infancy at the time of the study in 1994.

Table 1. **Transaction Costs of Lending as a Percentage of Loans Granted, India**

Bank	Model I	Model II	Model III	Model IV
Regional Rural Bank	4.05		2.45	
Public commercial bank	3.35	2.72	1.91	2.85
Private commercial bank	3.46		2.09	
All banks	3.68		2.19	

Source: Puhazhendhi (1995).

Puhazhendhi also analysed the viability of lending to the poor in the various bank branches by estimating net margins. The total cost of making funds available for lending was derived by summing the average interest rate paid on deposits, the percentage cost of mobilising deposits and the percentage cost of lending. This cost was then compared with the average interest rate earned on loans. The analysis indicated that the RRB branch's lending operations were conducted at a loss, whereas the lending operations of the two commercial bank branches were running at a profit. Had its entire loan portfolio been disbursed through intermediaries, it was estimated that the RRB branch would have reduced its loss, whilst the commercial banks would have been able to increase their profit margins.

Puhazhendhi found that involvement of NGOs and SHGs led to dramatic improvements in repayment performance, ranging from 81.32 per cent under Model II to 97.16 per cent under Models III and IV, as against 34.65 per cent under Model I.

A key conclusion from the Indian study is that intermediation by NGOs and SHGs leads to significant reductions in transaction costs facing banks in lending to the rural poor. In turn, these savings can be used for widening the outreach of credit to the poor. Hence identifying strong and effective NGOs and SHGs to act as intermediaries between banks and final borrowers is likely to yield considerable benefits in an appropriately supportive regulatory environment.

NGO Transaction Costs

The Philippines study (Llanto and Chua, 1996)[3] focused on two NGOs, denoted here as NGO X and NGO Y, which have lending programmes for micro- and small entrepreneurs who do not have access to formal credit. In terms of the Puhazhendhi study, these programmes fall within Model IV. The programmes of the two NGOs are similar, with the following key features:

—   a targeting mechanism for identifying the poor;

—   organisation of members into SHGs consisting of five members each as a requirement for loan eligibility, rather than the use of physical collateral. In turn, SHGs are organised into Centres comprising three to seven groups, with the plan to develop Centres eventually into independent people's organisations;

—   intensive supervision and motivation in terms of continuing group formation and training;

—   first loans ranging from Ps 500 ($18) to Ps 3 000 ($110), with the possibility of increasing subsequent loans, based on the borrower's performance;

—   an interest rate of 2.5 per cent per month calculated on the original loan principal, higher than commercial rates but substantially lower than rates charged by informal moneylenders. The loan term is 25 weeks for NGO X and 50 weeks for NGO Y, with weekly repayment;

—   compulsory group saving schemes.

Llanto and Chua compared the transaction costs of the two NGOs with those of other financial intermediaries. They took a broad definition of transaction costs. One component was lending operation costs proper, comprising planning and programming, advertising and promotions specific to lending, loan processing (i.e. screening credit applicants, credit investigation, evaluation and analysis), and loan recovery (i.e. monitoring, loan collection, record keeping, report writing and managing bad debts). They also considered fund mobilisation costs and costs associated with promoting SHGs.

Efficiency of the NGOs

Comparisons of transaction costs were complicated by the different types of intermediaries considered, and unlike in the Indian study, it was not possible to hold the loan size constant.

Notwithstanding these difficulties, the comparisons yielded some interesting insights. Table 2 provides data on transaction costs as a percentage of loans granted. In terms of transaction costs as a percentage of loans granted, NGO X was relatively efficient in providing loans to its clients. Its total transaction costs were only 14 per cent of loans granted, less than for any other type of intermediary except for the private commercial banks. The ratio was lower than for rural banks and specialised government banks, despite the fact that these intermediary types had much larger average loan sizes than NGO X.

Table 2. **Transaction Costs as a Percentage of (a) Loans Granted, and (b) Loans Outstanding**

Type of financial intermediary		Self help group promotion costs	Lending operations costs	Funds mobilisation costs	Total transactions costs
Private commercial banks	a	0.0	2.7	3.4	6.1
	b	0.0	3.5	4.5	8.0
Rural banks	a	0.0	10.5	4.6	15.1
	b	0.0	8.4	3.7	12.1
Co-operative Rural Banks	a	0.0	14.3	12.3	26.6
	b	0.0	4.0	3.5	7.5
Specialised Government	a	0.0	22.6	6.6	29.2
Banks	b	0.0	7.7	2.3	10.0
Credit Co-operatives	a	0.0	23.5	13.6	37.1
	b	0.0	4.0	2.3	6.3
Multi-purpose Co-operatives	a	0.0	16.4	2.1	18.5
	b	0.0	20.6	2.7	23.3
NGO X	a	3.8	7.6	2.6	14.0
	b	9.2	18.4	6.4	34.0
NGO Y	a	11.2	27.3	8.6	47.1
	b	19.8	48.4	15.3	83.5

Source: Llanto and Chua (1996).

On the other hand, the comparison is far less favourable to NGO X when transaction costs are considered as a percentage of loans outstanding, rather than as a percentage of loans granted. The poor comparative performance of the NGOs on this point partly reflects anomalies in the estimates of loans outstanding. Following the Casuga (1994) study, estimates relate to loans outstanding at the end of the period, rather than average loans outstanding over the period. More importantly, the estimates for credit co-operatives in particular, but also for some other types of intermediaries, appear to include a very large number of bad debts, significantly reducing the transaction cost ratios for these intermediaries. Hence the comparisons are more unfavourable to the NGOs than would otherwise be the case, and need to be treated with considerable caution. Nevertheless, the data also reflect the short loan maturities offered by the NGOs compared to the banks, which mean that loans outstanding at any given point in time are relatively low compared to loans granted.

Short loan maturities are an inherent feature of lending to the poor, and inevitably lead to higher transaction costs as a percentage of loans outstanding. There is also evidence that the NGOs provided better service to the poor in other ways than any of the other intermediaries did. The NGO programmes were more closely targeted to the poor, with a higher proportion of borrowers falling below the poverty threshold. Over 89 per cent of the NGO clients were women, compared with 37 per cent for the banks and 60 per cent for the co-operatives. Repayments were more frequent, weekly rather than monthly or quarterly, better addressing the needs of the poor. It should also be stressed that the NGOs had not been in operation for as long as the banks and credit co-operatives, with NGO Y's programme barely a year old and NGO X's programme around three years old.

Viability of the NGOs

Llanto and Chua also noted that to be viable, NGOs must earn at least enough revenue to cover all their costs, including transaction costs, the cost of funds and of bad loans/default. If they are to expand, they must earn a surplus from their operations to enable them to increase their lending.

Llanto and Chua used this simple framework to analyse NGO X's group lending operations. Given the very early stage of NGO Y's group lending programme, a similar analysis was not undertaken for it. NGO X's actual return on lending was calculated at 35 per cent, representing income from loans as a percentage of average loans outstanding.

Against this income, the following costs were identified.

— An effective annual interest rate on commercial borrowing of 12 per cent was assumed, based on market interest rates over the period. This compares to an actual cost of funds of around 2.3 per cent of average loans outstanding, reflecting the availability of concessional sources of finance.

— Transaction costs, excluding the costs of SHG promotion, were estimated at 35 per cent of average loans outstanding (including the costs of SHG promotion increased transaction costs to 48 per cent of loans outstanding).

— The cost of default was assumed to equal 10 per cent. This is conservative, in light of NGO X's repayment rate of 92 per cent and default rate of 3 per cent.

Therefore, the study estimated that if NGO X had to pay market interest rates for its funds and made greater allowance for bad debts, the total cost of lending would be around 57 per cent. This is some 22 percentage points above the current return on its lending. Hence NGO X's operations are not commercially viable at present, and it relies heavily on concessional funds.

Nevertheless, Llanto and Chua concluded that there was much potential for the NGOs to reduce their transaction costs further over time. For example, one way would be to increase the number of clients per field worker, which has been well below a stated "benchmark" of 200 to 300 clients per staff member (117 for NGO X and 65 for NGO Y). Another way would be to increase the number of repeat borrowers. To a large extent, this should occur naturally with time and the maturation of the programmes. Because NGO X had been operating longer in the linkage mode, it had more repeat borrowers than NGO Y. This significantly reduced the transaction costs of lending, with the approval process for repeat loans much simpler than for a first loan application. Moreover, the principal of a repeat loan could be as much as 50 per cent greater than a first loan.

The authors also made a number of other suggestions. They considered that because training costs formed a substantial part of the NGOs' budgets, it would be useful to find better, more cost-effective and faster ways of training and motivating field workers. It also argued that the NGOs could reduce costs by investing in improved computer technology for record keeping, report writing and loan monitoring.

Borrower Transaction Costs

The two studies also estimated transaction costs facing borrowers. In the study for India, estimates were derived from a random sample of 150 borrowers. Puhazhendhi identified three main components of borrower transaction costs: travel costs and incidentals, documentation expenses, and the opportunity cost of time spent in negotiating the loan. Borrower transaction costs were estimated at Rs 272 ($9.40) per loan account under Model I, of which 62 per cent involved cash expenditure and the remaining 38 per cent opportunity cost. Costs were much lower under the other three models; Rs 166 ($5.70) under Model II, Rs 40 ($1.40) under Model III and Rs 36 ($1.25) under Model IV.

Hence there was a reduction in borrower transaction costs of up to 85 per cent when the loan was delivered through NGOs and/or SHGs. Under these models, borrowers had no expenditure on documentation procedures and made fewer visits to the bank (although group members visited the bank on a rotation basis for depositing monies and withdrawing loan amounts on behalf of all members).

The Philippines study, which corresponded to Model IV in the Indian study, also considered borrower transaction costs, at the level of the individual borrower and of the SHG. Cash outlays consisted of loan application fees, loan insurance, transport costs for attending meetings, and a share of the cost of turning over weekly collections to the NGO office. Such costs ranged from 1.8 per cent to 5.1 per cent of the average loan value for NGO X borrowers, and 4.5 per cent to 6.3 per cent of average loan value for NGO Y borrowers. Llanto and Chua did not include an allowance for the opportunity cost of attending meetings, but noted that members considered that meetings provided positive benefits in terms of camaraderie, and mutual encouragement.

Conclusion

The two case studies are largely complementary. The Indian study compared the transaction costs to banks of lending to the poor through various channels, and found that transaction costs were much lower where banks used NGOs and SHGs as intermediaries. It also suggested that the use of such intermediaries significantly improved the commercial viability of lending to the poor for banks. While more research is needed looking at a larger number of cases and more mature programmes, the results support the central premise of the Banking with the Poor project that linkages with NGOs and SHGs can enable banks to provide credit to the poor on a commercial basis.

By contrast, the Philippines study looked at the question from the perspective of the NGOs. It found that NGOs could channel credit to the poor with lower transaction costs, as a proportion of loans granted, than most other institutions. This suggests an important role for NGOs in the intermediation process. Nevertheless, the small loans and short maturities inherent in lending to the poor inevitably lead to high transaction costs compared to the value of loans outstanding at any one point in time. This highlights the need for NGOs to minimise costs as far as possible if they are to achieve full financial sustainability. While the study offered a number of insights into how this might be done, it is an issue that would benefit from more research. More detailed case studies of the operations of NGOs acting as financial intermediaries over a longer time period, looking at a range of quantitative and qualitative indicators, would help to define much more precisely the critical factors which govern their efficiency and viability.

Another issue requiring further research concerns the activities of SHGs. Llanto and Chua noted that the costs incurred by NGO X and NGO Y in the Philippines in promoting SHGs had generally been met by grants from donors. The promotion of SHGs is likely to give rise to a range of benefits in addition to access to credit. Participants are likely to benefit from the training and skills that they acquire through participation in the groups. While it could be argued that they should pay for these benefits, their low income and the heavy subsidies typically given to other forms of education and training in many countries provide a strong argument for public support. Moreover, there are likely to be significant positive externalities in terms of community development, leadership, etc. which do not accrue to individual participants. In the absence of continued support from donors and governments, NGOs would tend to reduce expenditure on SHG promotion below the socially optimal level. Hence there is a strong argument for grants to NGOs to fund SHG formation and promotion for reasons of economic efficiency and equity. These issues need to be considered by researchers, donors and policy makers alike.

Most importantly, the results of the two studies also support a renewed focus on linkages between banks, NGOs and SHGs as a means of channelling credit to the poor. There remain a large number of impediments to the spread of linkages, and overcoming these will require active support from governments and central banks in the form of moral suasion, directives and changing inappropriate regulations. Although other aspects of microfinance have been emphasized in the recent period, donor agencies should not lose sight of the importance of fostering linkages. This will require support for institutional strengthening of banks, NGOs and SHGs alike, to provide grants for capitalisation (see the chapter by T. Feige in this volume) to enable NGOs to improve their sustainability and outreach, and to encourage policy reform where appropriate. Such measures are entirely consistent with the Guiding Principles for Selecting and Supporting Intermediaries agreed to by major donor agencies in June 1995, and with the recent Project Funding Announcement by the Consultative Group to Assist the Poorest (CGAP).

Notes and References

*   Respectively Programme Officer and Executive Director, Foundation for Development Cooperation, Brisbane, Australia.

1.   The Foundation for Development Cooperation commissioned these case studies. They were conducted during 1994 with the financial support of UNDP under its Asia-Pacific Regional Poverty Alleviation Programme, and involved BWTP Network members and other institutions, in India and the Philippines. Both studies attempted to quantify transaction costs of microfinance institutions, specifically, commercial banks and NGOs. The institutions selected were providing microcredit using a number of variants of the "linkage" approach.

2.   This study was conducted in 1994 by V. Puhazhendhi, now Manager of the Department of Economic Analysis and Research in the National Bank for Agriculture and Rural Development (NABARD).

3.   This study was carried out in 1994 by Gilberto M. Llanto, Fellow of the Philippine Institute for Development Studies, and Ronald T. Chua, Managing Director of the Center for Community Transformation in Manila.

Bibliography

CASUGA, M.S. (1994), "Transaction Costs under an Agrarian Reform Regime", in Llanto, G.M. and C.G. DINGCONG (eds.), *Financial Intermediation in an Agrarian Reform Regime, Agricultural Credit Policy Council*, Manila.

CHRISTEN, R.P., E. RHYNE, R.C. VOGEL AND C. MCKEAN (1994), *Maximising the Outreach of Microenterprise Finance: The Emerging Lessons of Successful Programs* (draft), Consulting Assistance for Economic Reform (CAER) Paper.

COMMITTEE OF DONOR AGENCIES FOR SMALL ENTERPRISE DEVELOPMENT AND DONORS' WORKING GROUP ON FINANCIAL SECTOR DEVELOPMENT (1995), *Micro and Small Enterprise Finance: Guiding Principles for Selecting and Supporting Intermediaries.*

CONSULTATIVE GROUP TO ASSIST THE POOREST (1996), CGAP Project Funding Announcement, World Bank, Washington, D.C.

FOUNDATION FOR DEVELOPMENT COOPERATION (1992a), *Banking with the Poor*, Brisbane, Australia.

FOUNDATION FOR DEVELOPMENT COOPERATION (1992b), *How to Build Self-Help Groups for Successful Banking with the Poor*, Brisbane, Australia.

FOUNDATION FOR DEVELOPMENT COOPERATION (1995), *Best Practice of Banking with the Poor*, Brisbane, Australia.

GALLARDO, J.S. AND B.K. RANDHAWA (1995), *Establishing a Subsidiary Bank for an NGO: The Philippines Case* (draft), Financial Sector Development Department, World Bank, Washington, D.C.

LLANTO, G.M. AND R.T. CHUA (1996), *Transaction Costs of Lending to the Poor: A Case Study of Two Philippine Non-Government Organizations*, Foundation for Development Cooperation, Brisbane, Australia.

PUHAZHENDHI, V. (1995), *Transaction Costs of Lending to the Rural Poor: Non-Governmental Organisations and Self-Help Groups of the Poor as Intermediaries for Banks in India*, Foundation for Development Cooperation, Brisbane, Australia.

WORLD BANK (1990), *World Development Report 1990: Poverty*, Oxford University Press, New York.

PART TWO. SELECTED CASES OF INSTITUTIONAL DEVELOPMENT

Developing Financial Services in Poor Regions: Self-Managed Village Savings and Loan Associations in the Dogon Region of Mali

*Renée Chao-Béroff**

A number of years ago, the Centre international de développement et de recherche (CIDR), a French non-governmental organisation (NGO), started a research programme with the objective of devising and implementing decentralised financial systems which would meet the needs of the poor in the South and which would be genuine tools for local development. This programme led to the creation of several networks of self-managed village savings and loan associations (*caisses villageoises d'épargne et de crédit autogérées* — CVECAs)[1]. The experiment has made the most progress in the Dogon region of Mali: in 1995, the network there comprised 54 *caisses villageoises* with 18 691 members, one-third of whom were women. It has mobilised CFAF 247.5 million in local savings, granted 11 218 loans for a total of CFAF 378 million and channelled more than CFAF 100 million in refinancing from banks. For nine years, the rate of repayment has always been over 98 per cent. Three unions of *caisses villageoises* and an autonomous support body called the common service have been created to ensure the permanence of the system. The results have surpassed expectations. No one would have imagined that such a savings and reimbursement capacity existed in a region with so many handicaps (geographic, economic, cultural and so on).

At a time when many donors are turning to the struggle against poverty, especially through the establishment of micro-financing programmes, it is important to agree on certain observations and realities. The fact is that the cost of creating financial structures in poor areas is certainly higher than that of creating the same services in cash-crop regions or urban areas. However, these higher costs are limited by the participation of the actor-beneficiaries in the success of their system. It is therefore possible to measure the real costs which developing-country decision makers and donors must agree to bear if they wish to create financial services for the poorest strata of the population. The two-fold challenge of reaching impoverished people while striving to make a savings and loan system financially autonomous calls for innovative measures (at the level of organisation, management, institutional integration and so on), which can have very concrete effects in terms of an increased capacity to mobilise and exploit local resources.

Lastly, the immediate environment — government, partner bank, monetary authority, donor country — plays a fundamental role in the institutionalisation of *caisses villageoises* as a truly decentralised financial system which is entirely in the hands of poor villagers.

Working in Poor Regions: Inevitable Supplementary Costs, Partly Offset by a Participatory Approach

Since the mid-1980s, the small farmers of the Dogon region have been making great efforts for the success of their network of savings and loan associations, in partnership with the CIDR; the *Direction nationale de l'action coopérative* (DNACOOP) of Mali; *the Banque nationale de développement agricole* (BNDA) of Mali; and the *Kreditanstalt für Wiederaufbau* (KFW), the German financial co-operation agency. The creation of the network was made possible by an external support project which is to terminate in June 1997, handing over to permanent — and technically and financially autonomous — Malian structures. During its eleven and a half years, the project will have borne some specific costs linked to working in a poor environment, costs which are partly offset by the participation of the beneficiaries.

The Supplementary Costs Borne by the Project

The purpose of the project is not to supply the savings and loan associations with funds; rather, it provides the villagers with professionals who help them to organise and run the *caisses villageoises*, as well as subsidies for their equipment. Costs have been higher than the "normal" costs of such a project, however, owing to the handicaps that generally afflict poor regions: specifically, the Dogon region is characterised by an arid climate, fragile agriculture, low household incomes, isolation, low population density and widely scattered villages, distant from economic centres, a low literacy rate and little participation by women.

To attenuate the effects of these handicaps on the success of the *caisses villageoises*, the project was obliged to make costly efforts, namely:

— to work with the *caisses villageoises* over a long period. First, a substantial amount of time was devoted to research and experimentation, since the project was one of the first to attempt to create a financial structure in a poor region with a low level of monetisation. The time devoted to these activities by the project team may be estimated at 20 per cent. Hence, with a well-tried methodology, the project could have lasted two and a half years less, or only nine years in all. Second, in poor areas, more time is needed for the network to become self-financing: loan portfolios are relatively small and transaction costs on small loans are proportionally higher than those on larger loans. The system of *caisses villageoises* in the Dogon region will have taken 12 years to attain financial autonomy;

— to bear equipment costs approximately 30 per cent higher than the norm (electrical generators, etc.);

— to bear high costs due to isolation and to the difficult terrain (wear on vehicles, transportation time, difficulty in exchanging experiences with other *caisses villageoises* and so on);

— to compensate for the lack of education. Before management training could begin, the project was compelled to set up programmes for literacy and learning how to use numbers, or refresher courses in writing and arithmetic for cashiers, which absorbed approximately 50 per cent of the project's training budget. Subsequently, more time was devoted to technical training than in other regions where the managers' educational level was higher (e.g. the Office in Niger, where the CIDR also has a programme);

— to encourage participation by women. The decision to have women participate in the membership and the management boards of the *caisses villageoises* involved a non-negligible cost. This effort was not motivated by a desire to make the network profitable, since women account for only a small share of deposits and loans (in number of deposits and loans, 22 and 33 per cent respectively; in volume, even less). Rather, the aim was social equity.

Table 1 sums up the supplementary costs borne by the project.

In total, the supplementary costs amounted to FF 7 140 000, in a total project budget of nearly FF 16 million over eleven and a half years. Thus, 45 per cent of the project budget can be attributed to working in a poor region.

Reduction of Costs through Participation

A strong sense of solidarity can be seen in the Dogon region, which may be due to the difficult living conditions. The people's determination to help themselves manifests itself in their complete commitment to the development activities of their villages. The costs which the actor-beneficiaries agree to bear by themselves are an essential contribution to the reduction of the project's costs. Similarly, the honesty of the village people has made it possible to economise on financial costs and expenditures related to security. Finally, some costs which the project bears directly are lower than in other contexts.

Table 1. **Supplementary Costs Borne by the Project**

Nature of supplementary costs	Basis for calculation	Amount (in FF)
Experimentation due to low levels of income	2.5 years x FF 1 385 000 a year[a]	3 462 500
Project equipment	30 per cent x FF 212 000	63 000
Amortisation of vehicles	1 year's amortization for 15 motorcycles and 2 years' amortization for 6 vehicles[b]	427 500
Transportation time, within and outside the region	20 per cent of the project team's working time[c]	1 150 000
Selection of villages	30 "unfruitful" surveys[d]	342 000
Supplementary training costs	65 per cent of the training budget[e]	1 120 000
Participation by women	10 per cent of the time worked	575 000
Total supplementary costs		**7 140 000**

a. The total cost of the project will be FF 15 938 000 for 11½ years, or an annual average of FF 1 385 000.
b. In 11 years, the project will have used and amortized 15 motorcycles and six vehicles. As a motorcycle costs approximately FF 18 000, its annual amortization, calculated over four years, is FF 4 500. By amortizing over three years, the project ran up extra costs of FF 4 500 x 15 = FF 67 500.
c. The project team grew from two to 12 persons. The average wage bill was FF 500 000 annually. The time spent in transportation thus represents: FF 500 000 x 20 per cent = FF 100 000 annually. Over the duration of the project FF 100 000 x 11,5 = FF 1 150 000.
d. A village survey lasts five days. It therefore costs FF 500 000/220 working days x 5 days = FF 11 400 = FF 342 000.
e. The project team devotes 20 per cent of its working time to training, or an annual budget of FF 100 000. To this must be added the training budget properly speaking, which includes the per diem of the trainees, pedagogical aids and materials, etc. This budget amounts on average to FF 50 000 a year. The total budget is thus FF 150 000 a year, or FF 1 725 000 over the duration of the project.

—   Village inhabitants participated in the construction of the *caisses villageoises* (20 people working for four days). This working time can be evaluated at FF 5 a day, which corresponds to the cost of agricultural labour. The construction materials are not expensive.

—   In a spirit of solidarity, village groups readily agree to make deposits in the *caisse villageoise*. The average volume of deposits for the duration of the project is estimated at FF 500 000 a year, and deposits made by groups account for about 10 per cent of this. The groups have thus given up a financial margin of 40 per cent (the difference between savings remunerated at 20 per cent interest and the possibility of lending at 60 per cent) on FF 50 000 francs a year.

—   Village inhabitants have agreed to pay relatively high interest rates to cover transaction costs and to ensure the profitability of the *caisses villageoises* and the accumulation of own funds. In the setting of lending rates, two elements were taken into account: the economic activities conducted with the funds lent generate very large economic margins; and the *caisse villageoise* must be able to cover its costs on small lending volumes. Some villages chose to begin with extremely high lending rates, as high as 120 per cent annually. Over the years, however, these *caisses villageoises* fell back to more reasonable rates, of the order of 40 per cent. On the other hand, deposit rates are also very high, generally half the lending rates. It may be estimated that on average over the last ten years, the banking margin has been 25 per cent per year.

— Managers are compensated at the end of the year on the basis of the year's results, depending on the decision of the village general assembly. In most *caisses villageoises*, managers' efforts will always be greater than the pay which they could expect to receive. Only in the most successful may their pay equal the annual salary of a teacher. Managers work one to one and a half days per week, plus the time spent in training and transportation. Table 2 allows us to measure the effort made by managers, by comparing what they should have received (theoretical pay) to what they actually did receive (real pay).

Table 2. **Savings on Managers' Remuneration**

	Phase 1	Phase 2	Phase 3[c]	Total
Number of years	3	5	3	11
Average number of managers	25	60	110	
Number of days worked per year (including training)	62	62	85	
Theoretical pay[a] (thousands of FF)	46	186	280	512
Real pay[b] (thousands of FF)	10	88	260	358
Savings (thousands of FF)	36	98	20	154

a. A day's work is evaluated at FF 10.
b. From the operating accounts of the network.
c. Estimations based on forecasts of a reasonable increase in the CVECAs' activity.

— Board members hold at least one meeting per week to analyse loan requests and to monitor loan repayments and the managers' performance. They lead consciousness-raising meetings on the advantages of the *caisse villageoise* in the village, monitor borrowers and participate in training and in inter-*caisse villageoise* meetings which can involve fairly long and costly travel. They are volunteers. Indeed, the villagers feel that the board members participate in village life in the same way as leaders of village associations or advisors do. After one or two terms (at most six years), they are replaced. The board members thus receive only a token payment at the end of the year, but the value of the work they do is quantified in Table 3. As a certain proportion of volunteer work may be considered normal for this type of participatory organisation, only 50 per cent of this effort, or FF 309 000, will be counted as a specific contribution due to the solidarity of the region.

— Provision for bad debts is very low, owing to the excellent repayment rate of nearly 99 per cent. With a total of FF 139 000 over ten years (1986-96), bad loans amount to only 1.5 per cent of the total loan portfolio (FF 9 400 000 over the same period). If the network had been obliged to make provision for 5 per cent of its outstanding loans every year — a level which is still considered low by experts in decentralised networks — this would have cost FF 517 000 for eleven years. It can thus be said that the network saved FF 378 000.

Table 3. Savings Resulting from Unpaid Work by Board Members

	Phase 1	Phase 2	Phase 3	Total
Average number of board members	80	200	360	
Number of days worked per year (including training)	56	56	70	
Theoretical pay[a] (thousands of francs)	67	280	378	725
Real pay (thousands of francs)	1	30	77	108
Differences (thousands of francs)	66	250	301	617

a.   A day's work is evaluated at FF 5.

—   In ten years of activity, the *caisses villageoises* of the Dogon region have recorded only four cases of embezzlement, for a total loss of FF 15 000. In almost all cases, family and village solidarity made it possible to recover these funds. It is difficult to quantify the gain brought about by the rarity of embezzlement. According to a rough estimate obtained by comparison to other networks in Mali, the *caisses villageoises* managed to "avoid" the equivalent of about FF 15 000 a year in misappropriation of funds, or FF 165 000 in total.

—   The *caisses villageoises* of the Dogon region have always managed to make do with management documents printed locally at very low cost. To be sure, these documents can be falsified, but the experience of other networks proves that this can also happen with more sophisticated and costly documents, printed on self-copy paper. On average, accounting documents cost the *caisses villageoises* FF 10 000 a year. Had more concern been shown for the quality of printing, the documents could have cost approximately FF 40 000.

—   The project pays for part of the initial investment needed to equip a *caisse villageoise*: a safe, reinforced metal doors and office equipment. This costs FF 5 000 per *caisse villageoise*, but in comparison to other networks, which operate in higher-risk areas, it may be estimated that the project and its beneficiaries saved FF 5 000 per *caisse villageoise* by using materials which are less strong but sufficient for their needs. For 56 *caisses villageoises*, this means a saving of FF 280 000.

—   The unions of *caisses villageoises* can cover all of their operating costs from the revenues which they generate. These costs stem from the organisation of meetings between *caisses villageoises* and between unions, meetings in villages experiencing difficulty, management of BNDA refinancing, bookkeeping and administrative paperwork, and so on. Operating costs, which amount to FF 83 000 for the duration of the project, are covered by an interest differential of the order of 9 per cent applied by the unions for refinancing. The *caisses villageoises* accept this differential out of solidarity, in order to promote the development of a strong union to represent them.

— The common service is an independent support unit which provides various services to *caisses villageoises* and unions, such as the training of *caisse villageoise* inspectors and union office inspectors, assistance in transactions with the BNDA, semi-annual inspections and unexpected checks, and so on. The idea of the common service arose from the joint thinking of the project and the peasant leaders. Very early on, the latter accepted the principle of contributing to the costs of the common service, on the basis of 15 per cent of the annual profits of all the *caisses villageoises*, in addition to 75 per cent of the unions' margin on BNDA refinancing, which is in fact the most usual contribution. The *caisses villageoises* and unions have been contributing to the operation of the common service since 1994. The total contribution of the *caisses villageoises* until the end of the project is estimated at FF 225 000). By 1997, the common service will be practically self-financing.

The contribution of the actors, through their investment in labour and their involvement, thus amounts to FF 1 895 000 of the system's costs. The savings realised by the project through the *caisses villageoises*' and unions' assumption of certain operating costs amount to FF 308 000. The total cost savings which can be attributed to working in a poor region are thus equivalent to FF 2 203 000 for the duration of the project (see Table 4).

Table 4. **Summary of Cost Savings**

Nature of the savings	Basis for calculation	Amount (in FF)
Participation by villagers in construction of the CVECAs	(80 working days x FF 5 + FF 500 for building materials) x 54 CVECAs	49 000
Groups' deposits	FF 20 000 x 11.5 years	230 000
Unpaid work by managers	See Table 2	154 000
Unpaid work by board members	See Table 3	309 000
Savings on provision for bad loans	See text.	378 000
Savings on embezzlement	FF 15 000 x 11 years	165 000
Savings on document production	FF 30 000 x 11 years	330 000
Savings on the CVECAs' equipment costs	FF 5 000 x 56	280 000
Total cost savings due to participation		**1 895 000**
Savings on costs borne directly by the project:		
Coverage of the operating costs of the unions	See text	83 000
Financing the common service	FF 225 000 by the CVECAs	225 000
Total cost savings		**2 203 000**

Order of Magnitude of the Cost of a Project to Create Financial Services in a Poor Region

The project for the *caisses villageoises* of the Dogon region to achieve autonomy has cost FF 15 938 000. The same project would probably have cost only FF 8 798 000 in a more central and well-off region with an organised and cohesive population. In other words, the supplementary costs linked to working in a poor region represent nearly half of the total project budget.

In the Dogon region, however, the solidarity of the people compensated for one-third of the supplementary financial outlays which the project had to make in order to reach them. If the cost reductions which amounted to "savings" for the project were added, the overall budget would have been FF 18 141 000. This would be the real cost in a poor environment lacking popular solidarity and involvement, in which the project had to take the place of the people.

Steps to Attain Financial Autonomy

The project may be divided into three phases. The first was that of research and of investment in setting up the system, starting up its dynamics and constructing the network of *caisses villageoises*. This was also the period in which the training effort at all levels was concentrated, and to which the greater part of the supplementary costs are attributable. It corresponds to the first six or seven years of the project, 1986 to 1992/93. The foreign donor and the Malian government bore all the external costs of this phase, such as project personnel (an expatriate advisor, Malian executives and organisers, guards, drivers), vehicles, training and so on. During this period, the local population bore only the costs of the individual *caisses villageoises*.

The second phase has been one of transition. Some of the functions and costs previously assumed by the project have been transferred to the *caisses villageoises* and the unions, but the project still bears certain costs for training and for structuring and following the rapid progress of the system. This period corresponds to the years 1993/94 to 1997, during which — in parallel with the permanent institutions (the common service and the unions), which began to function on their intended scale with their normal financing mechanisms — a reduced "project" structure, with seven organisers, has been maintained to finalise the material and intangible investments needed in this environment. It has been a period of cost sharing, in which both the donor and the people have taken part in financing the costs.

From 1997, the project structure is supposed to disappear, leaving behind permanent Malian institutions (three regional unions of *caisses villageoises* and a private common service) which will have full financial and technical autonomy. All costs should be covered by the system itself.

Innovations and Their Consequences for Cost Control and Growth of Resources

In very poor contexts such as that of the Dogon region, a traditional approach would not succeed in establishing a viable financial system. The more difficult the context, the poorer is the public to be reached and the more it is necessary to dare to innovate. These innovations, however, must be made with the people: the people are no longer the beneficiaries of innovations coming from outside, but are themselves the innovators. In these conditions, innovation makes it possible to reduce costs and to create new wealth and new dynamics. The innovations are presented in the order in which they were adopted: social innovations first, then economic, and lastly institutional. The first two categories correspond to the phase of research and experimentation, while the last occurred when the network had become fully operational.

Social Innovations of the Caisses villageoises of the Dogon Region

Finance being a job for professionals, with highly codified and very strict rules, the financial systems set up in Africa have almost always been transplanted from social and cultural contexts which are completely foreign to those in which the systems are supposed to take root. It is not surprising that this has made the appropriation of such systems by the local people more difficult.

The people of the Dogon region have a major advantage: ancestral values and social modes of functioning which they have managed to conserve over time and which give them strength in a difficult environment. The first innovation, at the methodological level, was therefore to start from the strengths and values of the Dogon people themselves and to conceive a system which enhances the value of these qualities and in which the people recognise themselves.

The Dogon people definitely draw strength from the social cohesiveness of their villages. In this context, a village savings and loan association[2] becomes the village's common property. It submits to the rules and values of the village and is protected by it: anyone who harms the *caisse villageoise* knows that he offends the entire village and the local authorities, and will have to answer for his acts and behaviour. Similarly, the managers of the *caisse villageoise* are appointed by the village and hence are accountable to it.

The promoters of the *caisses villageoises* encouraged the people concerned to establish the operating rules of their future savings and loan institutions by themselves, drawing much of their inspiration from local learning and know-how. The people were supposed to hold public meetings to define the rules concerning membership, savings, credit, management and so on. The promoters organise, monitor and accompany all these discussions, providing technical insights to draw the assembly's attention to the possible consequences of certain decisions, but it is the villagers who make the final decisions.

It is recommended that they regularly (e.g. at the end of each year) evaluate every aspect of these internal regulations and, if need be, profit from experience by modifying rules that have proved unenforceable or unjust, or that have undesirable effects. The operating rules of the *caisse villageoise* thus have some flexibility for adaptation and, being set by the villagers themselves in a public meeting, are in fact fairly well known to all, so that the *caisse villageoise* is not an exclusive club for a few privileged initiates.

After a training period, the village leaders promote the *caisse villageoise* among the non-members, hold meetings to encourage deposits and manage the association. When a crisis arises, the villagers often ask for external intervention to avoid having to settle sensitive matters among themselves, but the promoters managed to avoid this throughout, making the villagers assume their responsibilities. This firmness paid off, because it reinforced the people's sense of ownership (where such reinforcement was needed) and developed various capabilities.

Some Problems Resolved by Villagers

Case 1: A *caisse villageoise* was stagnating because the authoritarian and omnipresent village chief had taken it in hand himself. The union of the region's *caisses villageoises* met, analysed the situation and decided to send a delegation made up of village chiefs of the same rank as the chief in question, to reason with him and convince him that he should serve as a recourse if problems arose, and should let the board perform its function.

Case 2: A cashier who was also treasurer of the union of *caisses villageoises* was embezzling money from both his *caisse villageoise* and the union. The villagers held a meeting and decided that, to save the honour of their village, all family heads would have to contribute to repay the union immediately. This was done. As for the *caisse villageoise's* money, the chairman applied first to the parents of the cashier; not obtaining a satisfactory answer, he appealed for arbitration by the authority of the home village, which is located on the cliffs.

Case 3: A bad debtor was delaying repayment of a loan, and all the warnings issued had no effect. The board sent its women members to sit in front of his door in the morning. The whole village knew what this signified, and the bad debtor rapidly repaid his debt to rid himself of these women, whose presence called attention to him.

These social innovations had an appreciable impact, as the following indicators show:

— in nine years, only two of the 56 *caisses villageoises* created had to be closed. Most *caisses villageoises* in difficulty, or even moribund, were able to start up again on a new foundation and function normally today, following an accurate diagnosis by the managers of *caisses villageoises* in neighbouring villages and appropriate socio-cultural steps;

— during eight years and a total of CFAF 466 million in loans, provisions for bad loans have amounted to CFAF 1.39 million, an exceptionally low figure which reflects the effectiveness of social pressure;

— similarly, since the beginning of the project, only four cases of embezzlement have been recorded, for a total of CFAF 1.5 million — a very low volume in view of the sums of money involved.

These examples show that the social innovations, by very substantially reducing costs, have made an important and effective contribution to the financial viability of the system.

Economic Innovations

The economy of the Dogon region is precarious, being highly subject to climatic hazards. The villagers' purchasing power is very limited. To make a financial system viable and attain a sufficient volume in such a context, it was absolutely necessary to promote activities which are independent of climatic hazards and open to the national market — that is, it was necessary to act on the entire local economy. The project promoters chose to do research with local economic actors. In parallel with the *caisses villageoises*, which granted loans according to demand and often remained confined to small subsistence activities, a more voluntarist and systematic approach was set up, called the "diversification" segment of the project and endowed with an "innovation fund" and a "research fund". In six years, this part of the project conducted research on all the small economic channels that seemed promising, associating micro-entrepreneurs with its tests of economic innovation.

Overall, these tests were of three sorts:

— *technical tests*, combining traditional craftsmanship with industrial or technical elements to facilitate marketing or reduce costs. Examples are the fabrication of better-finished loincloths, or broadening the range of products made by local blacksmiths;

— *organisational tests*, in which village channels are set up whereby producers contract with a village wholesaler, who is responsible for gathering merchandise and selling it in external markets;

— *tests of geographical extension* to regional markets, so as to reach a larger clientele which has greater purchasing power and is less dependent on local constraints.

The research fund (FF 343 000) financed study trips, allowing groups of Dogon micro-entrepreneurs to see experiments in other regions, to speak with other entrepreneurs of their experiences and to get an idea of the various possibilities. It also served to finance some training in new techniques. The innovation fund (FF 215 000) was conceived as a venture capital fund, for granting loans at moderate interest to innovators wishing to try new methods (technical or organisational innovation, geographical extension). The risk of innovation was thus shared between the micro-entrepreneurs and the promoters of the approach without endangering the *caisses villageoises*, which work with the villagers' savings. These two funds were provided in the form of a grant from the project.

This approach had a strong impact in the traditionally conservative Dogon context. It upset customs and gave rise to discontent, but at the same time it created a true dynamic in which entrepreneurship, initiative and the affirmation of ambition progressively took hold in the society and were less marginalised than before. Background discussions were held with village leaders and authorities. From a solidarity oriented towards survival, there was a transformation to a *caisse villageoise* oriented towards economic development, which also offers business opportunities to those with the desire and the ability to become entrepreneurs.

The innovation triggered a surge of economic activity in the Dogon region, with many quantifiable impacts which contribute to the viability of the *caisse villageoise* system:

— When these innovations were introduced, the **volume of credit** doubled from one year to the next; in six years, it grew by a factor of 47, from CFAF 8 million to 378 million. Obviously, the new approach was not directly responsible for all of this growth, but it undoubtedly provided a boost which may be estimated at approximately 50 per cent of the results.

— The size of the **average loan** grew from CFAF 11 000 to 33 700 in eight years, with a very broad spread of CFAF 2 500 to 2 500 000. Since the effort to promote innovation, many applications for loans of CFAF 100 000 to 500 000 have been granted; these correspond to more significant economic activities with an impact on the local economy.

— The profile of **micro-entrepreneurs** changed: often, it was young micro-entrepreneurs who took advantage of the opportunity, either individually or in economic interest groups, so as to conduct a larger enterprise.

— The opening up of markets contributed greatly to **dividing the risks** of the loan portfolio; initially, the loans had been concentrated in small activities conducted in village markets, and thus totally dependent on climatic hazards and the related variations in purchasing power.

— Lastly, the **entry of money from outside**, spent and invested locally, had an overall impact on the local economy.

At the end of the project, the innovation fund is to be maintained, under the management of the three unions, to allow the financing of new financial products while limiting risk.

Institutional Innovations

Several observations, analyses and thoughts about past experiences of institutionalising savings and loan systems led to the development of "preventive" strategies, which underlie the institutional innovations of the *caisses villageoises*. First, it was noted that traditional systems (savings and loan co-operatives) are rendered fragile by their high degree of integration and the centralisation of financial resources and decision-making. Indeed, when there is a crisis, either at the intermediate level or at the top, the repercussions are felt throughout the system and serious malfunctions occur, even at the level of the individual *caisses villageoises*. Second, the tension between "technicians" and "elected officials" which exists in many systems provides a good illustration of the vulnerability of a large, highly structured federation endowed with substantial means and a large staff. Either party can, if it wishes, immobilise the other, causing substantial damage. How can this be avoided? In the Dogon region, the promoters tried another approach.

The "Firebreak" Strategy

A first innovation, in order to preserve the basic *caisses villageoises* even if other elements of the system collapse or disappear, was to opt for local use of all local resources. Money does not leave the village; there is no centralisation of liquid assets.

To avoid immobilising cash in the safe, all lending decisions are made by the village loan board, with no external presence regardless of the size of the loan considered. As the board members live in the village, the board can meet as frequently as necessary: at each repayment, it meets and makes a decision; in less than 24 hours, the money has left again in the form of a loan.

Lastly, to make this local self-management complete, all operating expenses of the *caisse villageoise* are covered, from the beginning, by the *caisse villageoise* itself, either from its earnings or through exceptional contributions from its members. Thus, even if the entire network disappeared, the remaining *caisse villageoise* could continue to function autonomously. It would suffer some loss, of course — financially, without access to external refinancing; technically, without the exchange of experiences, the advice and the support of other *caisses villageoises* — but it would survive in reduced form.

This preventive approach has also had appreciable financial effects on the viability of the system as a whole. Board members, aware of the entrepreneurial issues involved in running the *caisse villageoise*, have rapidly become good managers; they have reduced operating expenses to the real capacity of the *caisse villageoise*, but above all have been extremely efficient in managing loans. The "transformation rate", which indicates the speed of rotation of liquid assets and the level of investment of such assets, has always been above 80 per cent throughout the system and at times has been close to 100 per cent; whereas in most co-operative savings and loan networks the investment rate lies between 30 and 60 per cent. Obviously, this improved the financial results, especially the financial margin.

Externalisation of Central Services

The central services which are usual in traditional networks, such as the central fund and the technical unit (which includes the departments of inspection, training, legal and financial advice, research and development, and so on), are expensive, take a good deal of managing and become power strongholds, often bureaucratic or technocratic and cut off from the grassroots membership. The functions of these services are certainly indispensable, but their form is not necessarily so. The Dogon *caisses villageoises* have therefore externalised these two functions, entrusting them to two different enterprises.

—   The *central fund* function is entrusted to a partner bank, which holds and pays interest on the few "external" funds of the unions, such as their insurance funds, the innovation fund and the guarantee fund constituted on a case-by-case basis in order to obtain refinancing. Drawing on the money market and on donor countries, the bank mobilises the resources needed to refinance the unions.

—   The function of the *technical unit* is assumed by a local private enterprise, a service-providing economic interest group (EIG) created by three project executives. The EIG signs an annual contract with the three unions for paid services. Each year, the three unions meet; define the terms of reference for the services — audit, training, technical support and advice, contacts, representation and negotiation — that they wish the EIG to cover; and negotiate time (duration, schedule, deadlines) and budget with the EIG on this basis. At year-end, the unions and the EIG jointly evaluate the results of the fulfilled contract, with a view to signing a new one. At the same time, as a private enterprise, the EIG can contract with other interested organisations in the region, which has the two-fold advantage of continually renewing its capabilities through contact with different clients and of stimulating its competitive spirit. The network of *caisses villageoises*, for its part, pays only for the services used and has no fixed costs; it places the EIG in competition with other potential offers in order to maintain pressure on the quality of service and even on costs.

It is too early to measure the impact of this institutional innovation in financial terms, but one may already predict that it will help to maintain services at a reasonable cost.

The Governmental Environment with Respect to Innovation

The *caisses villageoises* of the Dogon region were set up as a project, in three phases over a period of about ten years. The sole financial backer during this period was the KFW, whereas the legal and administrative ties of the project changed over time. The first two phases, from 1986 to 1994, were carried out with the Direction nationale de l'action coopérative (DNACOOP) as designated director, while the third and last phase (1994 to 1997) was placed under the direction of the Banque nationale de développement agricole (BNDA), with the DNACOOP becoming project manager and the CIDR, technical operator. These changes corresponded to the evolution of the project: in the first two phases it had a strong element of research, while in the last phase, owing to the increasing volumes handled, it became more clearly a financial institution.

Finally, we should mention the legal vacuum in which these decentralised financial systems functioned in the Union monétaire ouest-africaine (UMOA) until 1994. As early as 1993, a series of discussions conducted by the Banque centrale des États d'Afrique de l'Ouest (BCEAO) led to a preliminary bill which, after being adopted by the Malian parliament in August 1994, created a single legal framework for all mutual savings and loan funds (*mutuelles d'épargne et de crédit* — MUTECs) in the country and gave the various systems two years to conform with the law and obtain official authorisation.

The DNACOOP: Partner of the Dogon Caisses villageoises

The DNACOOP provided protection from other decentralised administrations and from politicians. The fact that the director of the local co-operative movement served as the project's representative to the various local administrative authorities freed the project from this type of exercise, which is often cumbersome and tricky; in addition, it was this director who made the project report to his administrative superiors.

Six of the project's ten national-level executives are on secondment from the DNACOOP and its decentralised services. They are all Dogons and have proved to be highly committed civil servants and government agents, with an extraordinary sense of service to the people, an exceptional professional conscience and unimpeachable integrity. Of these six people, only two were civil servants to begin with. The DNACOOP agreed that the project would hire the workers it needed on the private labour market, freely and according to its own criteria.

Although the project had four successive national directors and four national co-ordinators as interlocutors over the ten-year period, there has nevertheless been some continuity in follow-up and dialogue, showing the DNACOOP's sincere interest in the work performed. The DNACOOP has shown trust in the *caisses villageoises'* management throughout the ten years, not hesitating to authorise adjustment of budget lines and modifications of programmes when this was justified and the arguments for it presented.

From the beginning of the project, the DNACOOP accepted and adopted the action-research approach, with all the flexibility which this requires. It accepted the underlying self-help approach in the *caisses villageoises'* governance, although it had been more familiar with methods of consciousness-raising and popularisation, as well as with subsidised rates of interest. It accepted the innovations to stimulate the local economy, which were very risky, controversial and uncertain. Lastly, it accepted and supported the final institutional innovation, which at first sight seems diametrically opposed to its own logic and operational methods: private enterprise and the use of auxiliaries under contract. Thus the DNACOOP has, in its own way, innovated with respect to its positions and partners in rural areas, which undoubtedly helped to facilitate innovation and hence the success of the overall approach.

The BNDA: A Partner in Realising the Project

The BNDA, which was at first an "interested observer" and then, from 1989, the partner bank for refinancing the *caisses villageoises*, became the designated director — a key job, representing the Malian part of this bilateral project — in 1994, at the final phase of the process. From the beginning, the majority of the BNDA's executives welcomed the approach of self-management and a high degree of possession of the *caisses villageoises* by the villagers, appropriate for poor and isolated regions (such as the Dogon region) and even for socially difficult regions (First region), although the general corporate culture of the BNDA considered these initiatives as gadgets of the donors, handling ridiculously small volumes in marginal sectors of banking activity, and hence not as partners or clients worthy of attention.

From 1994, the BNDA became more involved in methodological choices. For example, the BNDA co-ordinator took a clear-cut position concerning the operating methods of the common service EIG. Had the BNDA been placed in this position from the beginning of the project, debate over action-research options would probably have been more heated and the project would undoubtedly have had less flexibility to innovate. It must be recalled that the BNDA is first and foremost a bank, with all the rules and procedures required in that profession. At any rate, as a partner bank the BNDA has always behaved remarkably in refinancing operations, agreeing to consider the unions as its sole interlocutors and not trying to meddle with the management of the individual *caisses villageoises*. It agreed to help the growth of the network by increasing its refinancing from CFAF 1.5 million in 1989 to CFAF 100 million in 1995.

The following question should therefore be asked: are banks well suited to manage a decentralised, autonomous financial system, or rather, are they, by their nature and their purpose, complementary to such a system?

The Legal Environment

The *caisse villageoise* project of the Dogon region grew from 1986 to 1994 in a legal vacuum. The Banking Law covered the case of commercial and development banks, and a clause of the Co-operative Law governed that of savings and loan co-operatives. Highly decentralised financial activities were therefore able to develop without constraints, according to the methods which suited them best.

As early as 1993, however, the BCEAO was determined to legislate in this area, and in 1994 a law concerning MUTECs was submitted to the parliaments of the UMOA countries. In Mali, it was ratified in August 1994. This law regulates the procedures of mutual savings and loan institutions in minute detail, sometimes at the risk of being purely theoretical. In the matter of "governance", for example, it sets the configurations of all management boards, and it addresses some social issues without concerning itself with the impossibility of implementation in an under-

102

equipped rural area. As for the structure of these institutions, it provides for a traditional pyramid organisation, with a financial and technical organ in the centre. Existing systems were granted two years to conform to the law, request authorisation and become integrated in this structure. The deadlines were thus close at the time of writing.

Had this law been in force in 1986, the *caisses villageoises* could not have existed in their present form. If it remains the only legal form possible for decentralised financial systems in Africa, it will clearly be an enormous hindrance to many initiatives and to all innovation.

Decentralised financial networks must become institutionalised today, to ensure their long-term survival; but many systems which are very open, creative and successful must resort to extraordinary manoeuvres to fit into the framework of the MUTEC law, which obviously does not correspond to their histories, identities or purpose. An alternative has been found in the signature of a framework convention with the finance ministry which makes the necessary exceptions to the law, but this convention has the disadvantage of incorporating the most burdensome obligations without giving any rights in return, except the right to operate on a small scale.

Although the law on mutual financial systems is an incontestable advance, the work begun should be continued, so that a specific text for non-mutual systems may be established. Proposals to this end have been made, and negotiations are under way in Mali.

The Donor and Innovation

As mentioned above, the KFW, the financial co-operation agency of the German bilateral aid system, has been the sole backer of the project from its beginnings to 1996. It has been an advantage and a privilege for the project to have only one backer, and moreover to have continuity in dialogue over ten years. Decentralised savings and loan systems were a new field for the KFW, which previously had collaborated primarily with development banks; the agency was brought to this topic through the "struggle against poverty through self-help". The *caisse villageoise* project in the Dogon region was thus a pilot project, and this is what made a real flexibility possible.

The project's contacts at KFW headquarters have also showed exceptional continuity— two directors in ten years — and been open to action-research. Their commitment to and support for the project's operator and actors made possible a learning process, a rate of maturation and initiatives which are hardly possible in the standard framework of a bilateral project. In a sense, by playing the role of intermediary between the field and the central administration, they "protected" the project from pressure for rapid quantitative results, institutionalisation and expansion at top speed and from the pressure of unfair competition.

It has often been considered that working with a bilateral donor is linked to the constraint of having to work within a government framework, which is subject to certain priorities or to political trends. In this case, the project enjoyed both a very co-operative government partner and, in the beginning, a degree of discretion linked to the modest financial scope of the *caisses villageoises*, which were located in remote areas and thus not very visible.

On the other hand, the KFW's position as one of the largest bilateral donors in Mali allowed it to take a firm line with the government on matters of overall policy, such as the BCEAO law, and this was a large contribution to the project. At the same time, this helped to make the *caisse villageoise* approach widely known and recognised.

With respect to the innovative approaches, the programme directors of the KFW followed with interest and sometimes with enthusiasm the action-research attempted in the field, always showing a great deal of openness and tolerance, and probably at times going against the more strict and punctilious positions of their headquarters colleagues. This support proved to be very valuable in allowing the orderly progress and completion of the process.

Conclusion

Setting up a *caisse villageoise* involves several stages. First, the project holds a meeting with the village inhabitants and carries out a series of investigations to evaluate the village's economic potential, social cohesiveness and experience with credit, which lead to the signature of a contract between the project and the villages selected. The villagers then work out the internal rules of the *caisse villageoise* and choose the management board and cashiers. Payment of dues, collection of savings and lending can then begin. Interest rates on loans and savings are determined by the general assembly of the *caisse villageoise*. The *caisses villageoises* located in a given area can unite to form a union, which enables them to provide mutual support and obtain access to bank refinancing. A support apparatus is also created, in the form of an enterprise which provides services (verifying accounts, training and so on).

The success of a network of *caisses villageoises* is based on four principles:

— the villagers themselves decide how the *caisse villageoise* will function according to their own values, and they are entirely responsible for it;

— the system is autonomous on the technical level, owing to training and to the establishment of support bodies;

— the system is autonomous on the financial level, owing to rigorous management, links to the banking sector and an adequate interest rate differential (between loans and deposits; between banks, unions and *caisses villageoises*);

— economic and technical innovation allows the local economy to be developed, thanks to rapid distribution and, on site, to savings supplemented by refinancing and possibly the implementation of innovations to stimulate the local economy.

The entire process must be flexible, gradual and adapted to the context. Africa contains many difficult areas and poor, marginalised populations. Relying on the experience of the Dogon *caisses villageoises*, networks have been set up with the help of the CIDR in about a dozen regions of quite different countries: Burkina Faso, the Gambia, Madagascar, Cameroon, São Tomé and Principe, Ethiopia. These approaches have been evaluated, making it possible to put together a methodology which may today be used on a wider scale.

It is quite clear that some of the different decentralised financial systems for the poorest people are reaching maturity. It is now possible to define some fairly comprehensive principles of good management, and hence some indicators of performance that will be accepted by all. However, the 1990s witnessed the development of a "mainstream" which gives absolute priority to the profitability and self-financing capacity of the systems. As a result, norms, parameters and tools have been defined, like so many signposts for a forced march of these systems towards becoming banks. There is thus a great risk of diverting the newly created profession of the "people's banker" or of "micro-financing for the poor" from its proper objectives.

The fact is that if priority is given to making these networks profitable as quickly as possible, then the poorest people will automatically be marginalised in favour of populations which are supposed to be more creditworthy. Similarly, the rural areas, especially when isolated and subject to climatic hazards, will necessarily be abandoned in favour of the urban areas, which are more densely populated and provide better economic and commercial opportunities. This means that, once again, at least 60 to 70 per cent of Africans might not have access to financial services, because they are poor and far removed from economic centres.

The experience of the *caisses villageoises* of the Dogon region suggests another path. It shows that if all the partners give priority to placing viable and lasting financial services within the reach of poor rural populations, if they accept the consequences of this in terms of costs and time, it is quite possible to succeed, even in regions which are extremely remote and considered insolvent. It also shows that a too rapid normalization must be rejected. What can work in a given socio-cultural context with a certain economic environment is not necessarily suitable elsewhere. Each region may find an approach of its own, without necessarily importing formulas from afar.

Decision makers and donors who commit themselves to the struggle against poverty and exclusion in sub-Saharan Africa can see the Dogon experience as a clear signal that it is entirely possible to invest in the establishment and development of decentralised financial systems with a real hope of success in this part of the world — on condition that they are willing to listen to the grassroots actors, favour innovation and join with the people in seeking the path to permanence, including financial and institutional permanence.

Notes

* This chapter is based on a document by Renée Chao-Béroff, director of the study and research department of CIDR, which has supported and monitored the *caisses villageoises* of the Dogon region since their beginnings. The first section was written in collaboration with Cécile Fruman, field director of the project from 1991 to 1995.

1. The term *caisse villageoise d'épargne et de crédit autogérée* described in this chapter is specific to the CIDR's approach. It is substantially different from savings and loan co-operatives or people's banks. For several years, "village banks" and "self-managed banks" have been appearing in various contexts. They have no direct relationship to the *caisses villageoises*.

2. It is this whole social and cultural dimension which fundamentally differentiates the self-managed village savings and loan association from the "village banks" promoted by FINCA and other organisations in Latin America and elsewhere. In a *caisse villageoise*, membership is voluntary and massive. The penetration rate (defined as the percentage of the adult village population which belongs to the *caisse villageoise*) is often higher than 50 per cent, and may even reach 80-90 per cent. The *caisse villageoise* belongs to the village; it is not merely a bank based in the village.

Bibliography

CCCE/CIDR (1990), *Capitalisation d'une expérience de mise en place de Caisses villageoises d'épargne et de crédit autogérées. Cas du Burkina Faso, du Mali et de la Gambia*, Paris.

CIDR (1985), *Étude de faisabilité pour la mise en place de Caisses d'épargne et de crédit au Pays Dogon*, mission report, mimeo, Autrèches, France.

CIDR/DNACOOP (1986-94), *Rapports d'activité annuels du projet CVECA Pays Dogon*, Autrèches, France.

COLLECTIF (1993), Table ronde de réflexion sur les conséquences de l'application de la Loi portant règlementation des institutions mutualistes ou coopératives d'épargne et de crédit, Bamako.

OTERO, M. AND E. RHYNE (1994), *The New World of Microenterprise Finance*, Kumarian Press.

WEBSTER, L. AND P. FIDLER (1995), *Le secteur informel et les institutions de microfinancement en Afrique de l'Ouest*, World Bank, Washington, D.C.

WOMEN'S WORLD BANKING (1995), *Innovative Banking for Microbusiness*, New York.

Building up Capacity for Banking with the Poor: The Grameen Bank in Bangladesh

*Syed M. Hashemi**

Grameen Bank: The Rationale

The landscape of poverty, powerlessness and gender subordination in rural Bangladesh forms the context for the Grameen model. The famine of 1974 provided the stimulus for Professor Muhammad Yunus to look for alternatives. He discovered that while the credit market was the scene of the most brutal exploitation of the poor (with high interest rates resulting in chronic indebtedness, in turn, leading to forced sale of assets and destitution), it was also the arena where it was easiest for the poor to break out of their cycle of poverty. However, the conventional banking structure does not provide access for the poor because the poor can provide no collateral and the overheads for servicing loans are too high for the small loans that poor people require. Governmental loan programmes for rural areas get monopolised by the rich and powerful. Amongst the poor, women suffer even greater discrimination because patriarchal customs exclude their de facto ownership of assets and because the work that women generally engage in (home based) is not classified as economically productive[1]. Hence the need for targeted collateral-free credit for the poor and specifically for women, as developed by Grameen.

Since its inception as a pilot project in 1976 and becoming a chartered bank in 1983, Grameen has spread into 35 500 villages (more than half the villages in Bangladesh) and provided loans to 2.1 million members (more than 94 per cent of whom are women). By the end of 1995 it had disbursed over $1.6 billion in loans and has recorded a recovery rate exceeding 95 per cent. Grameen has provided loans to build 330 000 houses. The cumulative savings of members total $125 million. It currently has a paid-up capital of $5.4 million with 85 per cent of its shares owned by individual members. Nine of the 13 directors who constitute the board are Grameen clients elected by other clients as their representatives.

Building Capacity for Banking with the Poor

This chapter analyses the structure and operations of the Grameen Bank to understand the process and essential elements underlying the development of a sustainable system for providing the poor with effective access to credit. It seeks to explain how institutional capacity for ensuring targeted credit for the poor was built up in Bangladesh in the case of the Grameen Bank. This chapter therefore primarily focuses on the issue of capacity building. It addresses this at three levels. First, it looks at the capacity of the institution for reaching the poor and increasing their incomes or assets; secondly, it looks at the viability of the local office (branch office) for providing credit services to the poor; and thirdly, it looks at the programme's replication nationally for serving significant numbers of the poor. The evidence for this is based on long-term participant observation of bank functioning in two villages in Bangladesh, and an in-depth review of financial records of 20 branch offices, and finally a review of the financial statements of all 1 000 branches for one year. The paper first reviews the institutional mechanism for the delivery of credit and then provides some actual cost estimates of Grameen's path towards sustainability.

Grameen Bank: The Credit Delivery Model

Grameen targets credit to the rural poor, those who are functionally landless (owning less than half an acre of land) or have assets amounting to less than the value of an acre of medium quality land. Since collateral is not required, the Bank relies on the group mechanism to ensure effective repayments. The group mechanism transfers risks of non-repayment from the Bank to the group itself. The problem of asymmetrical information (the bank having limited information on borrowers) is resolved through selection of members by the group (screening out high risk borrowers), and through imposition of joint liability on the group. While individual borrowers receive loans, sanctions (in the form of suspension of new loans) are imposed on the group in the case of default by any individual borrower. Peer monitoring therefore reduces transaction costs and allows for successful implementation of targeted credit programmes (Stiglitz 1990; Besley *et al.* 1991; Aghion 1994; Matin 1995).

Groups of five (men and women separately) are formed by individuals themselves, selecting for those belonging to similar social and economic backgrounds (to eliminate unequal bargaining strength), from the same village and from those they have confidence in. Only one member is allowed per household. Generally a month of meetings dedicated to learning to sign one's name and learning about Grameen and memorising Grameen's "sixteen decisions" regarding social conduct, takes place before the group receives formal recognition. This period allows for group members to develop close relations with each other and be certain about their decision to join. It also instils a sense of importance and confidence in members who realise that they have "earned" membership only after a long process of screening.

Loans are disbursed to members only with the approval of the group and the final approval of the Bank. The disbursement schedule is staggered; two members receive loans followed by another two members in a month and the last member (usually the group chairperson) in another month. Six to eight groups are integrated together in a Centre. The Centre meets once a week (generally in the same premises in the village deemed as the "Centre") in the presence of a Bank worker. Credit transactions as well as discussions on Grameen or different social issues take place at these meetings. Repayments are made at these weekly meetings and attendance is compulsory. Savings mobilisation from group members in the form of weekly savings as a percentage of borrowed funds is also compulsory.

Grameen Bank: The Management and Organisational Structure

The Grameen's "branch" administrative structure (with day to day contact with members) and the "area office" function under direct management of the "zonal office". The twelve zonal offices are decentralised to the level where even strategic decisions are taken by them. In fact, all major policy decisions are taken at the zonal managers' conferences (held three times a year with the participation of senior head office staff) or in consultations with the zonal managers. The two-to-three day zonal managers' conference, with its extensive critical assessments of performance and intensive deliberations, provide the ideal format for participatory decision-making that keeps Grameen constantly revitalised. While Professor Yunus' role is still significant and important, for the most part Grameen has been able to institutionalise its management apparatus to ensure continuity and even development (Yunus, 1994, Holcombe, 1995).

Reaching the Poor

Most studies of the Grameen Bank (Hossain, 1988; World Bank, 1995) indicate that Grameen successfully targets the poor, most members being functionally landless with ownership of land below half an acre. Amongst the poor too, Grameen successfully targets women; 94 per cent of the membership are women. However, in rural Bangladesh there is significant differentiation even within the ranks of the poor. About half of the poor constitute what is referred to as the hard core poor, who are forced to subsist on a per capita income that is less than half that of the poverty line (Rahman, 1995). Sadly, Grameen has failed to target this group effectively, since most of them remain outside the Grameen net. For the most part these people are so destitute that they consider themselves not creditworthy. They do not feel they have enough resources to generate incomes to pay back loans. They therefore "self-select" themselves out of Grameen membership.

An exercise was conducted in the two villages that were exhaustively studied to determine who gets left out of the Grameen net. It was found that out of a total of 313 target group households (eligible for Grameen membership), women from 120 households (38 per cent) were not Grameen members (Table 1). It was revealed that 55 women did not join because they believed they could not "use" the money loaned and would therefore be stuck with debt for which they would eventually be forced to sell off what little possessions they still had. They refused to be burdened with still another debt. Thirty-five women did not join because joining and leaving the home for Grameen meetings with outside males would be a violation of social norms. Only eleven women said they actually wanted to join but were not accepted because other Grameen women felt they were high risks (their husbands were gamblers and would waste the money; they would migrate out of the village; they were not good money managers; or they did not get along with others). Surprisingly, 19 women said that the rules were too complicated and they couldn't memorise the 16 decisions (a prerequisite for membership).

Table 1. **Target Group Members Not Joining Grameen**

	Rangpur village	Faridpur village
Total households	246	189
Total target group households	173	130
Grameen members	99	84
Target group households not GB members	74	46
Reasons for not joining GB		
Cannot repay loan	41	14
Social/religious reasons	21	14
Cannot memorise the 16 decisions	9	10
GB members refuse to accept	3	8

Actually what this is indicative of is not so much that Grameen is unable to bring all poor women into their fold but that micro credit is not necessarily the way out for all the poor. In fact successful micro credit operations are strongly dependent on this screening to ensure that money that is borrowed can be repaid. Of course the weekly repayment schedule has been designed to specifically cater to this problem; it is easier to make small weekly payments rather than repaying all at one time. However for the really destitute even this weekly repayment schedule may be too difficult. In other words for the destitute and for others with difficulty in making good use of the loan (investing rather than meeting immediate consumption needs), credit programmes may not be the answer. Other targeted programmes would be required to address their specific needs.

This failure of all sections of the poor to use credit appropriately has specific implications regarding coverage of credit programmes. While village after village may be covered by credit programmes (extensive coverage) there would be great difficulty in ensuring intensive coverage of each village.

However, there is improvement in two specific situations. First, where there is an increase in demand at the local level and second, where other programmes are undertaken that cater to those who are not ready for credit programmes. The Grameen Bank has been active in easing demand constraints at the local level. The Grameen Bank is ensuring increased rural incomes through the "Grameen check" (handwoven cloth currently being used by local garment manufacturers for producing clothing for the export market) enabling poverty-stricken weavers, unable to compete locally with manufactured cloth, to be linked successfully with the international market; through the Agricultural Krishi Foundation which permits experiments with sustainable agricultural practices to increase agricultural productivity and hence local demand; and through the Fisheries (Motso) Foundation and the Venture Capital Fund, and recently the telecommunications project involving cellular phones to be run as business ventures by rural women, Grameen Bank is ensuring increased rural incomes. On the other hand, BRAC has been extremely successful with their Income Generation for Vulnerable Groups Development Programme in targeting the most destitute women and, over a two year period along with relief handouts creating a small asset base for them. This provides them with confidence and incomes to "graduate" into credit programmes (Hashemi 1995).

Member Level Sustainability

Numerous micro studies have attested to the positive impacts of the Grameen Bank in increasing incomes and asset ownership (Streefland *et al.*, 1989; F. Islam, 1992; Rahman, 1988; Todd, 1995). Moreover, there have been two major statistically representative sample surveys that confirm the micro level findings. The first one, undertaken in the mid-1980s by Mahabub Hossain (1988), reports that Grameen Bank had contributed to making members' household incomes 43 per cent greater than control group incomes. The Bank has contributed to generating new employment for a fifth of its members and increased the average level of employment from six to 18 working days per month. Working capital for Grameen-supported enterprises of members was shown to have increased from 743 to 2 811 taka (40 taka = $1), nearly a four-fold increase within about two years. About 87 per cent of members had also reported making investments in housing, education and sanitation of nearly 1 900 taka. Grameen has had an economic impact in the community also. Through increasing employment and incomes of members, Grameen had a positive impact on agricultural wages. The average wage rate in Grameen villages was shown to have increased by 19 per cent relative to non-Grameen villages.

The second study was based on an intensive survey conducted by the World Bank in the early 1990s. It found that, on average, it takes about five years for programme participants to rise above the poverty line and about eight years to reach a situation where they do not require loans from targeted credit programmes. Targeted credit also helps increase assets, savings, and net worth of households. Most importantly, by promoting a shift from land-based activities to non-traditional economic activities, targeted credit programmes promote productivity increases and employment generation in the rural economy. The study documents increases due to Grameen in overall employment, labour force participation among women, and self-employment (World Bank, 1995).

This economic impact at the household level ensures that members continue to retain membership. Since membership retention is so important to programme sustainability the World Bank study attempted to analyse the reasons for loan defaults. It was found that loan default was not erratic; factors influencing branch-level efficiency and local production conditions jointly explain 54 per cent of the variation in default behaviour for those having overdue loans of 52-72 weeks. Factors contributing to low default rates include benefits received by branch managers, staff and member training, rural electrification, roads, educational infrastructure and commercial bank density. This implies that members in an area with high economic and commercial activity and where motivation and training is high, perform better than members in other areas.

Economic welfare (contributing to sustainability) of members is also dependent on several other factors. It has already been mentioned that the absolutely destitute self-select themselves out of Grameen-type credit programmes. Initial levels of poverty are actually extremely important in determining success in loan utilisation. The very poor are in such a consumption crisis that loans are immediately used for meeting consumption needs or paying back loans. The "consumption space" required for purchasing assets or making investments with the credit funds is available only for those who are at a basic subsistence level.

For the most part, Grameen funds generate supplemental sources of income for the household. This supplemental income is of course critical in that it spells the difference between consuming two meals and one, between being able to acquire some assets and none. However, the fact that in most cases this is supplemental income assumes that there are other sources of income that can be used for meeting repayments, at least in the first couple of rounds in the credit programme. Subsequently, Grameen-funded assets may reach a level where income streams generated from them may indeed turn out to be the primary sources of income. About a third of Grameen's loan disbursement has been in livestock and fishery, and another quarter in agriculture. In both cases incomes from funded activities do not begin immediately after investments, although loan repayments (in small instalments) do. The majority of Grameen loans therefore presuppose the availability of alternative sources of income.

Grameen credit can fund activities directly only if such activities are in trading, processing and manufacturing, etc, where financial turnovers are daily, weekly or a couple of weeks, at most. In fact, Grameen credit works best in providing working capital for traditional artisan activities or petty trade. In the former, member households have a specific skill, a familiarity with the market, and in most cases a ready demand for their products. In rural Bangladesh most artisan families suffer from severe credit shortages that force them to borrow at high interest rates or buy raw materials on credit or buy only small quantities at a time. Grameen credit make a major difference for increasing incomes in these situations by reducing dependence on informal finance, by allowing larger purchases of raw materials (at lower prices), and by smoothing production levels.

Grameen Bank managers as well as members mention other non-economic factors which contribute significantly to successful use of credit. Such factors often serve as a basis for selection of new members. Women who are really disorganised and cannot "manage" their households, women who are considered foolish or lacking in common sense, women who are "belligerent" and cannot get along with others, women with many small children, with husbands who are "lazy" and gamble and waste money or are "bad", are generally considered "high risks". It is felt that these women will be unable to use loans "wisely"; they would be unable to save and invest and increase incomes. These women, even if provided with membership, would drop out and would have a negative influence on others.

The viability of credit programmes in terms of the sustainability of members therefore depends on a variety of economic and non-economic factors. In conditions of pervasive poverty and limited opportunities, the struggle to get out of poverty is slow and arduous. Grameen group dynamics is the essential element making this possible, even beyond the availability of credit.

Grameen's weekly Centre meeting is more than a mechanism for credit transactions. Women have to follow a strict code of discipline; they have to sit in straight rows of five, salute, chant slogans and do physical drills. They have to memorise the 16 decisions and repeat individual decisions when asked to. These rituals of participation and the regular contact with Grameen Bank officials and other members provide women with an identity outside of their family. In fact, for most of these women this is the first time that they have an identity other than being someone's daughter, wife or mother. Women coming to regular meetings also develop a sense of purpose, belonging to a public activity. This gives them a sense of self-respect. Participating in public, handling cash and keeping accounts builds their confidence. Many Grameen women have pointed out that joining Grameen allowed them to "see" their own village for the first time; they "learned" to speak to males and outsiders without fear; they could now handle finances; they have earned new respect within their homes and communities. It is this process of "empowerment" that most women go through that provides Grameen with its success, that ensures the continued support of its women, that allows for the sustainability of members, and therefore in turn the sustainability of the programme.

Branch Level Sustainability

Investigations into branch sustainability were conducted at several levels. In the first exercise, 20 branches were selected randomly (four each from five randomly selected zones) from all Grameen branches. The branches varied in age from three to 13 years. For each of the branches, membership and financial data were collected for each of the operating years of the branch. The results are presented in Table 2. The data represents averages of all 20 branches (or as many as were operating in any particular year). There seems to be a general pattern prevailing in terms of branch profitability and disbursements and years of operations. For the most part, branches seem to be running at a profit after the fourth or fifth year of operations, after disbursements exceed 10 to 11 million taka, and after membership reaches 1 600 to 1 700.

In the Grameen Bank's own idealised calculations of the financial sustainability of branches (different from Table 2), a typical branch is optimally considered to serve a little over 2 200 members. This figure is reached by the sixth year of operations. By the sixth year also, due to increases in membership as well as the increase in the average size of loans, branch incomes increase and profits are generated.

A second exercise was conducted to look at branch profitability over time but by region to account for regional variations. Financial statements were collected (all 1 055 branches of Grameen for the 1995 calendar year. Each branch was classified according to the number of years of its operations. Table 3 presents average net profits of branches for 1995 classified according to years of operations. The data shows wide variations in profitability by regions. Branches in Dhaka, Tangail and Chittagong zones show good profits whereas Sylhet, Rangpur and Patuakhali perform poorly. Rangpur and Patuakhali specifically indicate that irrespective of years of operations, most branches are running at a loss. In fact, of the 89 branches in Patuakhali and 110 branches in Rangpur, only 29 and 23 branches respectively are making profits. This compares with 73 branches out of 77 in Tangail, 59 out of 72 in Chittagong, and all 118 branches in the Dhaka zone making profits.

Such findings are illustrative of the importance of the economic context for the success of credit programmes. Dhaka, Tangail and Chittagong are all regions with high economic activity. This implies that high levels of employment prevail in these regions and relative incomes of poor households are higher than those prevailing in other regions. This is borne out by much higher agricultural wages than in depressed areas such as Rangpur. The implication of this is twofold. First, since even poor households have some cash incomes it is easier to meet weekly repayments and thereby accumulate assets through membership in the credit programmes. This, in turn, eventually leads to higher incomes from the income stream generated by such assets. Second, since income levels are higher, aggregate demand at the local level is higher, implying that there is a better market for products created through micro-finance funded enterprises. On the other hand, in the Rangpur area most people are unemployed for two to three months during the lean season. Economic situations deteriorate to

Table 2. Financial Data from 20 Randomly Selected Branches
(in thousand taka)

Year	Average No. of members	Average amount disbursed	Average branch revenue	Branch revenue as % of amount disbursed	Average branch expenditure	Average net profit
1	267	469	18	3.8	84	- 65.6
2	823	2 282	126	5.5	240	- 114.4
3	1 414	6 060	381	6.3	442	- 60.3
4	1 637	11 366	661	5.8	703	- 41.2
5	1 731	11 810	734	6.2	709	25.2
6	1 819	9 990	704	7.1	658	46.5
7	1 915	13 514	989	7.4	929	59.9
8	1 859	14 340	1 072	7.5	1 021	50.6
9	1 980	20 566	1 379	6.7	1 309	69.9
10	1 922	21 889	982	4.5	988	- 6.0
11	2 292	35 343	1 426	4.0	1 230	196.3
12	2 552	39 490	1 795	4.6	1 482	313.5
13+	2 469	37 306	2 007	5.4	1 760	247.8

Table3. Net Profit of Branches by Zone
(in thousand taka)

Year	Comilla	Dhaka	Chittagong	Sylhet	Mymensingh	Tangail
1	-21	-	15	-	-163	-
2	-287	-	-	-	-214	473
3	-307	-	-	-	-204	-
4	-60	355	130	-157	-31	-24
5	20	571	-44	-65	388	301
6	167	1 331	-	-34	354	412
7	95	952	-197	-121	-	430
8	48	1 062	180	-100	-	741
9	-	951	121	-164	-	307
10	-	1 019	87	-	-	523
11	-	1 000	507	-	-	683
12	-	841	489	-	-	738
13+	-	820	431	-	-	-

Year	Bogrra	Rangpur	Dinajpur	Rajshahi	Faridpur	Patuakhali
1	-	35	-319	-	193	-
2	-278	-	-85	-	-	-
3	-177	-	-160	-	-	-
4	32	-	-70	-159	-6	-148
5	49	95	-61	-50	42	-87
6	117	-151	-13	21	137	-11
7	94	-34	69	47	40	13
8	46	-12	-	152	78	23
9	-121	-66	-	-	-	65
10	-	-205	-	-	-	-185
11	-	-267	-	-	-	-197
12	-	-251	-	-	-	-61
13+	-	-229	-	-	-	-37

Note: $1 = 40 taka.

the point where localised famines are common. In such conditions, credit funds are often used to meet consumption needs or assets are sold to meet repayments. In a way, the situation mirrors that of the problems with destitute households. If households are very poor (if regions are economically depressed) normal credit programmes are insufficient to lead to greater income and economic well-being. This translates into continuing indebtedness at the individual level while at the programme level it means that branches do not make profits and suffer from defaults or from severe limits to expanding membership and credit disbursement.

This is not to imply that credit programmes should not be working with the poorest or should not be active in economically depressed areas. What is being pointed out is that credit programmes left to themselves to maximise profits would tend to stay away from economically depressed zones and from the poorest. There should be extra sensitivity to these issues which require special programmes to address them.

Grameen Bank branches do not have their own revolving credit funds. Branches borrow funds from the head office at 12 per cent interest rate to on-lend at a 20 per cent interest rate. This represents their largest source of earnings. Branches also earn a little from deposits of group funds, individual savings and other sources. Expenses include all branch expenses, from interest payments to the head office to all salaries, office rents, etc. Profits are sent back to the head office which also subsidises in the event of losses. Branches therefore are not independent operations and calculations on funding levels required to make a branch sustainable are not available. However, based on the figures from Table 2 it would seem that around year five, when branches become financially viable, they reach a level of disbursements of around 12 million taka. Given that fresh disbursements can be made from weekly repayments, funds can be far lower than the 12 million taka to reach a total annual disbursement of 12 million taka. However fresh disbursements cannot be made every week and the branch would need to retain some cash. Using a slightly conservative figure, one could easily assume an actual multiplier of two to determine the extent of disbursements possible from a given level of funds. Thus with a credit fund of 6 million taka, it would be possible to have disbursements of 12 million taka. Losses over the first four years should be added to it. Assuming that member savings as well as profits would assist in expansion of disbursements, one could estimate a fund requirement of 6.3 million taka as sufficient to set up branch level operations and carry it to sustainability.

Programme Level Sustainability

Since its inception as a bank, Grameen has had a phenomenal development, both in terms of membership as well as in terms of financial sustainability. Membership in the Grameen Bank has increased from 58 000 in 1983 to over 2 million at the end of 1995, with currently 94 per cent of the membership being women. During the same period, Grameen's activities have spread from 1 249 to 35 505 villages and

119

disbursements increased from 194 million taka to nearly 60 billion taka ($1.5 billion) Grameen has also provided housing loans to its members at an 8 per cent rate of interest payable over a ten to 15 year period. By December 1995, a total of 329 515 houses had been built with Grameen loans (Table 4).

Grameen encourages members to save. This is done both to help members cope with difficult times and to mobilise funds locally. Thus far members have generated cumulative savings equalling nearly 5 billion taka ($125 million). This is several times greater than that collectively mobilised by the top commercial banks in the country. It is interesting to note that poor rural women have saved enough to buy out the most expensive enterprise in Bangladesh.

In terms of financial sustainability Grameen's performance has also been impressive. It has managed to run at a profit for most years except for 1991 and 1992 (when salary increases decreed by the government suddenly increased costs across the board). Though the ratio of profits to equity is low, it still is impressive that a programme, targeting credit to the poor, could manage to be financially viable.

How has Grameen achieved this financial sustainability? The 1994 financial statements reveal that Grameen in that year had a total revenue of over 2 billion taka ($50 million) and made a profit of taka 21.7 million taka ($541 000). However, income includes interest on fixed deposits and three-month government treasury bills (262 million taka or 16 per cent of all interest income) that are not directly from the operation of the credit programme. It also includes (as part of "other income") a 76 million taka grant for head office monitoring, evaluation and training expenses. Thus 17 per cent of revenues were not generated internally from the credit operations. If these were to be excluded Grameen would not show a profit. However, portfolio diversification is common practice for reducing risks and therefore Grameen's decision to invest in short-term bills and deposits is acceptable. Grameen also likes to say that grant funds are not going to the members but to subsidise head office costs and therefore are not typically costs of loan operations. It should also be noted that the share of foreign grants as a percentage of income has been declining steadily from a high of 20 per cent in 1989 to 3.8 per cent in 1994.

The reporting of profits in the financial statements of the Bank provides a sense of its financial sustainability. However, this fails to give a notion of the subsidy enjoyed by the Bank in terms of subsidised credit and grants. Therefore, a measure of economic sustainability will be used that incorporates both the actual self-sustainability of the institution as well as its outreach. This measurement of economic self-sustainability is provided by Jacob Yaron (1992). He defines this sustainability as the "return on equity, net of any subsidy received, equalling or exceeding the opportunity cost of the equity funds." Yaron develops a Subsidy Dependence Index (SDI) to assess and quantify the subsidy dependence (defined as the inverse of self-sustainability) of financial institutions. The SDI is useful in "tracking progress made by financial institutions in reducing their subsidy dependence over time". "The SDI measures the percentage increase in the financial institution's average on-lending interest rate required to compensate for the elimination of subsidies."

Table 4. Growth of Operations
(monetary amounts in million taka)

Year	1983	1984	1985	1986	1987	1988	1989	1990	1991	1992	1993	1994
Total number of branches	86	152	226	295	369	501	641	781	915	1 015	1 040	1 045
Total number of villages	1 249	2 268	3 666	5 170	7 502	10 552	15 073	19 536	25 248	30 619	33 667	34 913
Total number of members	58 320	121 051	171 622	234 343	339 156	490 363	662 263	869 538	1 066 426	1 424 395	1 814 916	2 013 130
Total number of borrowers	46 955	106 943	152 463	209 467	328 557	472 430	648 267	852 622	955 031	1 385 324	1 682 914	1 860 674
Total loan disbursements	195	499	928	1 470	2 280	3 560	5 328	7 591	10 230	15 434	26 056	39 968
Total housing loan disbursements	-	4	21	27	167	338	574	799	1 100	1 660	3 333	4 671
Total member savings (Group Funds)	16	38	71	115	186	297	451	650	892	1 308	2 117	3 147
Total income	1	36	66	90	129	200	299	407	532	773	1 325	2 019
Total expenditure	4	31	65	90	128	198	297	404	540	778	1 316	1 997
Net profit for the year	- 3.1	4.9	0.5	0.4	0.4	1.2	2.3	3.1	- 8.3	- 5.7	9.6	21.7

The calculations of SDI for Grameen Bank suggests a decline over the years (Table 5). In 1994 the SDI was equal to 21 per cent, down from 170 per cent and 180 per cent in 1986 and 1987. This implies that though subsidies have been declining, Grameen Bank operations are still dependent on subsidised credit. If the Bank were paying market rates for the credit funds that they are receiving, it would have to be charging an additional 21 per cent interest to cover all expenses.

Strictly speaking therefore, Grameen is still being subsidised, though the subsidy is probably far less than that of the financial institutions for the wealthy (for financing industrial development in Bangladesh) where default rates are in excess of 80 per cent. However, it would not be possible to cover costs through increasing interest rates. The type of activities being funded by Grameen and the low level of economic activity in rural areas, combine to limit the return on investments. Incomes from funded activities are therefore low and could not sustain higher interest rates. It could be possible to increase the level of operations and lower costs, though currently Bank employees work extremely hard, for more than 12 hours a day and often seven days a week. As Grameen is now borrowing more and more from the money market at commercial interest rates and depending less and less on foreign funding, this would seem to indicate a decline in dependence on donor funds. As it is, donor funds are only being used for some head office activities such as training, monitoring and evaluation. It is therefore possible that the declining trend in subsidies will continue and make Grameen free of subsidies and economically viable, in addition to being financially viable.

Conclusion

The Grameen Bank has been extremely successful in reaching the poor, in ensuring that the poor do actually repay (much better than the wealthy do), in increasing incomes and economic welfare of the poor, in proving that programmes for the poor can actually be financially viable and in the long run even economically sustainable. In a generally enabling economic environment, Grameen has proved that branches servicing between 1 500 to 2 000 members can achieve viability in four, five or six years. The success of Grameen resides in the simplicity of the model: access to credit improves the lives of the poor; micro credit keeps overheads low and makes the programme financially viable. However, these results have been possible thanks to easy access to subsidised credit, albeit at a declining rate of subsidy dependence.

Table 5. **Estimation of Subsidy Dependence Index (SDI) for the Grameen Bank**
(in million taka)

Year	1983	1984	1985	1986	1987	1988	1989	1990	1991	1992	1993	1994
Average borrowing from banks and foreign institutions	85	198	373	575	836	1 094	1 501	1 803	1 857	1 877	3 674	6 843
SDI	85.20	0.68	1.06	1.70	1.80	1.31	1.25	1.16	0.86	0.43	0.25	0.21

123

The level of funding availability has not been an important constraint to the setting up of credit operations, nor indeed to the viability of the programme, though it may limit the extent of coverage. A close investigation of Grameen postulates the following essential elements in building credit capacity for the poor: peer monitoring to offset risks in information gaps and reduce transactions costs; group solidarity for building extra peer identity and loyalty to the programme; hiring of fresh university graduates who are motivated to work with the poor; close monitoring of all bank activities to ensure discipline; and a creatively open perspective to be always experimenting, learning and improvising. These have also proved to be the essential elements in replicating Grameen in other countries (Hulme, 1994; Gibbons, 1995).

Notes and References

*   Department of Economics, Jahangirnagar University, and Programme for Research on Poverty Alleviation, Grameen Trust

1.   Women's subordination in rural Bangladesh is embedded in the nexus of relationships defining the family as well as the underlying social arena. Within the family, a strict sexual division of labour is enforced through the system of "purdah", the practice of isolating women from men outside their immediate families. Purdah ensures women's separation from direct interactions with the money economy, thereby making it possible to ascribe low status to women's work. (Adnan, 1989; Cain *et al.*, 1979; Chen, 1989; Kabeer, 1988). The prevailing kinship system specifies that descent is patrilineal and residence patrilocal.

Table A1. **Balance Sheet**
(in million taka)

PROPERTY AND ASSETS	1983	1984	1985	1986	1987	1988	1989	1990	1991	1992	1993	1994
Cash in hand	0.1	0.0	0.0	0.0	0.3	0.3	0.5	0.0	0.1	0.0	0.1	0.1
Balance with other banks	12.7	20.0	19.1	19.4	22.3	34.6	49.1	60.1	67.1	151.7	339.9	328.9
Investment	26.5	146.5	218.5	435.5	408.3	399.3	642.0	1 077.7	1 450.8	1 301.2	1 744.8	3 201.9
Loans and advances	74.3	177.5	245.7	331.0	644.1	1 094.9	1 593.2	2 117.4	2 551.2	4 423.9	8 763.6	11 053.0
Fixed assets	1.4	4.8	9.7	32.1	68.5	122.6	161.8	264.3	344.0	421.1	497.1	551.2
Other assets	3.9	27.9	53.0	82.0	135.9	259.7	436.1	581.0	427.0	585.7	931.1	1 439.2
Total	118.8	376.6	546.0	900.0	1 279.3	1 911.3	2 882.7	4 100.4	4 840.1	6 883.7	12 276.6	16 574.1

CAPITAL & LIABILITIES	1983	1984	1985	1986	1987	1988	1989	1990	1991	1992	1993	1994
Capital - Paid up	18.0	25.2	30.0	35.5	42.1	56.9	72.0	72.0	114.4	149.5	150.0	216.5
General and other reserves		1.0	1.5	1.8	2.7	3.7	5.8	8.7	8.7	21.4	49.9	70.4
Revolving Funds	-3.1	0.6	0.5	0.5	7.7	10.3	307.6	1 025.0	1 278.1	2 383.5	2 827.8	3 089.2
Borrowings from banks/	85.4	311.3	433.9	716.9	954.7	1 232.9	1 720.0	1 838.2	1 876.1	1 878.2	5 470.0	8 215.7
Deposits and other funds	18.5	38.3	79.8	145.0	221.9	324.5	566.7	851.4	1 381.0	2 176.3	3 150.2	4 132.6
Other liabilities	0.0	0.2	0.3	0.4	38.2	215.9	91.6	168.7	183.0	274.8	628.8	849.7
SIDE Loan Payable Acct.					12.0	67.2	119.0	136.9				
Total	118.8	376.6	546.0	900.0	1 279.3	1 911.3	2 882.7	4 100.4	4 841.3	6 883.7	12 276.6	16 574.1

Table A2. **Profit and Loss Account**
(in million taka)

INCOME	1983	1984	1985	1986	1987	1988	1989	1990	1991	1992	1993	1994
Interest on:												
Loans and advances	0.2	23.4	35.1	42.6	65.1	112.7	162.0	213.7	315.7	522.2	1 055.6	1 646.4
Investments	0.0	0.1	0.8	1.6	59.7	51.6	74.0	112.9	133.6	176.4	165.6	262.1
Deposits	0.7	11.9	29.8	45.7	0.5	0.8	1.1	1.6	1.6	2.0	3.7	4.4
Other income	0.2	0.7	0.1	0.3	3.5	34.5	62.0	78.6	80.9	71.8	100.3	105.6
Total	1.1	36.0	65.7	90.2	128.7	199.6	299.0	406.8	531.8	772.4	1 325.2	2 018.5

EXPENSES	1983	1984	1985	1986	1987	1988	1989	1990	1991	1992	1993	1994
Interest on:												
Deposits	0.3	1.8	4.1	7.5	12.5	20.9	32.8	54.6	68.8	101.9	151.9	269.4
Borrowings	1.1	14.1	25.5	23.6	22.2	27.7	38.7	43.2	50.3	89.0	235.5	522.5
Salaries and other related	1.3	9.4	25.5	43.7	65.3	81.1	121.2	170.8	268.6	389.2	579.8	626.5
Directors remuneration	0.0	0.0	0.0	0.0	0.0	0.0	0.0	0.0	0.0	0.0	0.0	0.0
Other expenses	1.5	5.0	9.0	13.7	26.3	658.9	96.1	124.0	135.4	178.0	330.3	558.0
Depreciation	0.1	0.7	1.1	1.4	1.9	2.9	8.0	11.1	16.9	19.9	18.2	20.3
Total	4.2	31.1	65.3	89.9	128.3	198.4	296.8	403.7	540.1	778.1	1 315.7	1 996.8
Net Profit	-3.1	4.9	0.4	0.3	0.4	1.2	2.2	3.1	-8.3	-5.7	9.5	21.7

Bibliography

ADNAN, S. (1989), "Birds in a Cage: Institutional Change and Women's Position in Bangladesh", IUSSP, Dhaka.

AGHION, B. (1994), "On the Design of Credit Agreement with Peer Monitoring", DEP No.55, London School Of Economics.

BESLEY, T. *et al.* (1991), "Group Lending, Repayment Incentives and Social Collateral", Woodrow Wilson School of Public and International Affairs, Working Paper No.152, Princeton University, Princeton.

CAIN, M. *et al.*, (1979), "Class, Patriarch, and Women's Work in Bangladesh", *Population and Development Review*.

CHEN, M. (1989), "Developing Non-Craft Employment for Women's Work in the Third World", The Feminist Press, New York.

FUGLESANG, A. AND D. CHANDLER, (1993), *Participation as Process - Process as Growth: What We Can Learn From Grameen Bank, Bangladesh*, Grameen Trust, Dhaka.

GIBBONS, D. (1995), *The Grameen Reader*, Grameen Bank, Dhaka.

HASHEMI, S.M. (1995), IGVGD, "Vulnerable Groups Development: Report on the Surveys on Women Participating in the VGD Cycle", WFP, Dhaka.

HOLCOMBE, H.S. (1995), "Managing To Empower", University Press Limited, Dhaka.

HOSSAIN, M (1988), "Credit for Alleviation of Rural Poverty: The Grameen Bank in Bangladesh", Research Report 55, IFPRI, Washington, D.C.

HULME, D. (1993), "Replicating Finance Programmes in Malawi and Malaysia", *Small Enterprise Development*, Vol. 4, No. 4.

ISLAM, F., (1992), "A Study on the Viability of Grameen Bank Borrowers in Some Selected Areas of Tangail District", Department of Agricultural Finance, Bangladesh Agricultural University, Mymensingh.

JAHAN, R. (1989), "Women and Development in Bangladesh: Challenges and Opportunities". Dhaka: Ford Foundation.

JAIN, P.S. (1996), "Managing Credit for the Rural Poor: Lessons from the Grameen Bank", *World Development*, 24(1).

KABEER, N. (1988), "Subordination and Struggle: Women in Bangladesh", *New Left Review*.

MATIN, I. (1995), "Group Dynamics in Credit Groups: A Question of Context and/or Design?" University of Sussex. D. Phil. Project Outline.

RAHMAN, A. (1988), "Credit for the Rural Poor", A Study Prepared for the Agricultural Sector Review, 1988, UNDP, Dhaka.

RAHMAN, R.I. (1992), "Analysis of Labour Supply Function for Self Employed Workers". *The Bangladesh Development Studies,* Vol. XX, No. 1 (March 1992).

RAHMAN, H.Z. (1995), "Rethinking Rural Poverty", University Press Limited, Dhaka.

STIGLITZ, J.E. (1990), "Peer Monitoring and Credit Markets". *The World Bank Economic Review*, 4 (3).

STREEFLAND, P. *et al.* (1989), "Different Ways to Support the Rural Poor: Effects of Two Development Approaches in Bangladesh", Bangladesh: The Centre for Social Studies and the Netherlands: Royal Tropical Institute (2nd edition).

STREEFLAND, P. *et al.*(1995), "Women at the Centre: Grameen Bank Borrowers Ten Years On", mimeo.

WORLD BANK (1995), "Credit Programmes for the Poor: Household and Intrahousehold Impacts and Programme Sustainability".

YARON, J. (1992), "Successful Rural Finance Institutions", World Bank, Washington D.C.

YUNUS, M. (1994) "Grameen Bank As I See It", Grameen Bank, Dhaka.

BancoSol: The Challenge of Growth for Microfinance Organisations

Claudio Gonzalez-Vega*, Mark Schreiner, Richard L. Meyer,
Jorge Rodriguez and Sergio Navajas

Introduction: The Challenge of Growth

This chapter focuses on the difficulties inherent in the prudent management of growth of microfinance organisations and on the potential limits to increased efficiency, profitability and sustainability that may be expected from growth and large size[1].

The experience of Banco Solidario S.A. (BancoSol) in Bolivia is used to illustrate these questions. In the case of BancoSol, formalization as a bank brought with it the possibility of more rapid growth and thereby a number of challenges, unanticipated problems, new sources of cost and second-generation adjustments. Few Latin American microfinance organisations have grown so large, so fast, and important lessons can be learned from this case.

Growth has at least three positive implications for microfinance organisations. First, it is the main mechanism for improvement of one of the key criteria for success in microfinance: outreach (Yaron, 1994). Increasing numbers of clients improve the organisation's breadth of outreach. Given the very large numbers of poor, but creditworthy households/firms in developing countries who are potential clients but who do not have access to financial services, microfinance organisations should seek opportunities for sustainable growth (Rhyne and Otero, 1994).

Second, growth is an important mechanism for improving another criterion of success in microfinance: sustainability. Growth in the form of the addition of new and better products, such as deposit facilities, helps the intermediary satisfy more of the demands for financial services from existing and potential clientele. This improves the quality of outreach, and it enhances the image of the microfinance organisation. Sustainable growth is a signal to the intermediary's potential borrowers (microclients) and potential lenders (banks) about the program's strength and purpose. This image of permanency serves to attract loanable funds from banks for additional growth and to increase the borrowers' willingness to repay loans (Gonzalez-Vega, 1994).

Third, growth of assets can help reduce average operating costs. When fixed costs are significant and if microfinance organisations can take advantage of economies of scale, lower costs as a result of larger size can help increase both outreach and sustainability. Moreover, growth in the form of new products may generate economies of scope that may also lower costs and improve profits.

Growth is not easy, however, and it may be loaded with danger. First, expanding the portfolio too rapidly may increase loan arrears and losses. These losses may result from changes in the risk composition of the clientele as well as from more opportunities for mistakes in evaluating and managing risks. Rapid growth increases the share of new borrowers in the portfolio, and new clients are potentially riskier than older, well-established customers. Moreover, given a set of potential clients with heterogeneous risk profiles, expansion may require lending to riskier borrowers as a given market is gradually saturated.

Second, because clients located further from the lender usually cost more to monitor, accelerating growth may lead to higher costs or to reduced oversight of borrower behaviour and thus less effective prevention of default. If existing control systems become overloaded, risks and costs increase as growth accelerates[2].

Third, too fast a pace of growth may also bring about difficult-to-solve inconsistencies between, on the one hand, large size and a rapid expansion of operations (which require formalization of structures and depersonalisation of relationships) and, on the other hand, between existing organisational structures (which are largely based on informal relationships), the skills of available human resources (which may not be able to handle the new, more complex tasks of running a large organisation) and features of the lending technology (based on personal relationships between loan officers and borrowers). These inconsistencies may lead to a deterioration of communication, costly mistakes, and an increased vulnerability to fraud.

To address these issues properly and, at the same time, to experience healthy growth is one of the most difficult challenges faced by the management of self-sustainable microfinance organisations. An additional challenge is to avoid a process of "loan-size creep" (larger loans to wealthier clients, rather than growth via larger numbers of target customers). When loan size creep occurs, depth of outreach decreases, and the organisation may drift away from its original mission.

This chapter illustrates some of the main issues associated with rapid growth by reporting on the experience of BancoSol. The choice of this microfinance organisation is an acknowledgement of its outstanding overall performance. It also reflects the opportunity BancoSol offers to identify gains and dangers from brisk expansion, given the intensity of the challenges of growth at this organisation and the comparative success with which they have been addressed so far. This purpose is accomplished here by a brief evaluation of the history of BancoSol.

BancoSol: The Initial Conditions

Banco Solidario S.A. is a private, fully-chartered commercial bank. After a long gestation based on the earlier success of PRODEM (an NGO), BancoSol began operations in early 1992. Just as any other bank in Bolivia, it operates under the regulatory framework of the Central Bank and the prudential norms of the Superintendency of Banks and Financial Institutions. What sets it apart from other Bolivian banks is a portfolio built entirely of well-performing microloans. As such, BancoSol is an outstanding example of a financially viable microfinance banking venture.

Although chartered as a private bank, BancoSol has strong altruistic roots. Among its shareholders are leading NGOs and donor organisations (75 per cent of the shares) as well as prominent, successful and politically influential Bolivian businessmen (25 per cent)[3]. What makes it different from other microfinance organisations is its charter as a regulated private bank and the explicit pursuit of its altruistic mission through a profit-maximising strategy of commercial viability. BancoSol's shareholders expect profits and they will probably reinvest them in the quest for additional outreach, as they believe that a profitable operation best serves their altruistic goals. The accompanying strong concern for financial viability within its market niche is at the roots of BancoSol's successful performance.

BancoSol's ownership structure emerged from its NGO origins in PRODEM. This microfinance organisation began operations in 1987, and its rapid success made the emergence of BancoSol possible. Although PRODEM now owns about one-third of the shares of BancoSol, it has continued its own operations, with a new specialisation in rural microfinance.

By 1990 the belief had developed that the sustained growth of PRODEM was constrained by its NGO status and by its lack of access to sources of loanable funds that could be more flexible than from donors[4]. Market funds would allow the organisation to respond to substantial and clearly identifiable demands for credit and to manage its cash flows better in the presence of strong seasonal variations of such demands (Glosser, 1994). Thus, BancoSol was created as a response to anticipated constraints on the successful growth of PRODEM.

When BancoSol was established, PRODEM transferred a loan portfolio of $3 960 000, with about 14 300 active clients, some real estate from its network of urban branches, and a PL480 loan for $850 000 at 8 per cent per year (Agafonoff, 1994). Additional urban branches were transferred later. The total value of the outstanding loan portfolio eventually transferred was $6 477 029. More important, PRODEM transferred to BancoSol several intangible assets that represent initial conditions that gave BancoSol a head start toward success[5].

Among the important intangible assets transferred to BancoSol were:

a) a lending technology, proven and improved through the investment of several years of experimentation, development and adjustment of the programme's loan production activity;

b) a stock of information capital, accumulated over several years of working in its market niche and learning to understand the environment and the clientele;

c) the actual client relationships embodied in a large portfolio of active, well-performing clients;

d) the human capital embodied in an experienced staff, as a result of costly training and learning-by-doing;

e) a reputation as a serious organisation capable of sustaining long-term relationships with its clients[6];

f) well-established connections with international networks (particularly ACCION) and the resulting opportunities from technology transfers and sharing of experiences; and

g) a strong commitment to its mission, resulting from an unusual organisational culture (evolved by the leaders of PRODEM, most of whom moved into BancoSol) as well as the presence of strong shareholders with a clear vision about the role of the organisation.

Formalization and upgrading to a regulated bank brought additional advantages:

a) the capacity to mobilise funds in the market with greater flexibility, through deposits from the public, inter-bank loans, bonds placed in the domestic and international capital market or access to Central Bank rediscounts and other lines of credit;

b) any benefits realisable from larger size (scale and scope economies);

c) the intangible value of a bank charter in a financial market with severe restrictions on entry; and

d) the protection implicit in more professional and rigorous monitoring of its financial performance by the prudential supervisor (Superintendency of Banks and Financial Institutions), new lenders (other banks and bondholders), and shareholders (who may have more to lose in terms of reputation after the transformation into a bank).

Even though market funds typically have higher interest rates, shorter maturities and shorter grace periods than funds from donors, the overall management of BancoSol's liabilities has become more efficient. Access to the new sources of funds has helped to avoid the high transaction costs and lack of opportune disbursement sometimes experienced during the PRODEM days.

Although mobilising small deposits is expensive, BancoSol understands the social value of such an undertaking. The organisation is in the process of adopting more efficient technologies and procedures to reduce these costs to reasonable levels. It seems that deposit mobilisation is a wise investment for this microfinance organisation for preserving long-term relationships with its clientele, diversifying its liabilities and the independence that comes from commercial sources of funding (Gonzalez-Vega, 1994).

Breadth of Outreach

To judge the success of microfinance programmes, we have adopted the criteria of outreach and sustainability suggested by Yaron (1994). Outreach represents the provision of a wide array of financial services to large numbers of the poor.

At least six indicators show that, by Latin American standards, the breadth of outreach of BancoSol is remarkable. First, the average of the monthly loan portfolios outstanding from June 1994 to June 1995 was $30 million (Table 1)[7]. This indicator reflected very rapid portfolio growth from the date of conversion into a bank through mid-1994, followed by some reduction of the portfolio in 1995, as the organisation entered a period of consolidation. From the beginning of 1992 to the end of 1994, BancoSol's portfolio increased tenfold in real terms. This is even more remarkable because the portfolio inherited from PRODEM was already large by Latin American standards.

Second, the annual flow of loans disbursed shows a similar trend, with growth accelerating in 1993-94 and decelerating in 1995. As an indicator of the intensity of its lending activity, BancoSol disbursed $84 million during 1994, five times more than PRODEM disbursed in the year preceding the creation of BancoSol (Table 1).

Third, portfolio growth reflected a rapid expansion in the number of clients with active loans, from the original 14 300 transferred from PRODEM in February 1992 to over 60 000 by late 1994[8]. No other microfinance organisation in Latin America has a larger number of active clients[9].

Fourth, the number of loans disbursed each year increased rapidly, reaching 143 037 during 1994 (Table 1)[10].

Fifth, rapid growth allowed BancoSol to add continuously to its portfolio many new borrowers (23 510 in 1993 and 30 021 in 1994). From the start of PRODEM in 1987 to June 1995, the number of new clients was 100 539 (Table 1). Almost two-thirds of these clients were still active in the portfolio as of June 1995, reflecting the development of long-term relationships, based on the value for them of the services provided.

Table 1. BancoSol: Indicators of Breadth of Outreach, 1987-95[a]

For the 12-months ending as of	PRODEM					BANCOSOL					
	Dec. 87	Dec. 88	Dec. 89	Dec. 90	Dec. 91	Dec. 92	June 93	Dec. 93	June 94	Dec. 94	June 95
Portfolio outstanding[b] ('000)	69	359	693	1 855	3 245	4 577	7 804	13 962	23 288	29 645	30 200
Number of loans outstanding[b]	557	3 094	5 288	11 394	18 681	18 333	26 310	36 573	46 755	54 681	59 745
Amount outstanding per loan[b]	124	116	131	163	174	250	297	382	498	542	505
Amount disbursed ('000)	587	1 917	3 692	9 504	16 706	22 720	35 285	59 592	76 928	84 039	80 899
Number of loans disbursed	3 758	9 486	15 245	34 093	52 626	55 571	78 370	105 238	127 922	143 037	140 864
Amount disbursed per loan	156	202	242	279	317	409	450	566	601	588	574
Months to maturity[c]	1.8	3.9	4.2	4.0	4.3	4.0	4.0	4.2	4.4	4.6	5.1
Dollar-years outstanding per loan[d]	18	38	45	54	62	82	100	133	182	207	214
Number of new borrowers	1 737	1 816	3 539	8 984	10 475	11 056	16 006	23 510	30 814	30 021	23 200
Cumulative number of new borrowers	1 737	3 553	7 092	16 076	26 551	37 607	46 525	61 117	77 339	91 138	100 539

a. All currency figures are in US dollars, converted from bolivianos of constant purchasing power as of December 1995, at the exchange rate as of that date.
b. Average of the corresponding figures (monthly balances outstanding, or monthly numbers outstanding, or monthly balance outstanding per loan).
c. Estimated as the average amount outstanding divided by the amount disbursed for each period.
d. Dollar-years outstanding per loan are calculated as the average amount outstanding per loan multiplied by the average term of the loan, measured in months, and divided by 12.
Source: Computed by the authors from PRODEM and BancoSol records.

Sixth, BancoSol offers valuable voluntary deposit facilities to its clients. The number of depositors has grown rapidly. Between December 1994 and June 1995, the average of the number of outstanding passbook accounts was 29 753. These deposits come mostly from borrowers and have a small average balance ($69). The corresponding total outstanding balance was $2.1 million[11]. Another $3.2 million were generated by 1 049 time deposits, with an average balance of $3 092, probably held by wealthier individuals or institutions, including PRODEM. The addition of voluntary deposit facilities to the supply of BancoSol's microfinancial services represents an important improvement in the quality of its outreach.

Depth of Outreach

Depth rather than breadth of outreach connotes success in overcoming the difficulties of selling services to the target clientele. These difficulties are correlated with the poverty of the borrowers. From this perspective, the performance of BancoSol is also remarkable, as reflected by the small average size loan granted. This average loan is just over one-half of the Bolivian per capita gross domestic product.

Moreover, portfolio growth has been associated more with increases in the numbers of borrowers than in the average size of loan balance outstanding. Average balances increased from about $150 in the PRODEM days, to about $250 in the earlier days of BancoSol, to about $500 in recent years. Similarly, the amount disbursed per loan increased from just over $300 in the early days of BancoSol to over $600 in early 1994, but it declined to about $550 by mid-1995 (Table 1). This increase in average loan balance is one of the aspects of growth that requires an explanation. However, it appears that the increases have not been associated with a drift away from the target clientele of the poor.

Although BancoSol's clients are poor, they are not among the poorest of Bolivians. This may reflect, among other things, the precondition that the client must have operated an established business for at least one year before applying for a loan. The definition of the target market niche for BancoSol — how small the loans? how poor the clients? — has been the subject of constant debate among its owners in their evaluations of the organisation's mission. However, there is no doubt that most of BancoSol's clients could never expect to gain access to conventional formal financial institutions and that the clients prefer BancoSol over traditional sources of informal credit. BancoSol can legitimately claim to have expanded the frontier of microfinance.

According to survey data, about 78 per cent of BancoSol's borrowers are women (Table 2). As a result, only 42 per cent of the clients consider themselves as heads of household. This reflects the typical composition of poor households in La Paz and El Alto. In about 80 per cent of BancoSol's clients' households at least three members work, usually in different occupations, to address risks by occupational diversification. In a typical household the men may work in manufacturing or seasonal construction and the women in trade. Frequently, women market the output of their husband's industrial occupation, but they also diversify by marketing other products. Access to BancoSol's loans and deposits facilitates liquidity and risk management for the whole household.

The concentration of women in the portfolio is associated with the concentration of loans for trading. Trading was the main occupation of the borrowers interviewed in 63 per cent of the cases, while BancoSol's records indicate that 83 per cent of the loans in the portfolio were for trading. Thus, the sex distribution of BancoSol's portfolio is not the outcome of specific targeting. Indeed, BancoSol does not target loans to women. Rather, this distribution reflects the predominance of Bolivian women in trading. Moreover, the nature of the lending technology requires a rapid turnaround of borrower cash flows, which leads to the concentration on loans for trade. Rapid cash turnaround is needed to allow for the frequent payments required in order to facilitate the monitoring of loan repayment.

The BancoSol clients surveyed operate in the informal economy of La Paz and El Alto. In almost two-thirds of the cases they do not keep written accounts of their revenues and expenses. This in part reflects low levels of education. Only 34 per cent of the clients surveyed attended anything beyond primary school, while 33 per cent either had no schooling or did not progress beyond the third grade. Furthermore, there is no separation between household and business in almost half of the cases (Table 2). Lack of financial statements and other records constrains access to conventional formal financial services as much as does lack of traditional collateral (Sanchez, 1996). In this sense, the development of a lending technology that can be implemented by a bank but which does not rely on standard financial information and on collateral is a formidable innovation. This technological progress is at the root of BancoSol's outreach achievements.

For sustained implementation of this technology, it would be necessary to revise Bolivia's prudential regulatory framework further. Prudential regulations and supervisory norms are based mostly on ratios of the value of collateral to loan balances and on audited financial statements from the borrowers. A technological revolution in prudential practices would be required to match the innovations introduced by microfinance (Gonzalez-Vega, 1996a). For BancoSol, an unusual understanding of the nature of its operations by the Superintendent has allowed much progress, but in the long run this will not be sufficient without legal reforms (Trigo, 1996).

Quality of Outreach

Outreach must also be evaluated in terms of the quality of the services provided. Quality is mostly reflected in the transaction costs imposed on clients and in the appropriateness of contractual terms for the particular clientele. Borrower transaction costs were not measured for BancoSol's clients, so the present evaluation of the quality of services is based on qualitative observations.

Table 2. **BancoSol: Characteristics of Clients Surveyed, 1995**

a

Women	78
Client is head of household	42
Education level:	
No schooling	8
Up to grades 1-3	25
Up to grades 4-8	33
Up to grades 9-12	31
Beyond grade 12	3
Number of additional persons residing with client:	
0-3 persons	22
4-7 persons	69
8-14 persons	9
Number of additional household members who are employed:	
0-1	19
2-4	78
5 and above	3
Principal occupation:	
Trade	63
Production (industry and agriculture)	20
Services	17
Client has secondary occupation	56
Products marketed when the client is a trader:	
Domestically-produced goods	69
Foreign goods	36
Own production	31
Business is separate from household	44
Type of accounting system used:	
Uses accountant	1
Simple income and expense records	37
No written records	63
Clients are attracted because:	
Simpler guarantee requirements	65
Can borrow more	48
Can obtain group rather than individual loans	39
Less red tape	33
Interest rate is lower	28
Timeliness of loan	15
Proximity	13
Terms are longer	13
Clients are generally satisfied with:	
General relationship	91
Guarantee requirements	94
Term to maturity	69
Interest rate	55
Loan size	54

a All figures are in percentages.

Source: OSU survey of microfinance clients, 1995.

Two conflicting factors influence the quality of BancoSol's services. On the one hand, gains for borrowers from low transaction costs come from several aspects of the lending technology and the adaptation of BancoSol's services to the clientele's needs. On the other hand, the group-lending technology introduces transaction costs for the borrowers that do not exist in an individual loan. The costs for borrowers of participating in group loans result from the peer-monitoring efforts required by the joint liability rules. These efforts attempt to avert the obligation to pay another member's loan, when preventable difficulties are anticipated. Costs also result from the required co-ordination of the borrowing activities of all group members[12]. These transaction costs and the rigidities resulting from group transactions reduce the quality of the service provided, but many of BancoSol's clients may have no better alternatives, given the collateral requirements for borrowing elsewhere.

Simple procedures reduce transaction costs for borrowers. For the clients surveyed, on average it takes about eight minutes to reach a BancoSol branch. In addition, procedures have been designed to economise on the client's time. One-third of the clients indicated that an important reason that attracted them to BancoSol was less red tape. Furthermore, the absence of real collateral requirements is a highly appreciated attribute for one-third of these clients. As a result of these features, 91 per cent of BancoSol's borrowers surveyed are satisfied with its services (Table 2). Of course, there is room for additional improvement in the quality of these services, and BancoSol has been searching for ways to offer better financial products, including individual loans, to its most advanced clientele.

Loan Products

BancoSol offers its clients a number of loan products as well as three deposit products. Loans are denominated either in bolivianos or in US dollars. Loans in bolivianos are offered for shorter maturities and generally require more frequent instalment payments than loans in dollars. All loans are amortized in equal instalments, with interest charged only on the outstanding balance, and do not require compensating balances. Each of these attributes adds to the value of the contracts. For heuristic purposes, three types of loans in bolivianos are identified, according to payments every week, every two weeks, or every four weeks. Two types of loans in US dollars are identified, according to payments every two or every four weeks.

Loans in bolivianos with weekly repayments are typically for first-time borrowers, and have an average term of four months. These loans are granted for small amounts, with a median loan of $62 and an average of $82 (Table 3). The weekly repayment averages $5, and the average balance outstanding is $34. The nominal interest rate charged is 4 per cent per month, plus a flat up-front fee of 2.5 per cent of the loan. For the median loan, these terms imply effective interest rates of about 6.1 per cent per month in nominal terms and 4.9 per cent per month in real terms.

Table 3. **BancoSol: Terms and Conditions of Typical Loan Contracts, 1995**

mensions of loan product	Currency	Bs	Bs	Bs	Bs	$	$
	Weeks between repayments	1	2	4		2	4
	Average amount of repayment ($)	5	10	16		39	80
	Average amount outstanding ($)	34	42	50		338	467
nount disbursed	Median ($)	62	72	82		619	825
	Average ($)	82	93	103		1 031	1 340
ngth of term	Median (months)	3	4	6		9	12
	Average (months)	4	5	6		8	17
	Minimum (months)	1	4	4		6	6
	Maximum (months)	7	7	12		12	36
terest rates	Nominal monthly contractual rate	4.0	4.0	4.0		2.5	2.5
	Flat fees and commissions	2.5	2.5	2.5		1.0	1.0
	Nominal monthly effective rate[a]	6.1	5.6	5.2		3.0	2.9
	Monthly inflation rate	1.1	1.1	1.1		0.4	0.4
	Real monthly effective rate[a]	4.9	4.4	4.0		2.5	2.5

a Effective rates (internal rate of return) calculated using the median values of the amount disbursed and median length of term.

Source: Computed by the authors from PRODEM and BancoSol records.

As clients make progress in their relationship with the bank, the frequency of amortization may shift to every two weeks or even every four weeks, depending on the client's occupation and cash flow. For loans with payments every four weeks, terms may increase to an average of six months and up to one year, the average loan increases to about $103, and the effective interest rate declines to about 5.2 per cent per month in nominal terms and 4 per cent per month in real terms (Table 3). These real effective interest rates are still quite high, underscoring the importance of further reducing BancoSol's operating costs, as Schmidt and Zeitinger (1994, 1996) have argued for microfinance organisations in general.

Good repayment allows some clients to obtain larger loans, typically denominated in US dollars[13]. For these borrowers, the average loan then increases to about $1 000-$1 300 and the median to $600-$825. Maturities can increase to a maximum of three years and the effective interest rate can decline to 3 per cent per month in nominal terms and 2.5 per cent per month in real terms (Table 3).

The average size of loans at BancoSol masks a size distribution of a large number (about three-quarters of the total) of very small loans and a smaller number of somewhat larger loans. These diverse products generate different revenue streams and account for different shares of operating costs. It is likely that the larger loans are more profitable and, in this sense, they cross-subsidise the cost of making smaller loans. Very small loans are expensive for both the organisation and the client, but they may be a necessary investment for both to create the intangible asset of a long-term relationship. They lead to larger future loans and the totality of the relationship seems profitable for the bank. From the clients' perspective, moreover, continued relationships are strong evidence that such access is an improvement over their alternatives, despite the high costs of borrowing from BancoSol.

Sustainability

A viable microfinance organisation generates enough revenue over time to cover the costs of all factors of production and funds under its control, while being able to honour the contractual obligations implied by its liabilities at all points in time. This requires the ability to maintain the real value of equity. Organisations that can accomplish this without subsidies for their operational expenses, liabilities or equity are commercially profitable and, therefore, are potentially self-sustainable. Sustainability is important inasmuch as future and not only present outreach is important. Sustainability generates compatible incentives for all those with an interest in its survival, such as clients, managers, and staff, because it underpins perceptions of the microfinance organisation's permanency (Gonzalez-Vega, 1994).

Self-sustainability is frequently measured by some variation of Yaron's subsidy dependence index[14]. Under conventional definitions and assumptions, it can be claimed that BancoSol has been independent from subsidy since 1994[15]. Even before BancoSol was created, PRODEM had already made significant progress toward self-

Table 4. BancoSol: Subsidy Dependence Indicators, 1987-95

For the 12-months ending as of	PRODEM					BANCOSOL					
	Dec. 87	Dec. 88	Dec. 89	Dec. 90	Dec. 91	Dec. 92	June 93	Dec. 93	June 94	Dec. 94	June 95
Total subsidy ('000)[a]	231	296	571	681	1 046	1 314	837	1 486	106	(77)	313
Portfolio outstanding ('000)[a,b]	175	679	1 891	5 522	12 577	17 776	31 388	64 060	94 015	128 697	133 929
Nominal portfolio yield (%)	15	38	32	40	46	42	52	43	44	40	41
Interest revenue ('000)[a]	26	257	604	2 232	5 801	7 547	16 462	27 236	40 966	50 847	54 827
SDI[c]	898	115	94	30	18	17	5	5	0	(0)	1
Nominal subsidy-free yield (%)	147	82	62	53	54	50	55	45	44	39	41
Rate of inflation (%)	8	22	17	18	15	10	8	9	8	9	11
Real subsidy-free yield (%)[d]	129	49	39	29	35	36	44	33	33	28	27
Subsidy ('000)[e]	137	152	254	259	327	366	225	382	26	(18)	71
Number of loans outstanding[f]	557	2 810	5 288	11 394	18 681	18 333	26 310	36 573	46 755	54 681	59 745
Portfolio outstanding ('000)[c,f]	69	359	693	1 855	3 035	4 577	7 804	13 962	23 288	29 645	30 200
Number of loans disbursed	3 758	9 486	15 245	34 093	52 626	55 571	78 370	105 238	127 922	143 037	140 864
Amount disbursed ('000)[e]	587	1 917	3 692	9 504	16 706	22 720	35 285	59 592	76 928	84 039	80 899
Subsidy per loan-year outstanding[e]	246.84	54.24	48.10	22.72	17.50	19.99	8.54	10.44	0.56	-0.33	1.19
Subsidy per dollar-year outstanding[e]	1.987	0.425	0.367	0.140	0.108	0.080	0.029	0.027	0.001	-0.001	0.002
Subsidy per loan disbursed[e]	36.57	16.07	16.68	7.59	6.21	6.59	2.87	3.63	0.20	-0.13	0.51
Subsidy per dollar disbursed[e]	0.234	0.080	0.069	0.027	0.020	0.016	0.006	0.006	0.000	-0.000	0.001

a. Figures in unadjusted bolivianos.
b. Average of end-of-period and beginning-of-period net portfolio balances for 1987-1992 and end-of-period, middle-of-period, and beginning-of-period balances for 1992-1995.
c. Computed according to Yaron is (1994) methodology, as modified by Benjamin McDonald.
d. Real yields are computed as the difference between the nominal yields and the rate of inflation, divided by one plus the rate of inflation (Fisher formula).
e. Figures in December 1995 US dollars.
f. Average of the corresponding figures (monthly number of loans or of monthly balances outstanding).
Source: Computed by the authors from PRODEM and BancoSol records.

sustainability, as its subsidy dependence index declined from 115 per cent in 1988 to 18 per cent in 1991 (Table 4)[16]. That means that in 1988 it would have been necessary to more than double the yield on the loan portfolio in order to compensate for the subsidies received by PRODEM, while just before the transfer of the portfolio to BancoSol in 1991 yields would have had to increase by only 18 per cent[17].

It is important to note that PRODEM decreased its subsidy dependence not by increasing interest rates on loans but by reducing operating costs. Likewise, BancoSol decreased average costs through formalization and growth, without increasing the interest rates charged on loans. BancoSol also reduced subsidies by not seeking soft loans or operational grants[18]. Most of BancoSol's subsidy is derived from not earning enough to compensate for the opportunity cost of its equity. This subsidy poses little threat to its viability. The subsidy dependence of PRODEM, in contrast, sharply increased after the creation of BancoSol.

To compensate for all subsidies, in 1995 BancoSol needed to generate a real annual yield on its loan portfolio of 27 per cent. Given inflation in Bolivia, the required nominal yield was 41 per cent and BancoSol was able to produce it (Table 4). The interest rates on loans required to generate this yield may still be high, compared to the marginal rates of return of some microenterprise projects that are attractive in comparison to other investments in Bolivia. Thus, additional outreach is desirable and it will become possible if operating costs fall further. The impact of growth as a mechanism to reduce average costs and the potential limits to this profitability-enhancing role of growth are the main topics of this chapter.

Revenues, Costs and Returns on Assets

BancoSol had to face two challenges during its growth. First, nominal revenues as a proportion of average productive assets declined from 40 per cent at the time of conversion into BancoSol to about 33 per cent in the last 18 months (Table 5). This reduction in the average yield on productive assets is not surprising. It resulted in part from a portfolio made up increasingly of larger loans, made possible by the good repayment history of experienced clients. However, these loans generate lower effective interest rates than the smaller loans typical of new borrowers (Table 3). Furthermore, BancoSol has not received grants to cover operating expenses, unlike PRODEM. Lower average revenues also reflect an increasing share of non-loan assets, such as cash and reserves, which earn lower rates of return than loans. These non-loan assets may be necessary evils of formalization, which entails meeting legal reserve requirements, and of a larger organisational size, which increases the costs of funds in transit. After hiring experienced bankers, BancoSol significantly improved its management of non-loan assets.

Table 5. **BancoSol: Revenues, Expenses, and Returns. 1987-95**
(percentages)

For the 12-months ending as of date	PRODEM					BANCOSOL					
	Dec. 87	Dec. 88	Dec. 89	Dec. 90	Dec. 91	Dec. 92	June 93	Dec. 93	June 94	Dec. 94	June 95
Revenues/productive assets:											
Revenue from lending	8	27	24	31	34	34	41	34	32	29	30
Revenue from other operations	5	10	2	1	1	4	3	2	2	3	3
Grants and extraordinary revenues	58	31	12	8	4	0	(0)	0	0	0	0
Total revenue	71	67	38	40	40	39	44	36	34	32	33
Expenses/productive assets:											
Personnel	30	24	14	11	13	18	18	12	11	10	11
Administration	13	11	6	9	8	8	7	5	4	4	4
Depreciation	4	2	1	1	1	0	1	1	1	1	1
Taxes and other expenses	3	1	2	1	4	4	3	2	1	1	1
Loan-loss provision and write-off	0	1	0	1	1	1	1	1	1	2	1
Total operating expenses	49	39	23	23	27	31	30	21	18	18	19
Interest (cost of funds)	5	7	5	5	4	6	10	13	13	12	12
Inflation adjustments	10	6	14	9	5	0	1	0	0	0	0
Exceptional expenses	0	0	0	0	0	0	1	1	0	0	0
Total expenses	64	52	43	37	37	36	41	35	31	30	31
Retained earnings: current period	7	15	(5)	4	3	2	2	0	2	2	2
Return on assets	5.6	12.3	(4.1)	3.4	3.0	2.0	2.0	0.3	2.0	1.9	1.8
Return on equity	22.5	44.6	(18.1)	12.3	9.7	4.1	4.9	1.4	11.8	13.8	12.0
Return on assets without grants	(39.7)	(13.1)	(14.3)	(4.0)	(0.9)	2.0	3.4	1.7	2.4	1.9	1.8

Source: Computed by the authors from PRODEM and BancoSol records.

BancoSol had to face a second challenge as it switched from donor funding to market-based liabilities. This switch increased the annual average cost of funds from 4 per cent at the time of conversion to the present 12 per cent in nominal terms (Table 5). At the end of 1991, about 15 per cent of PRODEM's liabilities were deposits, 19 per cent were loans from private entities, and the remaining 68 per cent were loans from public entities. By the end of 1994, loans from public entities were only 2 per cent of total liabilities and equity, deposits were 66 per cent, and loans from private entities were 16 per cent (Gonzalez-Vega et al., 1996).

Declining average revenues and increasing average costs of funds reduced BancoSol's operating margin by about 13 percentage points. This challenge was met successfully by reducing operating expenses as a proportion of productive assets from 31 per cent in 1992 to 18 per cent in 1994. In this process, the share of operating expenses in total expenses declined from 84 per cent at the end of 1992 to 59 per cent at the end of 1994. This rapid substantial reduction in average operating costs enabled BancoSol to reinforce its financial sustainability. As a result, retained earnings continued to represent about 2 per cent of average productive assets throughout the whole period (Table 5).

In summary, the development of client relationships with the maturing of the portfolio, the formalization of operations and the switch to unsubsidised funds reduced BancoSol's intermediation margin, but the challenge was met through an even more dramatic reduction in average operating costs[19]. This reduction in operating costs resulted from economies of scale engendered by growth of total operations, increases in average loan size and some increases in average loan maturities. This allowed the bank to sustain the rate of return on its assets.

Transformation into a formal financial intermediary led to increased market funding via deposits and debt instruments. As a consequence of its bank charter and of its evident success, BancoSol was able to increase the ratio of its liabilities to equity from 1 at the end of 1992 to 6.2 at the end of 1994. With a constant rate of return on assets, the rate of return on equity increased sharply, from 4.1 per cent in 1992 to 13.8 per cent in 1994, reflecting this higher leverage (Gonzalez-Vega et al., 1996).

Another outstanding characteristic of BancoSol's sustainability is the comparatively low loan arrears and losses. The proportion of the portfolio represented by loans with at least one day of arrears was 4.5 per cent at the end of 1994. Only 1.3 per cent of the portfolio showed arrears of more than 60 days. Provisions for bad loans represented 3 per cent of the portfolio (Gonzalez-Vega et al., 1996). These low levels of delinquency are not typical of microfinance organisations, and they reflect BancoSol's commitment to its programme's sustainability and the strong incentives for repayment generated by its lending technology.

Incentive Structure of the Lending Technology

Most financial intermediaries find the costs and risks prohibitively high for lending to clients such as BancoSol's, namely poor households with highly risky and unstable informal businesses, obtaining small, short-term, non-collateralised loans (Gonzalez-Vega, 1996b). For many microfinance organisations, losses from lack of repayment and operating costs preclude self-sustainability. In some organisations, inadequate technologies lead to high levels of default, while in others keeping arrears at reasonable levels increases operating costs too much. BancoSol has been able to strike a balance between costs and risks at a level that allows self-sufficiency mostly by refining a lending technology appropriate for its market niche.

The strength of BancoSol's lending technology is reflected in a potent set of incentives to repay that can be implemented at comparatively low costs to the organisation[20]. These low costs reflect emphasis on contract design and enforcement[21] rather than intensive screening and monitoring. First, a strong incentive is that borrowers obtain access not just to a single loan but to a long-term relationship with a reliable and permanent lender, as BancoSol frequently emphasizes in communications with its clientele and corroborated by the clients. The value of this relationship is high, given its expected duration, the existing borrowing alternatives for a typical client and the features of loan contracts described below.

Second, the incentives include a sequential and substantial improvement in the terms and conditions of loan contracts for well-performing clients. Borrowers with impeccable repayment records not only have access to increasingly larger loans, but also to longer terms and less frequent repayments[22]. In turn, these changes imply a significant reduction in effective interest rates and in borrower transaction costs. This contract design introduces potent incentives, as the quality of the credit service substantially improves with the increasing duration of the client-organisation relationship. Even a few days of arrears, however, are sufficient to delay a client's progress along this sequence. This is a strong incentive for punctuality.

Third, BancoSol can monitor borrowers cheaply on the basis of frequent repayments, mostly through the immediate verification of arrears for the group. Loan officers do not make costly, deliberate visits to the borrower unless a problem has been detected. Instead, these trips are triggered by missed repayments, about which the loan officer is informed within one day. Moreover, given that BancoSol will not accept any payment from a group or any individual in the group unless the payment is enough to cover the entire amount owed by the whole group, group members are enlisted to monitor each other. Members are required to work close to each other to facilitate this delegated peer monitoring.

Fourth, timely disbursements increase the value of the client-organisation relationship by reducing borrower transaction costs. Applications from new borrowers are processed within a few days, and there is no interruption of service for repeat borrowers because applications for additional loans are received and processed before the earlier loan becomes due. Simple procedures, adapted to the clientele, also lower transaction costs.

Fifth, an additional determinant of the high value of the relationship with BancoSol is the limitation of the loan security requirement to joint liability of group members, at least for those clients who would not be able to offer the collateral required by other lenders. This feature of BancoSol's technology makes it possible to expand the frontier of microfinance by reaching a clientele that may not have better options.

However, joint liability, per se, does not guarantee repayment, as the incentives that it creates have ambiguous impacts on the group members' willingness to repay (Besley and Coate, 1995; Chaves, 1996). This results from two opposing externalities. In one case, non-defaulting members undertake repayment for defaulting members or harass delinquents to avoid the loss of their own relationship with BancoSol. In the other case, default by some members prompts default by others if the cost of repayment of the defaulter's loan are higher than the value of the relationship. Repayment depends on the stability of the groups, which may be enhanced or threatened by these conflicting effects. Understanding the net balance between these effects in the case of BancoSol would require additional research. In fact, however, loan arrears and losses have been very low.

The inevitable contract rigidities that accompany group borrowing may further reduce the value of this relationship for the client. These rigidities include, among others, a need for synchronous terms to maturity and repayment schedules, as well as the need to participate in group meetings. Joint liability may thus represent comparatively high costs and risks for borrowers who could otherwise have access to individual loans. Thus the inconvenience costs for the client from group credit must be added to the burdens of joint liability[23].

Sixth, the highly personalised service offered to the clients represents an additional strong incentive for repayment. A long-term personal connection is developed between the loan officer and the borrower, a bond which creates a powerful informal incentive to fulfil contract commitments. A similar personal allegiance (which may already exist) is further strengthened among the members of a borrowing group. Moreover, BancoSol has successfully adapted its culture to its operations, personalising the organisation's image.

Seventh, contract enforcement is also enhanced by the credibility of the threats of penalties in case of lack of fulfillment of loan obligations. This credibility is the result of:

a)   immediate reaction to arrears (as early as the next day), followed by involvement of both the loan officer and group in the search for a solution;

b)   interruption of the sequence of improvements in contract terms and conditions, as a consequence of arrears;

c)   denial of future loans to the whole group in case of default; and

d)   sharing of information on default among microfinance programmes, which prevents delinquent borrowers from switching to other organisations.

Determinants and Consolidation of Success

Several features of BancoSol's organisational design and technological development have contributed to its achievements. First, since BancoSol's creation its leaders have been deeply concerned with the organisation's financial viability. This attitude was reinforced by the confirmation of its own success. In practice, this attitude gradually led, through a search for formalization, to self-sustainability. The concern for viability was reflected in the adoption of interest rates that sought to cover the costs of lending and a resolute attitude toward loan collection. From the very beginning, BancoSol explicitly told its clients that it expected loans to be repaid.

Second, over the years the organisation developed a lending technology appropriate for its market niche. This allowed it to provide financial services to a clientele that other intermediaries find difficult to reach in a cost-effective way for both the organisation and borrowers. The success of this technology has been reflected in low rates of arrears and default.

Third, there was a fruitful investment in experimentation and learning during the PRODEM period. Success in the development of a microfinance programme rests on the accumulation of knowledge and experience about the environment in which it operates, relevant features of the clientele it serves, the individual creditworthiness of heterogeneous clients, and the comparative advantages of its own technology. This success requires constant fine-tuning and adjustment of the technology to varied local circumstances. External assistance mostly from ACCION, funded by USAID, was crucial for this purpose.

Finally, the transformation from an NGO into a formal financial intermediary also contributed to BancoSol's success. Even if PRODEM had remained a successful NGO, it could not have achieved the levels of outreach and sustainability that upgrading made possible for BancoSol. The accumulated tangible and intangible assets of PRODEM, moreover, gave BancoSol a head start. Had BancoSol started from scratch, it would have taken much longer to reach the present levels of profitability and self-sustainability. This must be recognised in any discussion of replicating BancoSol's success.

Moreover, if learning effects are important in microfinance, it may not be advisable to begin on a large scale. Gradual growth from small origins may be a preferable. This could allow for experimentation by trial and error while ensuring that mistakes are not extremely costly and that corrections are possible without leading to disintegration of the organisation (Chaves and Gonzalez-Vega, 1996). The organisation must also acquire the tools to deal with future problems effectively.

BancoSol's transformation into a formal financial intermediary consolidated the improvement in outreach and sustainability. Formalization as a bank made possible more flexible access to loanable funds. This relaxed the constraint experienced by PRODEM and encouraged a rapid expansion of the loan portfolio. Thus far this growth, critical for BancoSol's improved outreach, has been compatible with self-sustainability.

Growth has not been easy to manage, however, and opportunities for further rapid growth at the rates of the recent past may encounter severe limitations. BancoSol reduced its rate of expansion during 1995, partly because of the dangers of pressures on arrears and on internal control mechanisms, and partly because of the developing tensions between the existing culture and the new organisational structure required by rapid growth. Instead, it focused on improving its financial management, information systems and organisational structures.

The Challenge of Growth

The recent experience of BancoSol highlights the costs and benefits of a process of very rapid growth and suggests the nature of potential internal and external limits to gains in productivity and profitability that usually accompany growth.

The evolution of this organisation can be divided into two stages, each one characterised by a primary limit to growth. During the first stage (PRODEM period), growth was liability-constrained. Even at the high rates of interest needed for sustainability, a substantial demand for its credit services had been identified and a cost-effective technology had been developed. The organisation's NGO status, however, meant access to loanable funds was limited to donor finance. Moreover, its NGO status limited the extent to which equity could be leveraged with additional liabilities mobilised in financial markets (Rosenberg, 1994). Additional complications emerged from high seasonal variations in cash flows. Access to short-term money markets would have allowed a more efficient management of these cash flows.

Constraints were created by the lack of flexibility of donor funding, the microfinance organisation's lack of credibility due to the absence of a regulatory framework to protect potential lenders against its insolvency or illiquidity, and the limited leverage, due to the absence of a bank charter to mobilise deposits from the public. The resulting inability to grow and serve the clientele as desired frustrated PRODEM's leaders[24]. To a large extent, these constraints were removed with the creation of BancoSol and the accompanying formalization.

The second stage (BancoSol period) has been characterised by growth's threats to asset quality and by diminishing marginal economies of size and the resulting limits on opportunities to increase productivity as a consequence of growth. These limits are a challenge for microfinance organisations and are reflected in the evolution of key productivity and efficiency indicators.

The Evolution of Efficiency

Efficiency is defined here as the outputs per unit of cost. Costs are defined as expenses recorded in the organisation's accounts along with any unrecorded expenses or implicit subsidies. Outputs of a microfinance organisation may be the amount of the loan portfolio or the number of loans outstanding or the number and amount of loans disbursed.

Productivity, in turn, is defined as the outputs per unit of input. Inputs may be expressed in units such as branches, loan officers, or dollars of assets. The evolution of productivity helps understand changes in efficiency, and efficiency directly influences profitability.

The most critical indicator of efficiency is the average portfolio outstanding per unit of cost: portfolio efficiency. This is measured as the monthly average portfolio outstanding divided by total economic costs, which include the organisation's total expenditures, subsidy from not paying the total opportunity costs of its liabilities and equity, and other grants. For each $100 of cost, this indicator increased from 43 for 1987, during the early PRODEM days, to 140 by 1991, before the transformation. During the BancoSol period, this indicator increased from 167 in 1992 to 224 in 1994 (Table 6). These efficiency measures mean that in 1987 it cost $2.35 to keep an average balance of $1.00 in the portfolio for a year, but that this cost had declined to $0.72 by 1991. It further dropped to $0.60 in 1992 and $0.45 in 1994.

The sustained growth of portfolio efficiency reflected by these ratios allowed BancoSol to reduce its average portfolio costs sufficiently to remain profitable in the face of declining average revenues and of increasing costs of funds. To understand how this achievement was possible, it is necessary to examine the evolution of some components of this indicator.

Portfolio efficiency, measured as the ratio of the outstanding portfolio with respect to costs, can be expressed as the product of the number of loans per unit of cost (transactions efficiency) times the average size of loan balances outstanding:

Portfolio efficiency = (transactions efficiency) x (loan size)

$$L / C = (N / C)(L / N)$$

where L is the total portfolio outstanding, C are total costs, and N is the number of outstanding balances. Improvements in portfolio efficiency can then be interpreted as a result of increases in the number of loans outstanding per unit of cost or of increases in loan size.

Table 6. BancoSol: Indicators of Efficiency 1987-95

For the 12-months ending as of date	PRODEM						BANCOSOL				
	Dec. 87	Dec. 88	Dec. 89	Dec. 90	Dec. 91	Dec. 92	June 93	Dec. 93	June 94	Dec. 94	June 95
Accounting operational expenses[a] ('000)	93	192	257	629	1 415	1 880	3 360	4 640	5 895	7 365	8 012
Accounting financial expenses ('000)	27	67	221	373	511	357	1 101	2 725	4 194	5 029	4 903
Accounting total expenses ('000)	120	259	478	1 002	1 926	2 236	4 461	7 365	10 088	12 394	12 915
Operating grants not registered ('000)	0	0	0	0	0	0	0	0	9	17	8
Economic operational costs ('000)	93	192	257	629	1 415	1 880	3 360	4 640	5 903	7 382	8 020
Financial subsidies[b] ('000)	43	73	69	138	271	503	627	764	860	840	863
Economic total cost ('000)	163	332	547	1 140	2 197	2 739	5 089	8 129	10 958	13 250	13 787
Economic operational costs per:											
Number of loans outstanding	166	62	49	55	76	103	128	127	126	135	134
Portfolio outstanding	1.34	0.54	0.37	0.34	0.44	0.41	0.43	0.33	0.25	0.25	0.27
Number of loans disbursed	25	20	17	18	27	34	43	44	46	52	57
Amount disbursed	0.16	0.10	0.07	0.07	0.08	0.08	0.10	0.08	0.08	0.09	0.10
Economic total costs per:											
Number of loans outstanding	292	107	103	100	118	149	193	222	234	242	231
Portfolio outstanding	2.35	0.93	0.79	0.61	0.68	0.60	0.65	0.58	0.47	0.45	0.46
Number of loans disbursed	43	35	36	33	42	49	65	77	86	93	98
Amount disbursed	0.28	0.17	0.15	0.12	0.13	0.12	0.14	0.14	0.14	0.16	0.17
Product/economic operational cost:[c]											
Number of loans outstanding	0.60	1.61	2.06	1.81	1.32	0.98	0.78	0.79	0.79	0.74	0.74
Portfolio outstanding	75	187	270	295	229	244	232	301	394	402	377
Number of loans disbursed	406	494	594	542	372	296	233	227	217	194	176
Amount disbursed	633	998	1438	1512	1181	1209	1050	1284	1303	1138	1009
Product/economic total cost:[c]											
Number of loans outstanding	0.34	0.93	0.97	0.92	0.80	0.67	0.52	0.45	0.43	0.41	0.43
Portfolio outstanding	43	108	127	150	140	167	154	172	213	224	219
Loans disbursed	231	285	279	275	226	203	155	129	117	108	102
Amount disbursed	361	577	675	767	718	829	697	733	703	634	587

a. All currency figures are in US dollars, converted from bolivianos at constant purchasing power as of December 1995, at the exchange rate as of that date.
b. As per computation of the subsidy dependence index.
c. Product (either number or total amount of loans) per $100 of the corresponding category of expenses.

Source: Computed by the authors from PRODEM and BancoSol records.

Increases in loan size dilute fixed costs over a larger outstanding balance. Transactions efficiency reflects improvements in physical productivity, that is, in the number of transactions carried out at a given level of total expenditures. Increases in transactions efficiency can be achieved by several means, including a lengthening of the average term of outstanding loans. This means fewer procedures per outstanding balance over a period of time.

Two periods can be identified with respect to changes in transactions efficiency. During the PRODEM period, the monthly average number of loans held in the portfolio per $100 of economic cost increased from 0.34 in 1987 to 0.80 in 1991 (Table 6). During this period, the number of loans grew more rapidly (34-fold) than total costs (14-fold). This meant that the annual cost of holding one loan in the portfolio declined from $292 in 1987 to $118 in 1991.

During the BancoSol period, however, the number of loans per $100 of cost steadily declined, from 0.67 in 1992 to 0.41 in 1994 (Table 6). This represented a reduction in transactions efficiency, and the cost of holding one loan in the portfolio increased from $149 in 1992 to $242 in 1994. This was due to costs increasing 4.8-fold, while the number of loans grew only 2.8-fold[25].

Increases in Loan Size

BancoSol's portfolio efficiency improved steadily, despite reductions in transactions efficiency. This was possible because of increases in average loan balance outstanding. These increases began in the PRODEM period, when the average balance increased from $124 in 1987 to $162 in 1991, and then continued during the BancoSol period, when loan balances increased from $250 in 1992 to $542 in 1994 (Table 1)[26]. If it was this rise in average loan balance that allowed BancoSol to remain profitable despite reductions of transactions efficiency, it is important to examine the sources and consequences of growth of loan size as well as the causes of the decrease in transactions efficiency.

There are at least three reasons why loan sizes increase during a microfinance organisation's lifetime:

a) policy-induced increases, due to changes in the loan-supply criteria adopted by the organisation as a response to threats to its sustainability or redefinition of its market niche. These increases may reflect the search for wealthier clients who, *ceteris paribus*, demand larger loans than poorer clients;

b) information-induced increases, as accumulated knowledge and experience in the market and revised perceptions of risk make it possible to increase the initial loan size and/or accelerate the growth of size for additional loans along the sequence for a client with a given, imperfectly observed repayment capacity and level of poverty; and *c)*	client-induced increases, as individual customers improve their repayment capacity and demand larger loans. The share of these established clients among the total number of borrowers increases as the organisation's portfolio matures.

Client-induced and information-induced increases in loan size are not in conflict with outreach objectives, but policy-induced increases may be associated with mission drift. That is, if loan size increases (due to the information effect) for a client with a given repayment capacity, the wealth of the given client is unchanged[27]. Also, if loan sizes increase because the borrowers are becoming better off, this effect simply reflects the materialisation of the desired growth in the target clientele's wealth. However, policy-induced increases in loan size may in some cases reflect departures from the organisation's original mission and target clientele.

Policy-induced increases are usually reflected by changes in the average amount disbursed to new clients in a given year. Information-induced increases result in amounts disbursed which increase rapidly after the first few loans, but subsequently grow more slowly as loan size approaches the repayment capacity. Client-induced increases are reflected by continued growth of loan size after several loan cycles, when supply matches demand closely and demand growth causes the changes[28].

In the case of BancoSol, although there were policy-induced increases in loan size when constraints on the liability side were removed, most of the expansion of the portfolio appears to reflect client-induced and information-induced increases in loan size. This result is consistent with sustained attention to the same market niche and does not represent a deviation from the organisation's initial mission to assist the poor. Furthermore, increases in loan size as the client-organisation relationship evolves are critical to sustain strong incentives to repay. In this sense, opportunities for increasing loan size are needed for sustainability and greater outreach over time.

The size of the first loan disbursed to a new client increased rapidly in the early days of BancoSol and later decreased to almost the original level. For a sample of 259 borrowers surveyed, the average size of their first loan increased from $96 in 1991 to $170 in 1994, but then decreased to $108 in 1995 (Table 8). A similar behaviour was observed for each additional (second, third, etc.) loan. These changes in loan size, controlling for the number of repetitions, reflected policy revisions to the extent that, after the transformation into BancoSol, the organisation felt it could make larger loans to its clients once it had overcome the liquidity constraints typical of the PRODEM period. This attitude was revised in 1995, and the loan size decreased to historical levels.

Changes in policy were also reflected by an increase in the dispersion of loan sizes. That is, loans to larger customers grew even faster than the rest. Reductions in loan sizes in the most recent year also reflected policy revisions, as BancoSol prudently responded to the increasing pressures on loan arrears and losses that accompanied earlier increases of loan sizes, by becoming more cautious with its clients at all stages of the evolution of the organisation-client relationship.

Table 8. **BancoSol: Loan Size, by Repetition and Year when Loan was Granted, 1987-95**[a]

Repetition	Statistic	1987	1988	1989	1990	1991	1992	1993	1994	1995	Total
1	Mean	58	271	61	109	96	131	171	170	108	142
	Median	58	271	46	79	90	104	125	117	107	108
2	Mean	146	131	116	204	231	222	297	272	199	241
	Median	146	143	124	176	178	189	213	236	203	204
3	Mean	177	187	187	332	336	328	371	437	372	379
	Median	177	187	206	270	257	337	377	365	321	321
4	Mean	260	199	184	382	421	550	534	658	488	534
	Median	260	207	184	260	361	555	496	484	357	413
5	Mean		293	185	293	603	608	779	679	697	657
	Median		286	185	298	436	292	654	487	433	457
6	Mean		298	256	387	564	834	910	735	653	691
	Median		298	257	387	558	693	770	723	438	544
7	Mean		330	327	112	604	1 128	802	775	592	721
	Median		330	298	112	454	849	398	469	617	555
8	Mean			272	350	755	745	931	882	1 135	871
	Median			321	350	755	671	528	502	369	502
9	Mean			364	318	346	829	1 275	773	998	879
	Median			364	360	346	707	1 020	713	454	562
10	Mean				374	355	832	1 373	1 147	701	954
	Median				438	355	951	635	812	428	468
11-23	Mean				341	438	731	1 724	953	935	1 010
	Median				345	481	638	998	637	464	598
Total	Mean	129	225	208	262	392	547	582	486	460	477
	Median	119	215	206	245	319	351	301	302	260	286
	n	7	16	11	48	73	118	233	383	433	1 333

a. All currency figures from bolivianos of constant December, 1995 purchasing power, converted to US dollars at the exchange rate of that date.

n: number of observations.

Source: OSU microfinance client survey, 1995.

Growth of loan size with each repetition was particularly rapid for the earlier repetitions. For the sample, on the average the second loan was 70 per cent larger than the first, the third loan was 58 per cent larger than the second, and the fourth loan was 41 per cent larger than the third. This suggests that the information effect dominates the earlier growth of loan size. The rate of growth of loan size was 22 per cent for the fifth loan, however, and between the fifth and the sixth loan it was only 5 per cent. This suggests that the repayment capacity ceiling was being approached at about this time. Beyond this level, loan sizes increase mostly in response to demand growth due to client success.

By making it possible to dilute fixed costs, larger loan sizes increase portfolio efficiency. At BancoSol, the average balance for individual clients increases with additional loans. However, the average number of members in a borrowing group tends to decline over time, which has a negative impact on efficiency. Declining group size affects efficiency because some of the activities of loan officers deal with groups rather than individual clients. As of September 1995, almost 58 per cent of the groups had four members, 27 per cent had less than four, and 16 per cent had five to nine members (Gonzalez-Vega *et al.*, 1996).

To the extent that some of BancoSol's larger clients are attracted by more appealing contract terms and conditions offered at other microfinance organisations, the bank may be losing some of its most profitable clients to growing competition in the market. When they are willing and able to offer collateral, these customers may be attracted by the opportunity to obtain individual loans at lower interest rates.

Extensive and Intensive Growth

Portfolio growth may reflect two different processes:

a) extensive growth, the result of increased installed capacity, leading to a larger organisation and more sources of fixed cost, such as headquarters, branches, or loan officers; and

b) intensive growth, the result of increased productivity of existing capacity, such as larger balances and/or numbers of loans per branch or per loan officer. Intensive growth results from technological innovation, increased efficiency due to more effective incentives for staff performance, learning and the accumulation of experience, externalities due to having done a good job in the past, and improved capacity utilisation (economies of scale) either through larger numbers of loans or increased loan sizes.

Extensive growth can have a negative impact on the organisation's productivity, for at least four reasons. First, indivisible additions to existing installed capacity (larger headquarters, new branches, new employees) typically reduce the organisation's average productivity until the new capacity is fully utilised. New units cannot start at full capacity. For example, a new branch with the same fixed costs as an old branch initially has few borrowers to dilute costs.

Second, not all branches are equally productive, even after their installed capacity is fully utilised. The reason is that the branch's age is important for productivity. To the extent that learning effects count, *ceteris paribus*, older branches are more productive. Not only does it take time for a branch to reach capacity utilisation, but the passage of time itself increases productivity, as information is accumulated and lessons are learned from experience.

Third, not all branches are created equally productive because location matters for branch productivity. Market potential declines as the microfinance business moves from prime locations, densely populated with flourishing microenterprises, toward marginal locations. There are less potential borrowers, their wealth is smaller, and the risk-adjusted returns from their enterprises are lower at marginal branches, even at full capacity utilisation. Given fixed costs of branch operation, new but thinner markets reduce average productivity.

Fourth, communication costs increase as the organisation expands across space, and the headquarters finds it more difficult to monitor decentralised branches. These costs offset some of the gains from economies of scale.

Extensive growth via recruiting additional loan officers also tends to reduce the organisation's productivity because loan officers need time to develop their own clientele. Accumulating a complete loan portfolio requires about nine months. To the extent that on-the-job learning is important, more experienced loan officers are more productive than the new ones. Further, the average skill level of loan officers may decline with rapid recruitment. Finally, loan officers assigned to marginal locations must deal with a more difficult market.

The organisation's overall average productivity will tend to decline every time a new branch is created or a new loan officer is hired because of these Ricardian consequences of increases in the number of branches and the number of loan officers. Much of this reduction in productivity will be temporary, until full capacity utilisation is achieved at the new branch, but some will be permanent, as a consequence of smaller market potential at the new location. The larger the organisation already is, however, the smaller the negative marginal impact on average productivity of the new branches or loan officers will be, because the reduction will be diluted over a larger base.

The general trend under extensive growth appears to be for branch productivity to decline over time, as smaller branches are created in marginal areas, and for loan officer productivity to reach a natural limit. These potential limits to growth represent a challenge that the organisation must address by improving productivity via intensive growth. However, extensive growth may make it possible to dilute further the costs of the national headquarters and of other organisation-wide functions, thus reducing average costs, as long as the resulting economies of scale are not offset by the diseconomies of communication and internal control that eventually arise in large organisations.

BancoSol has experienced rapid extensive growth. In the five years before the transformation, PRODEM grew from one branch to four. In the four years after the transformation, BancoSol grew from four branches to 32. There was an exceptionally rapid creation of new branches in 1993 and 1994. Similarly, the number of employees increased from 13 to 97 during the PRODEM days and continued to grow at BancoSol, reaching 302 in 1995 (Table 7). The proportion of the total number of employees who are loan officers remained fairly constant at about two-thirds. The number of loan officers increased from six to 54 (1987-91) and from 59 to 183 (1992-95).

Table 7. **BancoSol: Indicators of Productivity, 1987-95.**[a,b]

For the 12-months ending as of date	PRODEM							BANCOSOL			
	Dec. 87	Dec. 88	Dec. 89	Dec. 90	Dec. 91	Dec. 92	June 93	Dec. 93	June 94	Dec. 94	June 95
Number of loan officers		10	20	31	54	59	86	116	133	159	183
Number of total employees	13	19	35	60	97	96	136	184	213	260	302
Number of branches[c]	1	1	2	3	4	5	9	13	20	25	29
Loan officers/employees	0.5	0.5	0.6	0.5	0.6	0.6	0.6	0.6	0.6	0.6	0.6
Employees/branch	13.2	19.3	17.5	21.0	27.1	18.9	16.0	13.7	10.9	10.5	10.4
Loan officers/branch	6.4	10.0	9.9	11.0	15.0	11.6	10.1	8.6	6.8	6.4	6.3
Number of loans outstanding/loan officer	87	309	267	367	346	312	307	316	351	344	326
Portfolio/loan officer ('000)	11	36	35	60	60	78	91	121	175	187	165
Number of loans disbursed/loan officer	591	949	769	1 097	976	946	915	909	960	901	768
Amount disbursed/loan officer ('000)	92	192	186	306	310	387	412	514	577	529	441
Number of loans outstanding/employee	42	160	151	191	192	191	194	199	219	210	198
Portfolio/employee ('000)	5	19	20	31	33	48	57	76	109	114	100
Number of loans disbursed/employee	285	491	437	572	542	579	577	573	600	549	467
Amount disbursed/employee ('000)	45	99	106	160	172	237	260	325	361	323	268
Number of loans outstanding/branch	557	3 094	2 644	4 022	5 213	3 606	3 095	2 726	2 387	2 202	2 066
Portfolio/branch ('000)	69	359	347	655	906	900	918	1 041	1 189	1 194	1 044
Number of loans disbursed/branch	3 758	9 486	7 623	12 033	14 686	10 932	9 220	7 844	6 532	5 760	4 871
Amount disbursed/branch ('000)	587	1 917	1 846	3 354	4 662	4 470	4 151	4 442	3 928	3 384	2 798

a. All currency figures are in US dollars, converted from bolivianos of constant purchasing power as of December 1995, at the exchange rate as of that date.
b. Averages of monthly figures.
Source: Computed by the authors from PRODEM and BancoSol records

156

Following transformation into BancoSol, rapid expansion of the branch network had some of the negative consequences of extensive growth on average productivity. Between 1987 and 1991, the average value of the monthly portfolio outstanding per branch increased from $69 150 to $905 669. As shown in Table 7, growth of the portfolio outstanding per branch has been modest since the creation of BancoSol. Measured as the annual amount disbursed per branch, productivity increased from $586 668 in 1987 to $4 662 133 in 1993, but it steadily declined afterwards, to $2 797 648 per branch in the twelve-month period ending on 30 June 1995. The lower level of disbursement per branch was compensated by some increase in the size and terms of the loans disbursed[29].

These reductions in branch productivity would be a cause of concern to the extent that large volumes of operations may be necessary to dilute the fixed costs of creating and operating a branch. How critical this is depends on the level of fixed costs of operating a branch, including security, office space, salaries, and equipment. Similar trends are observed with respect to BancoSol's employee and loan officer productivity[30].

In summary, while growth during the PRODEM period was mostly intensive, growth during the BancoSol period has been mostly extensive. This allowed the organisation to improve its outreach significantly, but it resulted in a slow growth of portfolio productivity per branch. Extensive growth has tended to dampen efficiency and profitability because the cost of operating a branch has not declined, in particular since the cost of hiring loan officers and other employees has increased. This is a serious problem if productivity gains run out of steam before the organisation reaches self-sustainability, but BancoSol has already become self-sustainable. Moreover, as already emphasized, reductions in productivity and efficiency do not necessarily represent poorer management. Instead, they may represent diminishing marginal gains from larger size and, therefore, consequences of the limits to growth. The challenge is to offset these trends with additional innovations, a task that the management of BancoSol understands.

Growth, Culture and Structure

Since the creation of PRODEM and then as BancoSol, the organisation has cultivated an idiosyncratic and unusually effective culture. This informal culture prevailed over PRODEM's formal structures. Indeed, to the extent the organisational structure was formally defined, it was fairly simple and flat. Instead of a rigid hierarchy, there was a conscious investment in the development of highly personalised relationships. This presumably resulted in a strong set of personal motivations, despite the absence of explicit pecuniary incentives, as well as a climate receptive to innovation, clear commitment to the organisation's mission and a style of self-management that emphasized recognition of individual contributions to the team's effort. This culture was well-adapted to the nature of the semi-formal lending technology and to the features of the clientele.

During the PRODEM period, personal affinity and informal attachments may have contributed to high staff productivity and low operating costs in ways that are only possible in a small organisation. An ardent and charismatic leadership promoted the development of a strong organisational ideology and encouraged devotion to an appealing goal: outreach via commercial viability. The approach, based on personal trust, applied to relationships among the organisation's staff and to those between the loan officer and the client. However, continued informality created a danger of waste and instability after the organisation grew rapidly into a large, regulated financial intermediary.

Moreover, the organisation believes in the importance of consistency between its personalised culture, based on trust, teamwork, and peer monitoring among branch employees, and its personalised lending technology, based on trust in the client and peer monitoring among borrowers in the group. This consistency is believed to be an essential determinant of BancoSol's success, and there has been concern that any transformation and depersonalisation of the organisation's culture may lead to reduced efficacy of the lending technology. Much of the success of BancoSol is due, however, to the structure of incentives embedded in the lending technology and its commitment to self-sufficiency, as described earlier. Such changes, therefore, may not necessarily threaten the organisation.

Nevertheless, rapid growth has introduced tensions in this system, reflecting the agency problems that typically develop as organisations grow[31]. A stronger foundation and structure became necessary to sustain the larger organisation; the links between the different parts of the system had to be defined more formally, and the lines of command and channels of communication had to be strengthened. Experienced businessmen on the Board of Directors perceived this need and a process of adjustment has been implemented during the past year[32]. The ensuing ideological debates within the organisation have been intense but fruitful. After transformation into BancoSol, PRODEM's original executive team (the visionaries) was complemented by experienced bankers and professionals in the management of human resources, assets and liabilities, information systems, and operations (the bankers).

With growth came the challenge of moving from the original informal culture to the new and more formal structure, without reducing the quality of service to the clientele or destroying the unified vision that had guided the organisation's evolution. High-quality service protects the value of the organisation-client relationship, the most important determinant of repayment and, therefore, of the organisation's self-sustainability. The challenge was to use an increasingly formal system to provide an inevitably quasi-informal service to a clientele that highly values personalised treatment and is bound by implicit rather than highly formalistic contracts.

The search for a solution has recognised the requirement for balancing, on the one hand, the need to solidify the formal structure, for the sake of efficiency within the organisation, via effective information flows, decision-making, security and communications, and, on the other hand, the need to preserve the personalised culture of contact with the clientele outside the organisation in order to preserve the incentives that result in low costs and low risks in lending.

Moreover, the heterogeneity of the clientele makes it difficult to adopt uniform standards for the development of the organisation-client relationship. Given this heterogeneity, it is impossible to anticipate all situations, and portfolio management will always require discretionary decision-making by loan officers. Decentralisation introduces problems of measuring and stimulating staff performance. The PRODEM-BancoSol tradition has been to encourage efficient staff performance via peer monitoring, a natural counterpart to the peer monitoring mechanisms used in the lending technology. However, the dangers of poor communications and inadequate oversight have been multiplied by the organisation's large size, the remoteness of decentralised units (such as branches opened in outlying parts of the country) and the greater distance between regional and central offices.

To address these challenges, the central office's divisions have been redesigned as service units responding on demand to the rest of the organisation. The concept of self-management has been redefined from a culture of "do as you like" to a system of "do well what you have been asked to do." This has paved the way for the introduction of performance indicators and a pecuniary incentive system based on employee and branch performance[33]. Introduction of these incentives may be critical to encourage productivity growth on the intensive margin, through more efficient effort on the part of the staff. In view of the limits to growth already noted, increased productivity is crucial.

In summary, rapid growth and large size have forced BancoSol to revise its original organisational design. Private owners in the board of directors, concerned with their reputation and the safety of their investment, have taken an active role in promoting key managerial reforms and in providing tighter internal control. Altruistic owners have insisted, in turn, on preserving the integrity of the original mission, as the only justification for the investment of public sector funds in a private bank. Among the executive staff, the visionaries from the PRODEM stage have become guardians of the consistency between organisational design and lending technology, while the bankers brought in by the board have been able to use their sophisticated professional skills in a more effective pursuit of the original mission. Only time will tell how successful this unique combination will be.

Conclusions

BancoSol's success in terms of outreach and sustainability can be attributed, among other things, to the strong concern of its leaders with the the organisation's financial viability, including the adoption of cost-covering interest rate policies and a firm commitment to enforcing loan repayment. Success can also be attributed to the development of a cost-effective lending technology that is appropriate for the target clientele, because it is based on the accumulation of information and experience about the organisation's market niche and its individual customers. The high value of the organisation-client relationships that were cultivated was further enhanced by the clear intention of permanence that was signalled by formalization as a private commercial bank.

In turn, success of the lending technology has resulted from a potent combination of incentives to repay that have been embedded in long-term implicit contracts with the clients. These contracts can be implemented at low costs to the organisation and also result in low transaction costs for the borrower. The possibility of obtaining better terms and conditions with successive loans adds value to the organisation-client relationships that are at the core of the bank's strategy. At least for the clients that continue purchasing its financial services, these terms and conditions are sufficient to compensate them for the added costs and risks of the joint liability required of the borrowers in each group.

Rapid growth at BancoSol has been based upon some unusual initial conditions, represented by the stock of tangible and intangible assets accumulated during the PRODEM stage. These intangible assets included information capital in the form of a lending technology, knowledge of its market niche and organisation-client relationships as well as the experience of its human capital at all levels of the organisation. It takes time to accumulate these assets.

From the head start made possible by these initial conditions, BancoSol managed to grow rapidly, due to formalization into a regulated financial intermediary. Upgrading increased its capacity to attract loanable funds and to manage its liabilities with greater flexibility. Indeed, further growth of PRODEM had been constrained by limits on the management of its liabilities that were removed with the creation of BancoSol.

Formalization, however, was not costless, as it introduced difficult second-generation adjustments[34]. The switch from donor funding to market-based liabilities significantly increased BancoSol's average cost of funds. At the same time, the maturing of the portfolio and the emergence of non-loan assets reduced the average revenue earned on productive assets. BancoSol responded to the challenge of a substantial reduction in its operating margin with an impressive reduction in average operating expenses. The behaviour of operating expenses resulted, in turn, from a number of either conflicting or complementary trends.

Decreasing average operating expenses reflected improvements in portfolio efficiency, measured as portfolio outstanding per unit of economic operating cost. Average economic costs had been $1.72 in 1987 and had declined to $0.63 by 1991, just before the transformation. This average cost further decreased to $0.42 in 1994 (Table 6). Such a reduction is difficult to achieve in any microfinance organisation.

Increased portfolio efficiency, however, was the result of two opposing forces: decreasing transactions efficiency and increasing loan size. The cost of keeping a client's balance in the portfolio for a year increased from $149 in 1992 to $242 in 1994, reflecting the Ricardian limits on the productivity-enhancing impact of growth. The cost per loan disbursed increased from $49 to $93 during the same period. The impact on costs was only partially compensated by some increase in average maturity terms.

Reductions in transactions efficiency reflected, in turn, a shift from intensive to extensive growth. While growth during the PRODEM period was mostly intensive, resulting from gains in productivity and from increasing capacity utilisation, growth during the BancoSol period was mostly extensive, resulting from rapid additions to the branch network. Accelerated creation of new branches and the accompanying hiring of new loan officers halted growth of average productivity or even decreased it. Smaller branch portfolios made it harder to dilute the fixed costs from branch operations, while the number of transactions per loan officer stopped growing. Thus, while extensive growth made major increases in outreach possible, the Ricardian limits to growth tended to dampen efficiency and profitability.

Thus, it was the increase in average balance outstanding that allowed BancoSol to reduce its average operating costs, despite reductions in transactions efficiency. Some of the increases in average loan size were policy-induced, with BancoSol encouraging its loan officers to grant larger loans to borrowers at all stages of the organisation-client relationship, before later reversing this policy in response to increasing arrears. Most of the increases in loan size, however, were due to accumulating experience about the clientele and increased demand from the clients themselves. These last two sources of increase in loan sizes are not in contradiction with the organisation's outreach objectives and do not represent a drift away from the original mission.

In addition to the limits on growth that naturally arise from the lending technology, during the process of accelerated expansion BancoSol had to face challenges resulting from tension between its original informal culture and the organisation's larger size and complexity. These tensions have been addressed by the complementarity of the earlier visionaries and the new bankers. BancoSol can take pride in the human and professional quality of its executive staff. The quality of these managerial personnel suggests that they will be up to the difficult challenges ahead.

Notes and References

*   Gonzalez-Vega is Professor of Agricultural Economics and of Economics and Director of the Rural Finance Program, Meyer is Professor Emeritus of Agricultural Economics, and Schreiner, Rodriguez and Navajas are Graduate Research Associates, all at The Ohio State University.

1.   This topic is equivalent to the questions raised in the finance literature about the existence of economies of scale and of scope in banking (Benston, Hanweck, and Humphrey, 1982; Berger, Hanweck, and Humphrey, 1987; Clark, 1988).

2.   For a detailed conceptual framework for evaluating the consequences of size and growth on the quality of the portfolio and on the structure of costs of microfinance organisations, see Gonzalez-Vega *et al.*, forthcoming.

3.   International shareholders include several NGOs and public organisations: ACCION International, Calmeadow Foundation, Société d'Investissement et de Développement International, the Rockefeller Foundation and the Inter-American Investment Corporation. Domestic shareholders initially included one non-governmental organisation (PRODEM) and three private banks, three private firms and five prominent individuals, including President Sanchez de Lozada. It was on the basis of the reputation of these prominent individuals that the prudential authorities were willing to issue a bank charter to BancoSol.

4.   The USAID Mission, however, had made substantial funds available to PRODEM and wanted to see its loan portfolio grow fast.

5.   These intangible assets are a source of implicit subsidies for BancoSol. If properly accounted for, they would increase the organisation's subsidy dependence (to be discussed below), as such considerations would raise the amount of equity and thus the level of the opportunity cost of the funds used by BancoSol. The implicit subsidy could have been eliminated had BancoSol paid a higher price for costs of organisation and other intangible assets at the time of founding and when additional branches were transferred.

6.   An image of serious concern with repayment and cost-covering pricing was critical for institutional survival in a country flooded with paternalistic NGOs unconcerned about their own viability. The subsidised interest rates charged by other organisations and their lack of discipline in collecting loans tended to create lax attitudes towards credit and made the job of serious microfinance organisations more difficult.

7.   Averages of monthly portfolios over the year are used to correct for sharp seasonality. These and all other figures reported here are in US dollars, converted from bolivianos of constant purchasing power as of December 1995, at the December 1995 exchange rate of 4.93 bolivianos per dollar. This corrects for the impact of domestic inflation and facilitates international comparisons.

8.   Table 1 shows averages of the monthly number of clients with balances outstanding for the corresponding twelve-month period. For the period ending June 1995, that number was 59 745.

9.   Compared to Grameen Bank in Bangladesh and Bank Rakyat Indonesia, however, BancoSol is small.

10.   Given the group-credit technology, the number of loans granted to clients is about four times larger than the number of group-loans processed. At BancoSol, loans are recorded as granted to individuals belonging to particular groups, but some of the tasks of the loan officer relate to working with groups and others to working with individuals. While these distinctions affect the structure of costs, from the perspective of outreach what matters is the number of individual clients reached.

11.   An additional 20 761 clients had compensating balances left over from earlier practices at PRODEM. Although these accounts are now, at least in theory, voluntary deposits, it is not clear that the clients have deliberately decided to maintain balances in those accounts.

12.   We cannot resolve here the debate about group versus individual lending technologies.

13.   This is a stylised version of actual practice, which does not follow a rigid standard sequence. In general, however, it appears that the terms and conditions of loan contracts improve as the organisation-client relationship ages. While BancoSol operates on the principle of making loans with more attractive terms to clients with more experience, there are no explicit guidelines about the implementation of this policy.

14.   Yaron's index is defined as the percentage change in the yield on the loan portfolio needed to compensate for existing subsidies (see also Yaron in this volume).

15.   Under more realistically stringent assumptions, BancoSol may still show a subsidy of $1.19 per loan outstanding per year (Table 4). By international standards for microfinance organisations, these subsidies are very small.

16.   This ignores a subsidy dependency index of 898 per cent in the initial year.

17.   This does not mean 18 additional percentage points but rather an eighteen-per cent increase of the existing yield level. Thus, if the yield was 46 per cent per year in 1991, it should have been 54 per cent (0.46 x 1.18).

18.   Calculation of the subsidy dependence index for PRODEM did not include the value of technical assistance funded mostly by USAID and provided largely through ACCION International. In the case of BancoSol, this analysis did not include the implicit subsidies that may have resulted from the transfer of assets from PRODEM. In addition, a USAID guarantee for BancoSol permitted the bank to issue bonds. USAID agreed to pay bondholders 50 per cent of the loss of principal in case of default, up to $2.5 million.

19.   The share of personnel costs in operating expenses remained fairly constant, at about 60 per cent, while the share of general administration expenses declined from 31 per cent at the end of 1991 to 22 per cent at the end of 1994, suggesting possible economies of scale in administration.

20.   This section describes features of the technology that may contribute to BancoSol's success. It does not address dynamic questions about the appropriateness of the technology for an evolving clientele, nor does it compare it to alternative technologies.

21.   The general principles represented by these incentives are incorporated in other successful microlending technologies, even when they use a different mix of activities to evaluate creditworthiness and to enforce loan contracts.

22.   As the clients progress, they may begin to demand a quality of services that may not be possible within the group-lending technology. This represents one of the most difficult challenges faced by BancoSol.

23.   We do not claim that group credit is superior to individual loan transactions nor that group joint liability is the key determinant of BancoSol's success. There are important advantages to the client (and presumably to the organisation) from individual transactions. As reported by Gonzalez-Vega *et al.* (1996), Caja Los ANDES and FIE have been able to show as good or even better repayment indicators as BancoSol, while still operating with individual clients. The argument here is only that, for a given subset of clients, the opportunity to borrow even if they do not possess collateralisable assets enhances the value of their relationship with BancoSol and thus contributes to repayment through this route, rather than through the peer monitoring emphasized elsewhere (Stiglitz, 1990). Increased competition in the market challenges BancoSol to improve the quality of its contracts beyond the constraints of group credit in order to protect the loyalty of its most advanced clientele.

24.   Limited access to funds in the early stages of the organisation may not be a curse, however, if learning and experimentation are critical to the achievement of self-sustainability.

25.   The reduction in transactions efficiency was even more pronounced when measured with respect to numbers and amounts of loans disbursed. The cost per loan disbursed increased from $49 in 1992 to $93 in 1994 (Table 6).

26.   At the same time, the average amount disbursed per loan increased from $156 in 1987 to $317 in 1991, and from $409 in 1992 to $588 in 1994 (Table 1).

27.   For example, if a client in the target group has a repayment capacity of $450, but BancoSol starts at $150 because it does not know enough about that repayment capacity, and then increases loan size to approach $450, this does not mean that it is leaving the target clientele behind. Over time, as the organisation learns more about the characteristics of its clientele, this generic information may also induce an increase in size of the first loan (e.g., to $200) for the same type of client.

28.   The figures are interpreted here on the basis of these non-testable assumptions, as repayment capacity is not known to the researchers and is only imperfectly observed by the lender.

29.   The decline of transactions productivity per branch was even more pronounced. The annual number of loans disbursed per branch increased from 3 758 in 1987 to 14 686 in 1991 and steadily declined to 4 871 in the twelve-month period ending on 30 June 1995 (Table 7).

30.   The number of balances outstanding per loan officer increased from 87 in 1987 to 346 by 1991. This indicator increased to 351 in 1994, but it declined to 326 for the twelve-month period ending on June 30, 1995 (Table 7). Despite declines in portfolio and transactions productivity per employee and per loan officer, however, BancoSol's levels of productivity are high compared to other Latin American microfinance organisations.

31.   Agency problems arise when those who devote resources to a particular purpose (the principals) surrender partial control over those resources to those in charge of implementing the purpose for them (the agents). The agents have their own objectives, and the principals need to monitor and constrain their behaviour to make sure that the original purpose is achieved. As the organisation grows, there is a reduced ability of BancoSol's board of directors (the principals) to monitor at low cost and to constrain the behaviour of central and regional offices and the bank's staff (the agents) effectively. Formal structures for internal control and formal incentives for improved staff and management performance must then be created.

32.   This was one instance when the presence of private bankers in the ownership of the organisation may have been important. These entrepreneurs recognised the need for more effective internal control mechanisms and better managerial skills to face the challenges of operating as a regulated commercial bank. Other owners in the board played the role of guardians of the mission, making sure that adjustment did not move BancoSol away from the target clientele.

33.   In the design of these incentives, BancoSol has been careful in assigning appropriate weights to individual as well as team performance at the branch, regional, and national levels. This reflects an effort to promote both local and global improvements in performance.

34.   This discussion ignores the additional operational costs that result from the reporting requirements imposed on regulated financial intermediaries by the Central Bank and the demands for additional formal administrative structures that result from application of the banking regulatory framework. It also ignores the constraints on portfolio composition (e.g., risk categories) and the associated costs (provisions for bad loans) that arise from the norms enforced by the prudential supervisor.

Bibliography

AGAFONOFF, A. (1994), "Banco Solidario S.A.: Microenterprise Financing on a Commercial Scale in Bolivia", Economics Division Working Papers 94/5, Research School of Pacific and Asian Studies, The Australian National University, Canberra.

BENJAMIN, MCDONALD P., JR. (1994), "Credit Schemes for Microenterprises: Motivation, Design, and Viability", Unpublished Ph.D. dissertation, Georgetown University, Washington, D.C.

BENSTON, G., G. HANWECK, AND D. HUMPHREY (1982), "Scale Economies in Banking: A Restructuring and Reassessment", Journal of Money, Credit and Banking, Vol. 14, No. 4 (November), Part I.

BERGER, A, G. HANWECK, AND D. HUMPHREY (1987), "Competitive Viability in Banking. Scale, Scope and Product Mix Economies", Journal of Monetary Economics, No. 20.

BESLEY, T. AND S. COATE (1995), "Group Lending, Repayment Incentives, and Social Collateral", Journal of Development Economics, Vol. 46 (February).

CHAVES, R.A. (1996), "Institutional Design: The Case of the Bancomunales", in C. GONZALEZ-VEGA, R. JIMENEZ, AND R.E. QUIROS (eds.), Financing Rural Microenterprises: FINCA-Costa Rica, Ohio State University, Academia de Centroamerica and the Inter-American Foundation, San Jose.

CHAVES, R.A. AND C. GONZALEZ-VEGA (1996), "The Design of Successful Rural Financial Intermediaries: Evidence from Indonesia", World Development, Vol. 24, No. 1 (January).

CLARK, J. (1988), "Economies of Scale and Scope at Depository Financial Institutions: A Review of the Literature", Economic Review, Federal Reserve Bank of Kansas City (October).

CHRISTEN, R.P., E. RHYNE, R.C. VOGEL, AND C. MCKEAN (1995), "Maximizing the Outreach of Microenterprise Finance: An Analysis of Successful Microfinance Programs", USAID Program and Operations Assessment Report No. 10, Agency for International Development, Washington, D.C.

GLOSSER, A. (1994), "The Creation of BancoSol in Bolivia", in M. OTERO AND E. RHYNE (eds.), The New World of Microenterprise Finance: Building Healthy Financial Institutions for the Poor, Kumarian Press, West Hartford, Connecticut.

GONZALEZ-VEGA, C. (1994), "Stages in the Evolution of Thought on Rural Finance: A Vision from The Ohio State University", Economics and Sociology Occasional Paper No. 2134, The Ohio State University, Columbus, Ohio.

GONZALEZ-VEGA, C. (1996a), "Non-Bank Financial Institutions and the Sequencing of Financial Reform", in Bruce L.R. Smith and Alison Harwood (eds.), *Sequencing Financial Sector Development and Reform*, The Brookings Institution, Washington, D.C.

GONZALEZ-VEGA, C. (1996b), *Microfinanzas en El Salvador: Lecciones y Perspectivas, Fundacion Dr. Guillermo Manuel Ungo*, San Salvador.

GONZALEZ-VEGA, C. *et al.* (1996), Progress in Microfinance: Lessons from Bolivia, forthcoming manuscript.

RHYNE, E. AND M. OTERO (1994), "Financial Services for Microenterprises: Principles and Institutions", in M. OTERO AND E. RHYNE (eds.),*The New World of Microenterprise Finance: Building Healthy Financial Institutions for the Poor*, Kumarian Press, West Hartford, Connecticut.

ROSENBERG, R. (1994), "Beyond Self-Sufficiency: Licensed Leverage and Microfinance Strategy", processed.

SANCHEZ, S. (1996), "Matching of Borrowers and Lenders: The Case of Rural Mexico", unpublished Ph.D. Dissertation, The Ohio State University.

SCHMIDT, R.H. AND C.-P. ZEITINGER (1994), "Critical Issues in Small and Microbusiness Finance", International Donor Conference of Financial Sector Development, Vienna, September.

SCHMIDT, R.H. AND C.-P. ZEITINGER (1996), "Prospects, Problems and Potential of Credit-Granting NGOs", *Journal of International Development*, Vol. 8, No. 2.

STIGLITZ, J.E. (1990), "Peer Monitoring and Credit Markets", *World Bank Economic Review*, Vol. 4, No. 3.

TRIGO LOUBIERE, J. (1996), "Regulation and Supervision of Microfinance Institutions: The Bolivian Experience", paper presented to the Conference on Regulation and Supervision of Microfinance Institutions, Washington, D.C., November 1995, in M. OTERO AND R. ROCK (eds.), *From Margin to Mainstream: The Regulation and Supervision of Microfinance*, Monograph No. 11, Cambridge, Mass.: ACCION International.

YARON, J. (1994), "What Makes Rural Financial Institutions Successful?" *The World Bank Research Observer*, Vol. 9, No. 1, January.

PART THREE. NEW MECHANISMS FOR ENHANCING SUSTAINABILITY AND RESOURCE BASE

Innovative Funding of Capacity Development: The "Self-administered Capital Fund" in German Bilateral Co-operation

Thomas Feige*

Preliminary Remark

The "self-administered capital fund" described below is a conceptually innovative approach in a pilot phase at the time of writing, which means that there is still no broadly effective application. This chapter focuses on the first tentative conclusions and is intended to encourage broader reflections on promoting NGOs in the microfinance sector.

Background of the Instrument

Self-administered capital funds are an instrument at the point of convergence of financial systems development, poverty alleviation, and private sector development. These funds are designed to strengthen the financial autonomy of target-group-oriented private financing institutions. Thus the aim is to make a direct contribution to reducing poverty by improving the financing for micro- and small enterprises, small farmers and women, especially in the informal sector. On the other hand, the capital funds are also based on the idea of a partnership between official development co-operation and NGOs, in which the NGOs' own responsibility and "ownership" is strengthened and their autonomy explicitly recognised by their administration of the capital funds. These funds are also meant to contribute to the internal organisational development of the institutions.

The ideas for establishing this instrument derive from discussions in Germany during the second half of the 1980s on redefining the state's role in development co-operation, especially by the working group "Poverty Alleviation through Help towards

Self-help", composed of representatives from the official and non-governmental (e.g. churches and political foundations) development co-operation sectors. During the debate on the role of official development co-operation, demands were made for increased co-operation with non-governmental agencies while recognising their autonomy.

At the same time, various models had been proposed for decentralised private financing institutions and self-help groups because the traditional development banks had failed to reach the poorer target groups and achieve economic sustainability. They were tested mainly in the field of technical co-operation. Examples include the linking of self-help groups with formal banks (see McGuire and Conroy in this volume), the Grameen Bank as a model, village savings banks and the strengthening of target-group-oriented financing NGOs. However, Germany's development co-operation policies accorded a central position to the financial sector in free-market reforms, private sector development and poverty alleviation since the beginning of the 1990s. Thus, the establishment of sustainable and efficient institutional structures in the financial sector became the focus of attention. This was the background to the creation of the self-administered capital fund in 1992, which thus far has been implemented in three pilot projects.

The Concept's Substance and Functioning

Self-administered capital funds are funds with equity features provided as a non-recurring, non-repayable grant to private agencies operating in the credit sector. The defining characteristic of this instrument is the creation of autonomous assets owned by the executing agency. The idea is not to promote projects or programmes, but rather executing agencies/institutions. At the same time, the donor is not the owner of the capital and does not participate in the executing agency's supervisory boards, unlike with the traditional participation in the equity capital. This will strengthen the agency's own responsibilities. Accordingly, there is no provision for extensive advisory services through long-term foreign experts.

The instrument is intended to serve several objectives:

— to enable the financing institutions to achieve sustainable income without jeopardising the equity, thus safeguarding competitiveness;

— to secure uninterrupted financing services at the target group level;

— to make the executing agency independent of external donor financing in the long term and facilitate refinancing on the national capital markets;

— to facilitate the formal establishment of banks by strengthening the equity base;

— to promote the mobilisation of savings capital.

Institutions considered eligible in particular are non-profit-oriented NGOs, financial self-help organisations, co-operative institutions, community financing institutions and target-group-oriented local private banks. The following are the criteria for eligibility:

— comprehensive experience by the executing agency in the financial support of micro- and small enterprises, women or self-help groups, including the offer of savings services, and in-depth know-how in the field of promoting small enterprises in general. In principle, advisory support is not envisaged to improve the skills of executing agencies;

— the executing agency is responsible for handling the credit business directly or with the help of a mediating institution (e.g. bank);

— there is access to the target group, preferably directly via an efficient field structure;

— the executing agency is gradually moving towards operating under formal rules determined by the central bank, the banking authorities and banking laws. The medium-term objective should be recognition as a bank;

— the executing agency's operations are autonomous, i.e. not functioning as a state instrument;

— operation on business principles, as applied by sound banks in the formal sector, in particular with regard to the terms and conditions for ultimate borrowers, which should take into account all banking costs and the maintenance of the real value of capital funds.

The capital funds can be used as investment funds or promotional funds for advisory services, depending upon the executing agency's requirements. Investment funds can serve to finance direct lending to target groups or as credit guarantees for other banks. Promotional funds can be used as credit support measures to finance information, training and advisory services for the ultimate borrower or for training and professionalisation of the executing agency's staff.

There is no limit on the scope of self-administered capital funds, except that they must be geared to the requirements and the absorptive capacity of the executing agency. Capital funds provided thus far have ranged between DM 0.4 million and DM 1.35 million.

The capital funds are allocated to the executing agencies directly through German technical co-operation (GTZ). There is a financing agreement between the GTZ and the executing agency on the use of the funds, implementation and the executing agency's obligation to verify and report on the use of the funds. Preferably, the proper utilisation will be supervised by internationally recognised local chartered accountants. In some cases monitoring by German technical co-operation is possible.

The Use of the Instrument

Due to the provisional nature of the instrument, self-administered capital funds have been provided only rather cautiously and on the basis of strictly applied criteria. They have been used in the following three pilot projects:

Philippines: NGO network CENDHRRA. Investment fund of DM 0.45 million. (Replenishment by another DM 0.9 million envisaged.) Used for direct lending and as a credit guarantee fund to secure lending operations of a private commercial bank with small farmers and small rural entrepreneurs via NGOs and self-help groups;

Uruguay: *Instituto de Promociòn Economico Social del Uruguay*/IPRU. A fund of DM 0.44 million, of which about two thirds is used as an investment fund and one third as a promotional fund for financing and providing advisory services to small entrepreneurs; and

Dominican Republic: *Asociaciòn Dominicana para el Desarrollo de la Mujer*/ ADOPEM. Capital funds of DM 0.65 million for direct lending to female urban micro-entrepreneurs.

Preliminary conclusions

It is premature to assess this instrument in a general way, given the limited scope of its application. Out of the three pilot projects, ADOPEM has not yet yielded any results, as the project was approved only in 1995. The project in the Philippines was evaluated with an overall positive result in terms of target achievement. Detailed evaluation reports from the Uruguayan project are not yet available. Therefore, this assessment will be confined to the following preliminary conclusions of a general nature on promoting more advanced financing of NGOs:

In principle, the instrument seems to be a promising tool for strengthening efficient NGOs and providing low-income people (having no other access to formal banks) with financial services. The funds were used in accordance with the purpose agreed upon, and the target groups were reached. Furthermore, the project in the Philippines contributes towards linking NGOs and micro-enterprises to a commercial bank.

The concept itself provides a framework which is meant to be very flexible about the potential institutional use of the funds. This facilitates adaptation to specific conditions of a country and/or the executing agency.

As the instrument grants an exceptionally high autonomy in the use of the funds by the executing agency, it is especially important that the credit operations be professional and sound. This means that the financing intermediary must be a relatively advanced institution so that no substantial supporting technical assistance is required.

Since the capital funds were introduced, experience has shown that very few institutions meet the strict allocation criteria. Moreover, existing financing intermediaries which are run on genuinely professional lines and are institutionally strong and target-group-oriented, quite often already have access to local capital markets.

Furthermore, it appears that the institutions presently supported still have weaknesses despite strict allocation criteria. Thus, two of the three institutions assisted show relatively high repayment defaults. Full cost recovery was reached by one institution, while another one might achieve this in the foreseeable future by enlarging the credit portfolio. By and large, the institutions assisted with the capital funds need additional external advisory support to ensure further professional qualifications and increased efficiency.

When promoting private executing agencies it is important to examine the investment and promotion fund ratio very carefully. The financing of investment and advisory activities tend to blur the clear delineation between financial services and general advice for the executing agency's ultimate borrower. For reasons of efficiency and lowering transaction costs, it is advisable that the executing agency clearly specialise in providing financial services. To ensure this concentration on financial intermediation, the promotional funds should be clearly subordinated to the investment funds in quantitative terms, and there should be an adequate ratio to the lending volume.

If the executing agency has sole responsibility for project planning, it must co-ordinate the ideas for implementation with the other actors concerned so that the stipulations of the financing agreement can be implemented. For example, in the Philippine project, a lack of co-ordination initially led to an unwillingness of the participating commercial bank to assume its envisaged share of the credit loss risk not covered by the guarantee fund.

Since the donor does not participate, the sanction mechanism for violations of the contractual stipulations is relatively weak. Therefore, ultimate transmission of ownership only occurs at the end of the project. Until that time the grant may be reclaimed in case of breach of contract. As this is possible only in extreme cases, special care must be taken when selecting the executing agency and planning the project.

The establishment of sustainable structures through capital funds means an abandonment of the "project approach" by the executing agencies, especially NGOs, and the donor. Under that approach, quite often a "new project" is requested from another donor in case of losses. Self-administered capital funds, by contrast, always address the overall institutional structure. This means that the executing agency must be willing to assume a real ownership responsibility in the sense of having an interest in maintaining the value of the equity funds. Therefore project appraisals must especially focus on the executing agency's self-assessment and its "governance".

Summary

Promoting private executing agencies, especially in the informal sector, has a large potential for development of the poverty-oriented financial sector. Self-administered capital funds are a comparatively new approach to co-operation in that sector, suitable only for rather advanced financing institutions. They cannot and should not replace other forms of institution-building of financial intermediaries (especially advice and training), for capital funds are the conclusion of a successful institution-building process.

Note

*   Private Sector Development Division, Federal Ministry for Economic Co-operation and Development (BMZ), Bonn, Germany

Debt-to-Development Conversions: Mechanisms, Experience and Potential

Marie-Hélène Libercier

In the 1980s, operations on the debt of developing countries were used by banks as a means of reducing their loan portfolios and spreading risk, or of making promising investments (debt-equity swaps[1]). The notion of using debt swaps to finance developmental, social, educational or environmental projects was formulated as early as 1984[2]. The exchange of debt for environmental conservation efforts (debt-for-nature swaps) was the first type to be implemented by non-governmental organisations (NGOs)[3]. We will examine debt-for- development swaps in a broad sense (conversions of debt into development projects), although it is true that steps to protect the environment may be a form of contribution to development. The principle of this type of debt swap is identical to that of debt-for-nature swaps: a debtor government establishes a fund in local currency to be spent on development projects in the country against a reduction in its debt. Only the end uses of the funds differ.

The advantage of debt-for-development swaps lies in their purpose, transforming debt into development capital, and in their means. This innovative treatment of debt supplements "traditional" forms of debt relief (unconditional cancellation of the debt and rescheduling reimbursement, on a basis defined unilaterally by organised groups of creditors). The idea is to introduce repayment or debt relief which is "creative"[4], in the sense that it frees resources for development and, moreover, is based on a participatory mechanism involving various actors from both North and South. In addition, this type of swap can be a new mode of financing for local development projects, worked out and implemented in collaboration with the grassroots populations and their organisations.

Debt swaps can be analysed as debt-relief instruments, in which case their impact is evaluated on the macroeconomic level (debtor countries enjoy renewed credibility and creditworthiness, and an easing of the pressure on the balance of payments and the budget). Our study concentrates more at the microeconomic level, trying to evaluate whether debt swaps can become a new mechanism for promoting lasting participatory development. We often refer to the debt swaps carried out under the Swiss debt-relief programme. This example illustrates the potential of swaps undertaken with the intention of favouring the participation of civil society and the people, in both the implementation of the swap mechanism and its benefits.

A priori, debt-for-development swaps present advantages for the governments of indebted developing countries and opportunities for grassroots participation. It is necessary, however, to have a thorough understanding of this mechanism, which is relatively simple in principle but complicated to implement, and to analyse the microeconomic impact of swaps before pronouncing on their potential as a new way of promoting participatory development[5].

The Mechanism of Debt-for-Development Swaps

The Principle

The idea is to reduce a country's external debt in exchange for a commitment to establish a budget line denominated in local currency for the financing of development projects. Foreign debt denominated in hard currency is thus effectively converted into domestic debt in local currency.

When an NGO carries out a debt swap, it buys up a debt denominated in foreign currency and discounted on the secondary market. It negotiates with the debtor country the cancellation of this debt against the establishment of a fund in local currency greater than the discounted value of the debt. This domestic currency fund is used to finance a development project carried out by the Northern NGO in collaboration with a local partner. The advantage of this operation is that all parties benefit: the creditor rids itself of a questionable asset; the debtor country repays its debt in a way which better corresponds to its abilities and needs (in local currency and benefitting the development of the debtor country and its population)[6]; the Northern NGO obtains a multiplier effect on the funds at its disposal and thus contributes more financial support to local organisations than if it had invested directly in development projects. The size of this multiplier effect depends on the secondary market discount and the payment terms negotiated with the government of the debtor country[7].

Variants on this basic model are possible. The model governing debt swaps carried out under the Swiss programme differs from that presented above in that NGOs do not contribute financially to swaps. Rather, it is the Swiss government which buys the debt instruments to be converted. It then cancels the debts (which are officially guaranteed, often arising from export credits) and asks the debtor in return to pay an amount in local currency, equivalent to a part of the canceled debt, into a fund managed jointly by private organisations and government agencies. This counterpart fund is supposed to support the projects of local NGOs and government agencies. The Swiss NGOs play an essential role in the conception and implementation of these debt-relief measures, being both the promoters of the process[8] and also participants in various stages, such as identification of partner organisations in developing countries, selection of development projects for financing by the counterpart fund and so on.

Unless specified otherwise, we will now study in greater detail the characteristics and methods of a typical swap managed by an NGO.

Actors

A swap brings together the following actors:

— a creditor, either a commercial bank or a government;

— an operator, usually a Northern NGO, which is ready to buy back the debt;

— a debtor country, particularly the financial authorities of this country (central bank, minister of finance or head of the treasury) and the local organisations responsible for implementing the development programme.

Intermediaries and counsellors, both financial and technical, are also needed to facilitate various transactions.

Stages of the Operation

Before the swap, as such, can begin, some prospecting work is needed, in order to identify the following: convertible debts and their buy-back terms; Northern NGOs interested by the swap mechanism with a view to undertaking projects in countries holding convertible debts. This work may take some time. It is not generally done by the NGOs which are the final beneficiaries of the swap but by intermediary organisations which put interested NGOs into contact with countries holding debts.

The swap of debt into development programmes can be broken down into four stages:

1) Negotiating the debt-swap agreement with the debtor country

At the end of the negotiations, the contracting parties — in the North, the operator of the swap, and in the South, the government of the debtor country[9] — must reach agreement on:

— the financial and legal terms of the swap (redemption price[10], conditions and schedule for making funds available); and

— the development projects suitable for such swaps and the local organisations responsible for implementation.

2) Acquiring debt on the secondary market at a lower price

Often an NGO buys the debt, and in that case the purchase is financed mostly by private donations to these NGOs and by their own resources. It is sometimes advantageous for several NGOs to pool their financial resources to increase the volume of the transaction and thus obtain a more favourable redemption price. Northern governments may also finance such operations, either in whole or in part. Exceptionally, creditors may simply cancel debts unconditionally. In the case of the Swiss programme, the government assumes the entire cost of buying back debt, so this programme corresponds more to conditional debt cancellations than to swaps.

3) Presentation of the debt at the debtor country's central bank and sale at a previously negotiated price

The amount paid in local currency by the debtor country is lower than the initial value of the debt but higher than its discounted value (as paid by the NGO). The NGO thus enjoys an attractive multiplier effect.

4) The swap, management of the proceeds and execution of the development programme

The debtor country's central bank can pay the negotiated amount directly in local currency or may prefer to emit treasury bonds, to be sold subsequently on the local secondary market to obtain cash[11]. The proceeds of the swap can be placed directly at the disposition of the organisation which is the beneficiary of the swap or invested in a local fund managed, in whole or in part, by local organisations.

The ways in which funds are made available and managed differ from one swap to another. The choice of one of these modes is not neutral, but reflects the spirit in which the swap is undertaken. In the Swiss debt-relief programme, the form and structure of this counterpart fund, and hence the role of local organisations, vary from one country to another, but the common principle is to promote constructive collaboration between the various actors (local organisations, the government of the debtor country, representatives of the Swiss government) to bring the administrators of the counterpart fund and the programme operators as close as possible. This involves adapting the counterpart fund instruments to local situations and guaranteeing that the activities thus financed will be appropriate to the needs and goals of the grassroots.

Finally, the counterpart in local currency can be used as a fund for immediate financing of projects or can provision a long-term capital fund (in the latter case, only the interest on this capital is used to finance the projects selected). The advantage of the latter scheme is to guarantee to the organisations undertaking projects that the financial contributions will be lasting.

Conditions for This Type of Operation to be Feasible and Worthwhile

— The debtor country must have a transferable external debt which is eligible for a swap on the basis of the underlying loan contract and of the laws and regulations in force.

— This debt must also be subject to an attractive discount and must represent a non-negligible amount. The Northern NGO should make enough to cover the various costs and commissions for legal and technical assistance and to justify the investment in time taken up by various procedures, even if financial return should not be the only criterion used to assess the appropriateness of swaps.

— The debtor country must intend to pay its debt. If it has already stopped making repayments, there is no direct financial advantage in converting and paying its debt, even in local currency. Nevertheless, undertaking a swap can be motivated by the wish to improve its image in the eyes of its creditors.

— Inflation must not be too high (a high rate of inflation would quickly "melt" the local-currency proceeds of the swap), the exchange rate must be relatively stable and the local currency must not have been abandoned in favour of a foreign currency (in certain countries, such as Cuba, the dollarisation of the economy partly explains the local NGOs' lack of interest in the swap mechanism, which would place a local currency fund at their disposition).

— The debtor government must approve the development projects to be financed and thereby express its confidence in the local organisations responsible for implementation. Some authoritarian governments may show a certain reticence, particularly if the local-currency fund finances organisations which promote human rights, or any other activity aimed at giving more power to the grassroots. Whatever the destination of the funds, debt swaps hold a special interest for governments which favour the increased participation of civil society in the formulation and implementation of development programmes.

— Northern NGOs must wish to launch development programmes in the debtor countries concerned and have partners there among the local development organisations.

— These NGOs must have sufficient financial means to envisage buying up the debt. The size of the initial amounts needed to realise swaps of official debt can be an obstacle to NGO participation in this type of operation.

Swaps Already Carried Out

Quantitative Evaluation

The amount of debt converted into development programmes was estimated in 1994 at between $750 million and $1 billion (World Bank, 1994). Although this figure has increased in the last two years, it remains relatively modest. Indeed, debt-for-development swaps may have reduced the indebtedness of the South by only 0.05 per cent. Moreover, this type of swap accounts for only a little over 1 per cent of the total volume of debt swaps, as against 40 per cent for debt-equity swaps. The latter, at $35 billion for the 1985-93 period, were the leading form of swap, although they have tended to fall in volume since 1990.

Debt-for-development swaps can be negotiated at the bilateral or at the multilateral level.

At the Bilateral Level

Some of these swaps have taken place under programmes for the swap of official debt (mostly debt resulting from official development assistance, or ODA), such as those set up by the German, Canadian, Swiss, French, Belgian and US governments. Some governments, including some of those just mentioned, have also participated in selective swap operations.

Among the swap programmes, measures and incentives used by countries of the North to encourage such operations, we refer to the diverse experiences of three countries: Switzerland, which has shown a marked orientation towards creative debt relief, i.e. debt relief which favours the poor; Belgium, which has shown a certain dynamism in this field since 1987; and France, which has taken some initiatives, although it appears to have no single, well-defined policy of promoting debt-for-development swaps[12].

Switzerland

In 1991, the Swiss government set up a debt-relief facility of SF 500 million to reduce the debts of low-income or highly indebted countries. These funds made debt-relief measures possible at the bilateral level, such as the debt-for-development swaps examined here, and also at the multilateral level[13]. The Swiss initiative is one of the most generous and innovative in the domain of debt swaps, since it is based on the Swiss government's cancellation of the debt. This cancellation leads to the debtor country's establishment of a counterpart fund in local currency, which is supposed to help promote the social and economic development of disadvantaged populations. By mid-1995, the Swiss government had signed debt-relief agreements which provided for the creation of counterpart funds with 11 countries (Bolivia, Honduras, Peru,

Ecuador, Tanzania, Zambia, Jordan, Senegal, Côte d'Ivoire, the Philippines and Egypt). The debt forgiveness for these countries totals more than SF 1 billion and the counterpart funds to SF 266 million ($706 million and $180 million respectively).

Table 1 presents the figures for nominal canceled debt and the volume of the counterpart funds, as well as for ODA received by the countries. It highlights the potential of swaps. Although the amount of debt canceled is negligible in comparison to the total outstanding debt of the beneficiaries of the Swiss facility[14], it is much higher than Swiss ODA flows to these same countries. Debt cancellation thus involves a substantial financial effort for Switzerland, a sign of its desire to contribute to the recovery of the debtor countries by carrying out constructive debt restructuring. The amounts of the counterpart funds are also significant: for those countries which benefit from debt swaps, they represent on average 2.5 times the amount of Swiss ODA. These funds in local currency also have many advantages over classic aid flows, in particular because of the system for managing the counterpart funds, where financed projects must address needs identified as priorities in the beneficiary country and must guarantee the participation of people's organisations and their grassroots supporters. The priority sectors chosen are usually social infrastructure, the environment, promotion of small enterprises, health and education. The debt-relief agreement signed with Zambia also provides for a contribution to a financial institution which supports women in starting up micro-enterprises (the idea is to use the counterpart fund to endow this institution with capital). Five of the eleven counterpart funds were operational in August 1995: the projects to be supported have been chosen (or are being chosen) and financing has begun. On average, 57 per cent of the available resources has been committed, but the rate of utilisation varies greatly from one fund to another.

Belgium

Debt swaps are also a form of debt relief under Belgium's bilateral co-operation policy. Some of these swaps were carried out unofficially before 1990 (that is, before the Paris Club approved some swaps of official debt[15]) with the intention of consolidating the accounts of the Office National du Ducroire (OND), the export insurance agency. The government aid agency buys some developing country debt from the OND. Cancellation of this debt leads to the debtor country's establishing a counterpart fund in local currency, allocated to the financing of a social development project to be managed jointly by the Belgian aid agency and the government of the debtor country. These swaps of official debt began in 1987. At the end of 1993, sales of bilateral debt amounted to approximately $170 million, of which 46 per cent was sold with a view to promoting development (through the projects financed in this way). Although initially debt was sold at its nominal value, a discount rate has been introduced, based on financial and economic criteria used by the OND to estimate risk when insuring new transactions. Institutions other than the co-operation ministry have been able to buy such debt.

Table 1. **Debt Reduction Operations with Counterpart Funds under the Swiss Debt Relief Programme**

Country/ (date of agreement)	Nominal debt cancelled $ million	Counterpart Fund		Total ODA in 1993 $ million	ODA from Switzerland in 1993 $ million	Cancelled debt/ODA (percentage)		Counterpart fund/ODA (percentage)	
		$ million	In percentage of cancelled debt			Cancelled debt/total ODA	Cancelled debt/Swiss ODA	Counterpart fund/total ODA	Counterpart fund/Swiss ODA
Bolivia (04/93)	35.8	3.9	11	564.7	11.9	6.3	300.8	0.7	32.8
Honduras (09/93)	42.8	8.6	20	333	3.7	12.8	1 157.5	2.6	232.4
Jordan (11/93)	23.8	6.4	27	311.6	14.9	7.6	159.7	2.1	43
Tanzania (11/93)	22.5	3.4	15	948.1	11.9	2.4	189	0.4	28.6
Peru (12/93)	132.6	33.1	25	560.5	7.2	23.6	1 841.6	5.9	460
Zambia (01/94)	18.2	1.5	8	874.6	0.5	20.8	3 640	0.2	300
Côte d'Ivoire (06/94)	244.6	34.3	14	765.7	6.1	31.9	4 009.8	4.5	562
Senegal (07/94)	15.5	3.1	20	496.7	3.5	3.1	442.8	0.6	88.6
Ecuador (09/94)	40.7	10.2	25	240.3	4.6	16.9	884.8	4.2	221.8
Philippines (08/95)	28.6	14.3	50	1 490.7	3.1	1.9	922.6	0.9	461.3
Egypt (05/95)	101.4	60.8	60	2 304	7.8	4.4	1 300	2.6	779.5
Totals or averages	T = 706.5	T = 179.6	A = 25	T = 8889.9	T = 75.2	A = 12	A=1349.9	A = 2.2	M=291.8

Sources : Blesse-Venitz, Gugler et Helbling (1995).
OECD (1995).

Since 1992, the Belgian government has been trying to extend swap operations to other categories of debt, especially to debts held by commercial banks. These new creditors are asked to make a special effort, as the buy-back price for debt (set after discussions in October 1993) is 50 per cent of the value estimated by the OND. In addition, the Belgian government recognises the need to extend the involvement of Belgian NGOs and debtor countries in the formation and management of counterpart funds.

France

The French government promotes debt-for-development swaps in two ways, by opening a line of credit which offers a financial incentive for swaps, and making available FF 4 billion in ODA debt for swaps exclusively for four countries.

A credit line of FF 20 million established in 1992 was intended to make available an amount in French francs equivalent to that invested by the Northern NGO in buying back debt to co-finance the development project associated with the swap. The mechanism was highly advantageous for the NGO, which enjoyed a doubling of its initial stake, in addition to the multiplier effect linked to all such swaps. Some operations (fewer than ten) have indeed obtained this co-financing, but part of the FF 20 million was used for "classic" co-financing of projects not financed through debt swaps. This initiative proved to be somewhat in advance of the needs expressed by NGOs, which had not yet formulated more than a few swap projects.

During the same period, the French government decided to establish a debt-for-development swap fund (called the Libreville fund), endowed with FF 4 billion in ODA debt and intended for four middle-income countries of sub-Saharan Africa, all in the franc zone: Cameroon, Congo, Gabon and Côte d'Ivoire. This fund offers a premium for the realisation of priority development projects which the indebted state has undertaken, permitting the cancellation of a certain amount of official debt against the beneficiary country's expenditure on development projects. This swap mechanism is not a tool to provide supplementary financing, as the counterpart projects must find financing elsewhere. To be accepted as counterparts, projects must contribute to sustainable development; initially, they had to support basic productive activities, local development projects, social projects or environmental protection projects. The beneficiary state's outlay should have a quantifiable cost, but its estimated value — which is used to calculate the amount of debt to be canceled — can include non-monetary elements, missed opportunities or expenditure not directly linked to the establishment of the project. Utilisation of this fund was suspended when the CFA franc was devalued in 1994. In September 1995, a reform broadened the range of projects which could serve as counterparts. Specifically, the following are now taken into account: privatisation or restructuring of the parapublic sector, as well as projects financed by donors other than France and the European Union. Further cancellations were made at the end of 1995, bringing the amount of debt cancellation approved by France to FF 1.2 billion, over a quarter of the total sum available for this purpose.

At the Multilateral Level

In the 1980s, there were major changes in the aims of multilateral mechanisms for consolidating debt (official and commercial), shifting from rescheduling to reducing outstanding debt and debt service. In 1990, under the so-called 10 per cent clause, the Paris Club authorised the swap of 10 per cent of a country's official or state-guaranteed debt (or $10 million if this amount is higher than 10 per cent of non-concessional bilateral debt) and of 100 per cent of ODA loans. At first, the clause applied to heavily indebted middle income countries, but it was extended in 1991 to low income countries. Several Northern countries (United Kingdom, France, Norway, Sweden) have carried out swaps of official debt under this clause.

As for bank debt, in 1989 under the aegis of the International Development Association (IDA), the World Bank established a debt-relief facility for the poorest countries (those which can qualify for IDA loans). This facility finances in part[16], and co-ordinates at the international level, the buy-back of these countries' bank debt at a large discount (the minimum discount was fixed at 70 per cent of the nominal value of the debt). A new option added in 1994 extended the initial purpose of this facility (debt buy-backs) by authorising the allocation of all or part of the funds provided by the IDA to operations in which debt is exchanged for funds for the development of the debtor country. In 1995, with the financial support of the IDA, debt-relief operations were carried out in seven countries (Niger, Mozambique, Guyana, Uganda, Bolivia, Zambia, São Tomé and Principe). These operations reduced the commercial debt of these countries by $814 million. Only the programmes for Bolivia and Zambia included a debt swap option. In Bolivia, the operation carried out in 1993 reduced that country's commercial debt by $32 million. The Bolivian organisation PROCOSI[17], which bought up this debt at an 84 per cent discount, obtained the equivalent of $7.5 million in local currency to finance health-care projects for children. For Zambia, the debt relief resulting from the swap amounted to $96.5 million. Here again the premium was 50 per cent (the initial cost of buying back debt was $10.6 million, and a development fund of $15.9 million was obtained) (World Bank, 1994).

These different measures, programmes and options have been in effect for several years, but the amounts of debt converted are still low in comparison to the total stock of the developing countries' debt. Thus debt swaps do not appear to be a preferred tool for reducing debt. Although their impact on debt relief has not been significant, swaps eliminate interest-bearing debt denominated in hard currency, with no loss of hard currency for the debtor country. By freeing budget resources to finance the social development sector, swaps can counter-balance reduced public expenditure under structural adjustment programmes (austerity measures which in any case are partly the result of unsustainable indebtedness).

Qualitative Assessment: Results in Terms of Capacity Development

This study of debt-for-development swaps should not be limited to their financial advantages. Another advantage of the swap mechanism lies in the fact that it involves a dialogue between actors who are often unaccustomed to collaborating: government institutions of creditor and debtor countries, associations and other local groups in the South, and the Northern NGOs (the "operators"). Swaps give rise to beneficial exchanges of skills and know-how. They also offer the opportunity for Northern NGOs to increase the ability of local organisations to respond to requests and initiatives.

To evaluate the effective use of swaps as instruments for promoting participatory and sustainable development, apart from the amount of debt involved and the size of the multiplier effects obtained on invested funds, it is necessary to study in more detail how swaps are organised, the management of counterpart funds, the beneficiary organisations and the allocation of funds at their level.

As for the first point, it is advisable to consider the participation of grassroots organisations and Southern NGOs in the **operational organising of the swap**. The risk is that, owing to the technical difficulty of swap operations, individuals or institutions in the North, or at the very top of the ladder, may be the only ones capable of undertaking them. Similarly, the grassroots organisations which wish to benefit from local funds very rarely have the funds to initiate such operations. In some cases, they can approach Northern partners directly, explaining their needs. The partners then have the choice of whether to launch a swap on their behalf, but is not the decision-making power then concentrated in the hands of foreign NGOs? Then in the negotiations with the debtor country, do these NGOs not determine the development actions to be undertaken, their goals and so on?

The **form of management** of the counterpart fund varies greatly from one swap to another. Under the Swiss debt-relief programme alone, five types of counterpart funds can be distinguished. These funds differ in form, management structure (simple or multi-levelled) and by the roles of the governmental authorities (of the debtor country and of Switzerland) and the representatives of local organisations in the fund's management. However, the form and structure of the fund partly determine whether debt swaps will serve to promote participation.

Furthermore, the potential for supporting an endogenous dynamic of development is greater when pre-existing organisations which have already developed project proposals are chosen as the privileged **beneficiaries** of swaps. An error to be avoided is giving financial support to fictive groups which have no dynamics of their own and are constituted solely to attract the financial windfall resulting from the swap.

Finally, to be capable of starting up or maintaining a process of participatory development, the beneficiary organisations must have some autonomy and flexibility in **allocating the funds** they obtain. The advantage of debt-for-development swaps is in part linked to the possibility for local organisations and their grassroots bases to allocate the funds according to their own objectives and projects, and thus to limit external intervention in the management of funds. It should also be possible to use this allocatory freedom to reinforce civil society in the South by strengthening the capacities of its constituent organisations, in particular by making them financially autonomous.

Among the debt swaps carried out under the Swiss programme, the Philippine counterpart fund is worth examining. Its originality lies, first, in the model's development, since it was the result of a series of long, intense debates in which Philippine NGOs took part. Second, the model holds many advantages for helping strengthen independent government structures. It was decided to use the counterpart funds to constitute the capital for a foundation, the Foundation for a Sustainable Society, Inc. In contrast to the funds for immediate financing of projects set up in the majority of the other countries supported by the Swiss programme[18], only the interest earned on the fund's capital can be used to finance projects. The goal is to provide lasting financial support (through loans, equity participation, guarantees and, in certain cases, grants) to local NGOs and grassroots organisations involved in productive activities which favour the empowerment (especially economic) of marginal or disadvantaged populations. This model also offers the government the possibility of provisioning the counterpart fund by emitting treasury bonds instead of paying cash, thus reducing the pressure on public finances. Finally, it provides for a counterpart fund controlled by local NGOs, as the foundation will be managed mostly by federations of Philippine NGOs. The Philippine government will have a non-voting seat on the foundation's board of directors, which is responsible for defining policy concerning the fund's investments. Switzerland will only have observer status. Philippine NGOs will also be the exclusive beneficiaries of the counterpart fund[19]. It may be supposed that giving responsibility for the fund to local NGOs will bring the entire process closer to the grassroots and make it more respectful of local conditions.

Converting Debt into Development Programmes: A Financing Method for the Future?

Potential

The future volume of debt-for-development swaps and their place among the various modes of aid principally depend on the evolution of the advantage which this mechanism presents for the various actors and of the regulatory context in which these operations take place.

Interest in swaps is mainly linked to the various parties' expectations concerning the profitability of these operations. For the creditor, getting rid of bad debts, even at a price well below their face value, can prove to be the best operation possible in financial terms. Moreover, the creditor may regard the discounted sale or forgiveness of a debt as a means of participating in a previously identified development project in what the creditor perceives as a priority sector. By adopting such an attitude, displaying its environmental or social concerns (real or apparent), the creditor improves its image.

The "profitability" of debt swaps for the operator (the NGO) depends essentially on the differential between the price of the debt on the secondary market and the buy-back price in local currency negotiated by the debtor country. The evolution of the discount rate in part governs the attractiveness and thus the "success" of debt swaps. However, the secondary market price of the commercial debt of Latin American countries has already risen substantially, and a similar trend can be observed for other countries. This appreciation of the value of foreign debt is generally a sign that the situation of the indebted country has improved. It can also follow debt swaps by this country. Whatever its cause, the appreciation of the debt redemption price, by reducing the multiplier effect on the invested funds, reduces the operator's interest in launching further swaps. The situation for official debt presents sharp contrasts: some Northern governments favour NGOs over enterprises, selling them debt at lower prices; while others behave according to the sole objective of obtaining the greatest amount of money for the debt instruments they hold. In the latter case, the debtor countries must offer a substantial counterpart for NGOs to participate in swaps.

With respect to the **regulatory framework**, the quantitative assessment above already mentioned the recent changes in the terms and procedures of the Paris Club on behalf of official debt swaps. These principles could be revised again to increase the scope of multilateral mechanisms for restructuring debt: the list of eligible countries could be lengthened, the ceiling on convertible debt raised and so on. National regulatory and legislative frameworks can also be changed. Creditor countries could adopt new measures to support swaps. Moreover, all decisions concerning the treatment of debt have a direct influence on the stock of convertible debt. For example, this stock has been reduced by the cancellation in recent years of all or part of the debt of certain developing countries or categories of them.

For the moment, although they are authorised, few swaps of official debt have taken place. One problem raised by this type of swap is linked to the lack of a secondary market for official debt and, consequently, to the choice of criteria for setting the discount. Creditors use various procedures to dispose of the debts they hold: some negotiate with buyers by mutual agreement, others set up a bidding system. Moreover, swaps of official debt involve large amounts of debt, which the creditor country is not always prepared to sell at a price the NGOs can pay. These swaps are thus more often organised by enterprises than by NGOs. To be able to respond to a call for bids, several NGOs can join together or an NGO can find a place in an enterprise's project.

The possibility of converting official debt nevertheless offers interesting prospects, given the weight of this debt in the total debt of some developing countries. The indebtedness of all developing countries to official creditors rose markedly between 1982 and 1987. In contrast, debts owed to multilateral organisations cannot be restructured, as a matter of principle. However, multilateral debt in 1992 amounted to about 17 per cent of the total indebtedness of developing countries, and this share has steadily risen in recent years for low-income countries in general and for the lowest income countries in particular. In a region such as sub-Saharan Africa, the majority of the countries are in debt to the multilateral institutions (the region's multilateral debt was more than 30 per cent of its total foreign debt in 1992, as against 20 per cent in 1982). The growing volume of this type of non-renegotiable debt can cause problems.

Thus it seems that the scope of debt swaps could be expanded, but certain political and technical limits remain, and they need to be well understood for dealing with or even overcoming them.

The Limits Encountered

We may distinguish between **limits on the capacity or the willingness to undertake swaps** and **limits on the implementation and the success of the mechanism.**

The former limits arise mostly in the debtor country, which does not always see the advantage of participating in a swap or because of institutional limits or monetary and budgetary constraints.

The first question is that of the **motivation of debtor countries**, which may be affected by the increasing possibilities of having their debts canceled without any compensating outlays or counterpart. These debt cancellations have two effects on swaps: they discourage any effort by the indebted developing country and also reduce the volume of debt available for this type of operation. Nevertheless, if the debtor country agrees to provide a counterpart for the reduction of its debt (by establishing a fund in local currency), it will expect certain advantages. However, this raises the problem of **whether debt swaps are to be an additional mode of financing** of development projects. Concretely, for a swap carried out by a Northern NGO, is the supplement in local currency obtained by the NGO (through the multiplier effect on the initial investment) to be added to the funds the NGO had earmarked for development activities in the beneficiary country, or is it to be substituted for them? This question is quite difficult to answer. Even if an NGO is questioned directly on this matter, it can state that it took advantage of this supplement to invest more in the debtor country concerned, although is it not possible to compare this investment with its initial intentions.

In theory, two scenarios are possible. In the first, the NGO takes advantage of the supplementary money to carry out a project on a larger scale. The benefit of the swap for the debtor country is then real in terms of resources for development. In the second case, the NGO has planned to carry out a given development project which requires a certain sum of money. In anticipation of the multiplier effect, it invests a smaller amount in the project than initially planned. The money saved in this way is allocated to other projects or to financing other costs. This allocation of the supplement is not necessarily reprehensible, but it deprives the debtor country of the advantage it might have obtained from the financing of counterpart funds and by the multiplier effect from which the NGO benefitted.

It may also be asked whether there is a "risk" that swaps of official debt will be accompanied by reductions of aid to the debtor countries concerned. As many factors affect ODA volume, simple comparison of the amounts from one year to the next does not suffice to show a causal relationship between the realisation of a swap and a fall in ODA. When the Swiss government began its programme, it made clear that the debt-relief facility (SF 500 million) would be added to the aid budget. At first, this principle was respected, but today it seems that the two are only partly additive. When negotiating an agreement, debtor countries do not have the power to insist that the Northern funds dedicated to the swap actually be additional or that the NGOs actually implement larger projects, nevertheless this "demand" seems justified and could be laid down as a principle in swaps. The swap mechanism does imply an outlay on the part of the debtor country. Some even consider that the debtor subsidises the operator by placing at the latter's disposal an amount in local currency which is higher than the amount of foreign currency invested in buying back debt. This effort should not be discouraged by a concomitant drop in aid flows.

Apart from the inherent interest of the swap, the **lack of sufficient skills in the debtor country** can be an obstacle to such operations: for example, the government does not always have departments specialised in debt management, with competent personnel capable of mastering the techniques required for carrying out swaps; local organisations, owing to certain internal weaknesses and limited capacities for action, cannot manage the funds obtained through the swap and invest them efficiently in development projects. Before launching swaps, therefore, it is advisable to examine the skills of local organisations, as well as their own dynamics and the possibility of harnessing them in the service of participatory development. Moreover, some debtor governments may refuse to allow development projects be implemented by independent local organisations, which otherwise are perfectly capable of taking relevant action.

Monetary and budgetary constraints can also limit the volume and frequency of swaps in debtor countries. Many such countries are trying to control the growth of the local money supply (some even place annual ceilings on the emission of local currency) to protect themselves from inflation. In some cases the counterpart funds in local currency are financed by money creation, but the debt swaps carried out by NGOs involve amounts which are too small for a real risk of inflation. Moreover, the details of "payment" can be modulated so as to reduce the risks (the central bank can emit treasury bonds, payment can be made by *tranche* or be deferred to a later date, and so on). The swaps carried out under the Swiss programme highlighted certain countries' narrow margin for manoeuvre in establishing the counterpart fund (owing to budget constraints in particular) and thus confirmed the need for adapting the fund's form and structure to local conditions.

Lastly, the obstacles to the success of swaps stem mostly from the **complexity of implementing the swap mechanism**. Among other things, this complexity is linked to the number and diversity of parties involved and to the intent to begin a participatory programme. The negotiating process among the various actors and the subsequent co-operation can be burdensome. In the Swiss case, co-operation between government and NGOs, one of the strong points of this initiative, can sometimes be difficult in practice. Tensions may arise between the relevant bodies of the Swiss government (the Directorate of Development and Co-operation and the Federal Bureau of Foreign Economic Affairs) and NGOs, owing to different views about the procedures to be followed and to the temptation felt by each side to appropriate the process for itself. Thus a debt-for-development swap can be a long and hazardous business. Indeed, to carry out such an operation successfully requires that at the same time all of the following must exist:

— debt which is both available and not too expensive;

— a financial flow making it possible to buy back the debt;

— an agreement or understanding between the debtor country and the operator on the terms of the swap;

— identification of development projects eligible to be financed by the proceeds from the swap; and

— local skills, both at the level of the local organisations responsible for the development projects and within the debtor government.

The realisation of a swap also requires some political stability in the debtor country as a guarantee of the continuity of the government's position over time and its respect for the commitments made under the swap agreement. The Swiss debt-relief programme has a supplementary condition, namely that the debtor country must be engaged in a structural adjustment programme with the World Bank and the IMF.

Conclusion

Debt-for-development swaps have the advantage of reconciling two objectives: the battle against debt overhang of developing countries and the search for new resources for their development. Although this instrument cannot solve the overindebtedness of developing countries, as it can affect only a marginal fraction of debt, it tries to limit the burden of indebtedness on their economies. Moreover, it is an ethically and socially acceptable way of treating debt. Debt-for-development swaps are also a means of extending resources for development, with the particularity of providing opportunities for promoting participatory development. This makes them all the more advantageous for debtor countries, since NGOs use them with the intention of exploiting these opportunities. These swaps are thus innovative from that standpoint and also in the techniques used, the partnerships created and so on. For this reason, they have a pedagogical interest, which stems in particular from the necessity for development actors which usually work in isolation (governments, organisations of Northern and Southern civil society, banks and so on) to undertake joint discussions and "actions". The sharing and transfer of responsibilities, particularly in favour of local organisations, is also accompanied by a learning process.

Past experiences have highlighted certain limits to the use of this mechanism, stemming from the large number of conditions which must be met in order for a debt-for-development swap to be *1)* attractive to the various protagonists, *2)* feasible and *3)* actually carried out. The result of these conditions is that the debt-swap mechanism can be reproduced but not generalised (as it cannot be applied to all types of debt, in all countries or in all circumstances), and that its use as an instrument in support of sustainable development remains marginal.

Some of the limits encountered in the course of swaps can be overcome if the actors wish to do so and make commitments to this end. The initiation of such operations depends principally on strong political will in the debtor and creditor countries. The expression of such a political will in debtor countries implies, as a prerequisite, that the swap mechanism is well understood, not feared, and that domestic capacity is sufficient to implement it. It appears that a first swap favours further operations for the same country, by attenuating fears and allowing the beneficiary country's government to master the swap mechanism better[20].

Intermediary organisations can also facilitate the setting up of swaps[21]. These organisations offer advice and assistance to Northern NGOs and developing country governments in the preparation and management of swap programmes. They play a technical role (identifying convertible debts and Northern NGOs which might be interested, participating in the negotiations with the debtor country and so on) and more generally provide information to raise awareness about swaps among the various people concerned. Their mobilising ability and dynamism play a determining role in whether a swap actually occurs. The prospects of debt-for-development swaps thus partly depends on the future actions of these organisations.

New perspectives have appeared with the possibility of converting official debt (at a time when the stock of convertible bank debt is dwindling) and with the launching of innovative programmes at various levels. The introduction of a swap option in the debt-relief facility of the IDA, for example, offers NGOs new opportunities to participate in debt-for-development swaps in poor countries. The Swiss initiative is a particularly encouraging example in the field of debt swap, although it is not yet possible to judge the impact in terms of participatory development of projects supported by the counterpart funds. This initiative is characterised by a strong political determination to transform residual debt into development capital, a determination inspired and maintained by the Swiss NGO community. This programme has the advantage of being based on debt cancellation by Switzerland. Under these conditions, it is easier to motivate Northern NGOs and indebted developing countries to participate in swaps, as the governments of debtor countries are not subject to excessive pressure on the amount of the counterpart. It can remain "modest and bearable", and there is no requirement that it cover, at a minimum, the cost of debt buy-back[22]. Moreover, the Swiss programme tries to involve local organisations in the establishment and management of the counterpart funds, and works to strengthen the organisations institutionally. The programme's long-term perspective is exemplified by the introduction of counterpart funds in the form of capital funds, as in the Philippines, and using counterpart funds for projects supporting local financing systems.

Debt-for-development swaps such as those carried out under the Swiss initiative therefore seem to correspond to a balanced sharing of costs and advantages linked to debt relief, freely agreed to by the various actors. Other possibilities can be envisaged, which require firm commitments from the parties involved, a definite conviction and sometimes an innovative spirit. Irrespective of context, these new debt-for-development swaps should be guided by a determination that the debt-relief measures should benefit the populations and environments of developing countries, and involve a participatory process.

Notes

1. For creditors, debt-equity swaps consist of an exchange of debt for equity in the public or private enterprises of the indebted country. They have often been used in privatisation programmes.

2. By Thomas Lovejoy, then Vice-President of the World Wildlife Fund.

3. The first debt-for-environment swap dates from 1987. It was carried out in Bolivia by the US environmental NGO Conservation International.

4. The notion of creative repayment (or the 3-D formula — debt, development, democracy) was developed by George (1988). Swiss NGOs supported the principle of creative debt relief on which the Swiss debt-relief programme is based today; the characteristics and principal results of the programme are presented throughout this chapter.

5. For a definition of participatory development and an analysis of ways of promoting participatory approaches, see Schneider and Libercier (1995).

6. This is one advantage of the swap, as a debt-relief instrument, over unconditional cancellation of debt. Cancellation can be considered as a bonus for leaders who mismanaged the borrowed capital. Moreover, it does not help to improve the "image" of the debtor country in the eyes of its other creditors. Finally, reduction of a country's debt is not sufficient to promote economic and social development.

7. A quantitative example will serve to illustrate this effect. An NGO buys a debt with a nominal value of $1 million for $400 000 on the secondary market (thus at a 60 per cent discount). The central bank of the debtor country buys back this debt at a 40 per cent discount on its nominal value, and thus pays the equivalent of $600 000 in local currency. Thus the NGO has invested $400000 (the initial cost of the operation, to which commissions must be added) and obtained the local-currency equivalent of $600 000. The net gain for the NGO, as compared to direct financing of a development project through a traditional currency exchange, amounts to the local-currency equivalent of $200 000. In other words, the funds invested by the NGO have been multiplied by a factor of 1.5.

8. Swiss NGOs were at the origin of the debt-relief programme by launching a national awareness-raising campaign in 1989 concerning the debt problem and its consequences for Southern populations.

9. Although there are really only two parties, each is composed of many elements, which sometimes makes negotiations difficult.

10. The redemption price (i.e. the swap price) is the price at which the debtor country "buys back" its debt in local currency from the operator. A redemption price of 100 per cent corresponds to the provision of an amount in local currency equivalent to the nominal value of the debt.

11. For the moment, the vast majority of counterparts are monetary, but counterparts in kind could be imagined (provision of land, of equipment and so on).

12. These three experiences were also chosen because they are well documented. The presentation of the US swap programme called the "Enterprise for the Americas Initiative", which is supposed to finance environmental protection projects managed by NGOs, was less relevant to the subject of our study.

13. Through this facility, Switzerland has co-financed some buy-back operations carried out under the aegis of the IDA.

14. Switzerland is a small creditor, and swaps on the debt which it holds would reduce the overall debt of the beneficiary countries by only 0.5 per cent.

15. See the paragraph below on multilateral mechanisms for restructuring debt.

16. Debt buy-back can be co-financed by bilateral funds (grants or loans accompanied by liberal conditions accorded by donors). In 1995, Switzerland agreed to provide SF 28 million in co-financing for these operations under its debt-relief programme

17. This organisation oversees CARE and Save the Children.

18. The form selected for the counterpart fund depends on the purpose for which it is established. In some countries, it responds to the short-term logic of implementing anti-poverty actions by financing immediate development projects. In others (such as the Philippines), the goal is to guarantee that the projects supported will be long-lived.

19. Public institutions and multilateral agencies can also take advantage of the proceeds of the swaps carried out under the Swiss programme, but in 1995 the vast majority of projects approved (80 per cent) were placed under the responsibility of private organisations.

20. We may refer to the example of Madagascar, where NGOs have carried out, through the Association conversion de dette pour le développement (ACDD), 11 debt-for-development swaps since the end of 1992. These swaps have cancelled a little over $2 million of the country's foreign debt and have generated resources of the order of FF 5.5 million for the Malagasy partners of the French NGOs. The government's favourable attitude towards this mechanism has been constant over time, despite some political turbulence.

21. The ACDE in France or the Debt-for-Development Coalition in the United States may be cited as examples. The European Network on Debt and Development, which co-ordinates the activities of NGOs working on the issues of debt and structural adjustment, also issue information on the swap mechanism in the NGO community.

22. The average redemption price for operations carried out under the Swiss programme is 25 per cent of the nominal value of the debt.

Bibliography

Auriault, A. (1991), « Intervention des ONG dans la réduction de la dette des pays du Tiers-Monde », in *Techniques Financières et Développement*, No. 25, December, Paris.

Auriault, A. (1994), « Les conversions de dette », in *Pour de nouvelles approches de l'aide au développement* », SOS FAIM and COTA, Proceedings of a colloquium held 7-9 March, Brussels.

Blesse-Venitz, J., A. Gugler and R. Helbling (1995), *Mesures de désendettement prises par la Suisse, bilan intermédiare*, Swiss Coalition of Development Organisations, Berne.

Bouchet, M.H. (1994), *Les expériences des pays de l'OCDE en matière de conversion et d'abandon de créances*, CNUCED Seminar, Geneva.

Demain Le Monde (1992), *Dette du Tiers Monde : 10 ans de crise*, Supplement, July, Brussels.

Eurodad (1993), *Third World Debt in the 1990s*, No. 4, June/July.

George, S. (1988), *Jusqu'au cou, enquête sur la dette du Tiers-Monde*, Editions la Découverte, Paris.

Griffith-Jones, S. (1993), "Conversion of Official Bilateral Debt: The Opportunities and the Issues", proceedings of the 1992 World Bank Annual Conference on Development Economics, Washington, D.C.

Gugler, A. (1994), *Creative Debt Relief: The Swiss Debt Reduction Facility*, Berne.

Martin, M. (1994), « La dette publique bilatérale : nouvelles voies d'action », EURODAD policy document, Brussels.

Oecd (1995), *Geographical Distribution of Financial Resources Allocated to Countries Receiving Aid*, Development Assistance Committee, Paris.

Oecd (1996), *Development Co-operation: 1995 Report*, Development Assistance Committee, Paris.

Pfister, G. and A. Gugler (1992), *Les fonds de contrepartie dans le contexte du désendettement*, Berne.

Schneider, H. with the assistance of M.H. Libercier (1995), *Participatory Development*, OECD Development Centre, Paris.

Service de désendettement des ONG suisses (1993), *L'initiative suisse en faveur du désendettement*, Berne.

Swiss Coalition of Development Organisations (1994), *Swiss Coalition News*, No. 1, June; No. 2, September.

Tanzania-Swiss Trust Fund (1994), *Guidelines for the Submission of Project Proposals to the Board of Trustees*, Dar es Salaam University Press, Dar es Salaam.

Van Der Horst, K. (1994), *Debt Buybacks by Western NGOs*, ADA Dialogue No. 1, September, Luxembourg.

World Bank (1994), *World Debt Tables 1994-95*, Washington, D.C.

List of Participants

FINANCIAL MECHANISMS IN SUPPORT OF PARTICIPATION OF THE POOR

Paris, 9-10 April 1996

Luis Noel Alfaro Gramajo	Instituto Centroamericano de Administracion de Empresas, Managua, Nicaragua
Paul Armbruster	Head, International Relations Department, Deutscher Genossenschafts- und Raiffeisen-verband e.V., Bonn, Germany
Corinne Beyer Reymond	International Catholic Migration Commission, Geneva, Switzerland
Jill Burnett	Consultant, Heidelberg, Germany
I. Fane Camara	Consultant, Dakar, Senegal
Renée Chao-Béroff	Centre international de développement et de recherche (CIDR), Autrèches, France
Shafiqual Haque Choudhury	Chief Executive, Association for Social Advancement (ASA), Dhaka, Bangladesh
John D. Conroy	Executive Director, The Foundation for Development Co-operation, Queensland, Australia
Mario Davalos	Executive Director, FondoMicro, Dominican Republic
Henry Dommel	United Nations Capital Development Fund (UNCDF), New York, United States
Robert Dhonte	Commission européenne, Direction générale du développement, Brussels, Belgium
Sidy Modibo Diop	Chef du service des Études générales et de la communication, Banque nationale de développement agricole (BNDA), Bamako, Mali
José Garson	Credit Advisor, United Nations Capital Development Fund (UNCDF), New York, United States
Dominique Gentil	Secteur financement, IRAM, Paris, France

Eugenio M. Gonzales	Foundation for a Sustainable Society, Inc., Quezon City, Philippines
Claudio Gonzalez-Vega	Ohio State University, Columbus, Ohio, United States
Alfred Gugler	Swiss Coalition of Development Organisations, Berne, Switzerland
Anne Guillaume-Gentil	Secrétaire exécutive, ACDE, Paris, France
Syed Hashemi	Department of Economics, Jahangirnagar University and Programme for Research on Poverty Alleviation, Grameen Trust, Dhaka, Bangladesh
S.I. Ijioma	Secretary General, African Rural and Agricultural Credit Association (AFRACA), Nairobi, Kenya
Lucy Izumi Ito	World Council of Credit Unions, Madison, Wisconsin, United States
Andreas Kappes	International Relations Department, Deutscher Genossenschafts- und Raiffeisenverband e.V., Bonn, Germany
P.A. Kiriwandeniya	President, Federation of Thrift and Credit Co-operative Societies, SANASA Colombo, Sri Lanka
Fernando Lucano	Chargé d'affaires, SIDI, Paris, France
Mohammed R. Mustafa	Secretary General, Near East and North African Rural and Agricultural Credit Association (NENARACA), Amman, Jordan
Zulkifli Noor	General Manager, The Asia-Pacific Rural and Agricultural Credit Association (APRACA), Bangkok, Thailand
Sayeeda Rahman	Chief, Micro-credit System and UNESCO-GRAMEEN Co-operation Unit, UNESCO, Paris, France

K. Vanderweele	Regional Director for Central Europe, Opportunity International, Vienna, Austria
Luc Vandeweerd	Programme d'appui-SMEC, BIT-BCEAO, Dakar, Senegal
Fernand Vincent	Recherches et applications de financements alternatifs au développement (RAFAD), Geneva, Switzerland
J.D. Von Pischke	Consultant, Reston, Virginia, United States
Jacob Yaron	Rural Finance Advisor, World Bank, Washington D.C., United States
Regula Züger Caceres	Swiss Coalition of Development Organisations, Berne, Switzerland

DAC Members

Belgium

| Robert Clemens | Belgian Administration for Development Co-operation, Brussels, Belgium |

Canada

| Gilles Lessard | Senior Advisor, Enterprise Development, Policy Branch, Canadian International Development Agency (CIDA), Hull, Quebec, Canada |

Finland

| Kirsti Aarnio | Counsellor, Development and Economic Co-operation, Finnish Delegation to the OECD, Paris, France |

Germany

| Thomas Feige | Federal Ministry for Economic Co-operation and Development, Bonn, Germany |

Italy

Eugenio d'Auria

Premier Conseiller, Délégation de l'Italie auprès de l'OCDE, Paris, France

Antonio Bandini

Ministère des Affaires étrangères, Direction générale de la Co-opération de développement, Rome, Italy

Korea
Kyong-Yul Lee

Second Secretary, Korean Embassy, Paris, France

Mexico

Carlos Hurtado

Ambassador, Permanent Representative, Mexican Delegation to the OECD, Paris, France

David Topete

Counsellor for Economic & Financial Affairs, Mexican Delegation to the OECD, Paris, France

Switzerland

Roger Pasquier

Conseiller d'Ambassade, Développement, Agriculture, Délégation de la Suisse auprès de l'OCDE, Paris, France

Michel Gressot

West Africa Region, Swiss Agency for Development Co-operation, Federal Department of Foreign Affairs, Berne, Switzerland

United States

Lee Roussel

Minister-Counsellor, Representative to the Development Assistance Committee, United States Delegation to the OECD, Paris, France

International Fund for Agricultural Development (FIDA)

Rauno Zander	Technical Advisor, Rural Credit and Institutions, Technical Advisory Division
Jean-Philippe Audinet	Associate Evaluator, Office of Evaluation and Studies

OECD Development Co-operation Directorate

Aid Management Division

Elena Borghese	Head of Section

Elisabeth Thioleron

Aid Review Division

Ruth Stock

Financial Policies and Private Sector Division

Raundi Halvorson-Quevedo

OECD Development Centre

Giulio Fossi	Head of External Co-operation Programme

Henny Helmich

Hartmut Schneider

Marie-Hélène Libercier

MAIN SALES OUTLETS OF OECD PUBLICATIONS
PRINCIPAUX POINTS DE VENTE DES PUBLICATIONS DE L'OCDE

AUSTRALIA – AUSTRALIE
D.A. Information Services
648 Whitehorse Road, P.O.B 163
Mitcham, Victoria 3132   Tel. (03) 9210.7777
Fax: (03) 9210.7788

AUSTRIA – AUTRICHE
Gerold & Co.
Graben 31
Wien I   Tel. (0222) 533.50.14
Fax: (0222) 512.47.31.29

BELGIUM – BELGIQUE
Jean De Lannoy
Avenue du Roi, Koningslaan 202
B-1060 Bruxelles Tel. (02) 538.51.69/538.08.41
Fax: (02) 538.08.41

CANADA
Renouf Publishing Company Ltd.
5369 Canotek Road
Unit 1
Ottawa, Ont. K1J 9J3   Tel. (613) 745.2665
Fax: (613) 745.7660
Stores:
71 1/2 Sparks Street
Ottawa, Ont. K1P 5R1   Tel. (613) 238.8985
Fax: (613) 238.6041

12 Adelaide Street West
Toronto, QN M5H 1L6   Tel. (416) 363.3171
Fax: (416) 363.5963

Les Éditions La Liberté Inc.
3020 Chemin Sainte-Foy
Sainte-Foy, PQ G1X 3V6 Tel. (418) 658.3763
Fax: (418) 658.3763

Federal Publications Inc.
165 University Avenue, Suite 701
Toronto, ON M5H 3B8   Tel. (416) 860.1611
Fax: (416) 860.1608

Les Publications Fédérales
1185 Université
Montréal, QC H3B 3A7   Tel. (514) 954.1633
Fax: (514) 954.1635

CHINA – CHINE
Book Dept., China Natinal Publications
Import and Export Corporation (CNPIEC)
16 Gongti E. Road, Chaoyang District
Beijing 100020 Tel. (10) 6506-6688 Ext. 8402
(10) 6506-3101

CHINESE TAIPEI – TAIPEI CHINOIS
Good Faith Worldwide Int'l. Co. Ltd.
9th Floor, No. 118, Sec. 2
Chung Hsiao E. Road
Taipei   Tel. (02) 391.7396/391.7397
Fax: (02) 394.9176

**CZECH REPUBLIC –
RÉPUBLIQUE TCHÈQUE**
National Information Centre
NIS – prodejna
Konviktská 5
Praha 1 – 113 57   Tel. (02) 24.23.09.07
Fax: (02) 24.22.94.33
E-mail: nkposp@dec.niz.cz
Internet: http://www.nis.cz

DENMARK – DANEMARK
Munksgaard Book and Subscription Service
35, Nørre Søgade, P.O. Box 2148
DK-1016 København K   Tel. (33) 12.85.70
Fax: (33) 12.93.87

J. H. Schultz Information A/S,
Herstedvang 12,
DK – 2620 Albertslung   Tel. 43 63 23 00
Fax: 43 63 19 69
Internet: s-info@inet.uni-c.dk

EGYPT – ÉGYPTE
The Middle East Observer
41 Sherif Street
Cairo   Tel. (2) 392.6919
Fax: (2) 360.6804

FINLAND – FINLANDE
Akateeminen Kirjakauppa
Keskuskatu 1, P.O. Box 128
00100 Helsinki

Subscription Services/Agence d'abonnements :
P.O. Box 23
00100 Helsinki   Tel. (358) 9.121.4403
Fax: (358) 9.121.4450

*FRANCE
OECD/OCDE
Mail Orders/Commandes par correspondance :
2, rue André-Pascal
75775 Paris Cedex 16 Tel. 33 (0)1.45.24.82.00
Fax: 33 (0)1.49.10.42.76
Telex: 640048 OCDE
Internet: Compte.PUBSINQ@oecd.org

Orders via Minitel, France only/
Commandes par Minitel, France
exclusivement : 36 15 OCDE

OECD Bookshop/Librairie de l'OCDE :
33, rue Octave-Feuillet
75016 Paris   Tel. 33 (0)1.45.24.81.81
33 (0)1.45.24.81.67
Dawson
B.P. 40
91121 Palaiseau Cedex   Tel. 01.89.10.47.00
Fax: 01.64.54.83.26

Documentation Française
29, quai Voltaire
75007 Paris   Tel. 01.40.15.70.00

Economica
49, rue Héricart
75015 Paris   Tel. 01.45.78.12.92
Fax: 01.45.75.05.67

Gibert Jeune (Droit-Économie)
6, place Saint-Michel
75006 Paris   Tel. 01.43.25.91.19

Librairie du Commerce International
10, avenue d'Iéna
75016 Paris   Tel. 01.40.73.34.60

Librairie Dunod
Université Paris-Dauphine
Place du Maréchal-de-Lattre-de-Tassigny
75016 Paris   Tel. 01.44.05.40.13

Librairie Lavoisier
11, rue Lavoisier
75008 Paris   Tel. 01.42.65.39.95

Librairie des Sciences Politiques
30, rue Saint-Guillaume
75007 Paris   Tel. 01.45.48.36.02

P.U.F.
49, boulevard Saint-Michel
75005 Paris   Tel. 01.43.25.83.40

Librairie de l'Université
12a, rue Nazareth
13100 Aix-en-Provence   Tel. 04.42.26.18.08

Documentation Française
165, rue Garibaldi
69003 Lyon   Tel. 04.78.63.32.23

Librairie Decitre
29, place Bellecour
69002 Lyon   Tel. 04.72.40.54.54

Librairie Sauramps
Le Triangle
34967 Montpellier Cedex 2 Tel. 04.67.58.85.15
Fax: 04.67.58.27.36

A la Sorbonne Actual
23, rue de l'Hôtel-des-Postes
06000 Nice   Tel. 04.93.13.77.75
Fax: 04.93.80.75.69

GERMANY – ALLEMAGNE
OECD Bonn Centre
August-Bebel-Allee 6
D-53175 Bonn   Tel. (0228) 959.120
Fax: (0228) 959.12.17

GREECE – GRÈCE
Librairie Kauffmann
Stadiou 28
10564 Athens   Tel. (01) 32.55.321
Fax: (01) 32.30.320

HONG-KONG
Swindon Book Co. Ltd.
Astoria Bldg. 3F
34 Ashley Road, Tsimshatsui
Kowloon, Hong Kong   Tel. 2376.2062
Fax: 2376.0685

HUNGARY – HONGRIE
Euro Info Service
Margitsziget, Európa Ház
1138 Budapest   Tel. (1) 111.60.61
Fax: (1) 302.50.35
E-mail: euroinfo@mail.matav.hu
Internet: http://www.euroinfo.hu//index.html

ICELAND – ISLANDE
Mál og Menning
Laugavegi 18, Pósthólf 392
121 Reykjavik   Tel. (1) 552.4240
Fax: (1) 562.3523

INDIA – INDE
Oxford Book and Stationery Co.
Scindia House
New Delhi 110001   Tel. (11) 331.5896/5308
Fax: (11) 332.2639
E-mail: oxford.publ@axcess.net.in

17 Park Street
Calcutta 700016   Tel. 240832

INDONESIA – INDONÉSIE
Pdii-Lipi
P.O. Box 4298
Jakarta 12042   Tel. (21) 573.34.67
Fax: (21) 573.34.67

IRELAND – IRLANDE
Government Supplies Agency
Publications Section
4/5 Harcourt Road
Dublin 2   Tel. 661.31.11
Fax: 475.27.60

ISRAEL – ISRAËL
Praedicta
5 Shatner Street
P.O. Box 34030
Jerusalem 91430   Tel. (2) 652.84.90/1/2
Fax: (2) 652.84.93

R.O.Y. International
P.O. Box 13056
Tel Aviv 61130   Tel. (3) 546 1423
Fax: (3) 546 1442
E-mail: royil@netvision.net.il

Palestinian Authority/Middle East:
INDEX Information Services
P.O.B. 19502
Jerusalem   Tel. (2) 627.16.34
Fax: (2) 627.12.19

ITALY – ITALIE
Libreria Commissionaria Sansoni
Via Duca di Calabria, 1/1
50125 Firenze   Tel. (055) 64.54.15
Fax: (055) 64.12.57
E-mail: licosa@ftbcc.it

Via Bartolini 29
20155 Milano   Tel. (02) 36.50.83

Editrice e Libreria Herder
Piazza Montecitorio 120
00186 Roma   Tel. 679.46.28
Fax: 678.47.51

OECD PUBLICATIONS, 2, rue André-Pascal, 75775 PARIS CEDEX 16
PRINTED IN FRANCE
(41 97 03 1) ISBN 92-64-15415-9 – No. 49247 1997